Friendship

Friendship

Michael Jackson

PENN

UNIVERSITY OF PENNSYLVANIA PRESS

PHILADELPHIA

Published by
University of Pennsylvania Press
Philadelphia, Pennsylvania 19104-4112
www.upenn.edu/pennpress

Printed in the United States of America on acid-free paper
10 9 8 7 6 5 4 3 2 1

Paperback ISBN: 978-1-5128-2412-4
Hardcover ISBN: 978-1-5128-2428-5
eBook ISBN: 978-1-5128-2429-2

A Cataloging-in-Publication record is
available from the Library of Congress

To Howard Eiland
in friendship

Friendship, it would seem, remains a bit of a riddle: we
know it is important, but as to why people become friends
and remain friends we can only guess.
        —J. M. Coetzee, letter to Paul Auster, July 14–15, 2008

And yet friendships endure, often for many decades, in this
ambiguous zone of not-knowing.
        —Paul Auster, letter to J. M. Coetzee, July 29, 2008

CONTENTS

PROLOGUE

It was a time of separation and a time of loss. When I learned of the death of an old friend in England, I was stunned and incredulous, for in his recent emails, Keith had given no hint of being ill or in distress. For several days, everything was a blur, and in a vain attempt to bring my friend back to life, I began writing a memoir of the times we had spent together in New Zealand two decades ago. This did nothing to assuage my grief, which, I now realized, was as much for Keith's untimely passing as for my estrangement from the country where our friendship first flourished.

Though we often think of friendship as a meeting of hearts or minds, every friendship is associated with specific objects, events, times, and places, so when I think of Keith's joie de vivre and boon companionship, I immediately picture him standing in an open doorway with a hand-rolled cigarette between his fingers and an espresso cup in his left hand, or he is at the stove, stirring a pot of green-lipped mussels in tomato sauce or quaffing a glass of chilled white wine as we listen to Pat Metheny's and Lyle Mays's collaborative album, *As Falls Wichita, So Falls Wichita Falls*. The smell of Drum tobacco or the mussels simmering on the back burner, like Mays's jazz piano or Italo Calvino's books, call him to mind, and I think of what Pat Metheny said when Mays died in Los Angeles on February 10, 2020: "He was one of the greatest musicians I have ever known. From the first notes we played together, we had an immediate bond."[1]

As spring segued into summer, I received an email from another friend, who had moved from Boston to western Massachusetts in early 2020. Despite the challenges of settling into a new home during a pandemic, Howard and his wife, Julia, had found time to resume their academic projects. Howard was writing about the "philosophical friendship" between Walter Benjamin and Theodor W. Adorno and had become intrigued by the tidal pull in this relationship between affirmations of solidarity and declarations of independence, the tension between admiration and criticism, and the incompatibility of Benjamin's philosophy of immediacy and Adorno's infinite dialectics.[2]

Howard's emails sharpened my sense of the complexities of friendship. Though frequently idealized, friendship shares with kinship a shadow side and is notoriously fickle and uncertain. Just as it waxes and wanes over time, it sometimes ends when friends move apart or survives and is revived in unexpected ways. And although Howard and I became acquainted through a shared interest in, if not identification with, Walter Benjamin, neither of us romanticized the philosopher to whom we had been intellectually drawn.

As our emails about Benjamin, Adorno, and Hannah Arendt continued through the summer and the idea of this book began to form in my mind, I felt that I was writing in the presence of Keith and Howard, as well as other friends who had passed away. When I refreshed my memory of Adorno's dedication to Max Horkheimer in *Minima Moralia*, I was struck by the fact that the "immediate occasion for writing this book" had been Horkheimer's 50th birthday on February 14, 1945, and that Adorno considered his work an homage to a collaboration interrupted by war and enforced emigration. As such, it was an interior dialogue in which the friendship was sustained despite distance, and a testimony to what separation and loss could not destroy.[3]

For Jacques Derrida, every friendship carries with it the inevitability of its ending and is haunted by a sense that one friend will outlive the other.[4] Derrida's words uncannily echo one of Raymond Carver's last essays, simply called "Friendship." In part, it is about Carver's close friendships with Tobias Wolff and Richard Ford, and it begins with a photograph of the three writers, taken in London, where they were giving a fiction reading together. The three friends are having a good time, and when life is full and you are with people you love, it is easy to let yourself be fooled into thinking that the halcyon days will never end. But, says Carver, who may have been facing death when he wrote these lines: "Things wind down. Things do come to an end. People stop living. Chances are that two of the three friends in this picture will have to gaze upon the remains—the *remains* of the third friend, when that time comes. The thought is grievous, and terrifying. But the only alternative to burying your friends is that they will bury you."[5]

If death is foreshadowed in our closest friendships, so too is a life beyond death, since in our recollections of lifelong friends, we celebrate the small gestures and shared gifts that are the quintessence of hope and the source of our greatest happiness. What we talk about when we talk about friendship is the mystery that we are never more fully ourselves than when we are in the company of our friends.

While every friendship may be experienced as unique, it possesses characteristics that are common to all intimate human relationships—the trust that someone cares for us as deeply as we care for them, the recognition in another human being of a life we wish to have or a world to which we would like to belong, and the fear that this trust and recognition may be lost.

Are there limits to the possibilities of friendship between people of different cultural or ethnic backgrounds, genders, and ages? Is a shared worldview essential to friendship? Is there a fundamental difference between friendship at a distance and friendship face-to-face? In what ways does friendship differ from kinship and marriage? Do we choose our friends, while our relations with kith and kin are not ours to choose? And what of the distinction Aristotle made between personal and political friendships, both of which are informed by a spirit of goodwill, though the latter extend this goodwill from one to one and all?

While this book touches on these questions, it does so by deconstructing them, which is to say by exploring the contexts in which the very possibility of such questions arises. This strategy involves interleaving narratives of personal friendships with reflections on friendship as a "way of life [that] can yield a culture and an ethics."[6] This counterpointing of particular and general perspectives allows each to illuminate the complexities of the other in the same way that friends bring to light latent potentialities in each other.

Thinking Friendship

Although many classical accounts of friendship cite exemplary pairings—such as David and Jonathan in the books of Samuel, and Damon and Pythias in Aristotle's *Nicomachean Ethics*—their focus is on friendship as a social virtue (*arête*). Friendship is construed as an ideal form of collective well-being (*philia politike*) rather than a mode of dyadic togetherness, though Aristotle is careful to explain that both are based on the "same standard of measurement."[7] As Mary Wollstonecraft put it in 1792, "The most holy bond of society is friendship."[8] But was she thinking of communities and city states, or close companions?

While Michel de Montaigne's 1580 essay on friendship (*amitié*) extols the virtues of friendship, its inspiration is a single friendship from the author's own life, and Montaigne makes it clear that, for him, the *emotional* truth of his friendship with Etienne de la Boéthie is far more important than any *idea* one might entertain as to how friendship may be defined, though he echoes Aristotle's conception of a friend as "another self," a soulmate.[9] For Alan Bray, this "modern" conception of friendship as an essentially private relationship that is "necessarily set apart from the commerce and practice of the world" can be glimpsed in fourteenth-century tomb monuments in which "sworn" male friends are buried together, their faces turned to each other rather than to the altar.[10] But any attempt to draw a hard-and-fast line between traditional and modern notions of friendship, or between friendship, love, and eros, may be less edifying than acknowledging the multiple and metaphorical potentialities of the terms.

For the ancient Greeks, *philia* could apply to people with whom one cooperated, members of one's family, companions, and passing acquaintances—anyone, in fact, who was not an enemy.[11] To friends, one owed well-being (*eudaimonia*); to guests, one owed hospitality (*xenia*); but to enemies, one owed nothing.

What was true for the Greeks is true in many societies. Consider the Māori concept of *whakahoanga* (friendship). The word *hoa*, "friend," can be used of a companion, ally, partner, and even a spouse, and *whakahoanga* can connote fellowship, conviviality, and sociability, depending on context. It is possible, however, that friendship was traditionally assimilated to kinship (*whanautanga*), which can refer, metaphorically, to any close relationship that is born of working together and sharing experience. What is crucial to friendship and kinship in the eyes of many Māori is filial love (*aroha*).[12]

For the Kuranko, among whom I have done fieldwork for many years, friendship (*dianye*) connotes the spirit of togetherness and acting in concert that comes from moving "as one body" in work or in dance. Even when used to express personal liking or love, *dianye* carries a sense of mutual indebtedness, as in a political alliance that is sealed by a marriage, a business partnership based on equal shares, or the traditional system of work cooperatives (*kere*) that enabled labor-intensive farming to be done enjoyably, efficiently, and together to the accompaniment of drums or flutes. As with the Māori, friendship was ideally more inclusive than exclusive and often morphed into affinity and kinship, as when men expressed their amity by marrying one another's sisters.[13]

Rather than decide what friendship essentially *is* or isn't, it may be more edifying to reflect on who one's friends are; and rather than identify differences between premodern and modern conceptions of friendship, it may be more enlightening to examine the word *friendship* situationally and see how it is deployed to assign an ethical or emotional value to certain relationships. Thus, to call someone a friend is analogous to calling God "father" or a comrade in arms "brother." Its meaning emerges from its moral and tactical use. It is, therefore, important to observe the effects of friendship rather than search for its essence, for while we may argue about the inherent qualities of friendship, whether affective, political, or moral, we seldom have any doubts that with certain friends we feel more alive, more hopeful, more intellectually inspired, and more secure in ourselves than we would otherwise feel.

Certainly, this perspective helps us see beyond the idealistic or reified conceptions of friendship as mutual trust and affection, and better appreciate its dynamic character. Friendships can sometimes be one-sided, competitive, erotic, or exclusive, and sometimes quite the opposite. As with families and communities, whether secular or religious, friendships may be a source of fulfillment or disappointment, admiration or resentment. Moreover, as Socrates observed, friendship is often born of neediness not altruism, and is a sign of some deficiency in ourselves.[14]

For me, the semantic ambiguity of the term *friendship* is less interesting than the existential ambiguity that friendship shares with all intersubjective relationships.

As R. D. Laing pointed out many years ago, "Each and every [person] is at the same time separate from [others] and related to them. Such separateness and relatedness are mutually necessary postulates." Accordingly, Laing concludes, our being with another can never be completely physical, any more than our being apart from another can ever be psychologically viable. We, therefore, find ourselves in the "potentially tragic paradox, that our relatedness to others is an essential part of our *being*, as is our separateness, but my particular person is not a necessary part of our being."[15] In this vein, Maurice Merleau-Ponty speaks of intersubjectivity as "a shared operation" in which neither self nor other is the sole creator. "We borrow ourselves from others," he writes. "We have a dual being. . . . We are collaborators for each other in consummate reciprocity. Our perspectives merge into each other and we coexist through a common world."[16] In friendship, the line between self and other blurs but is never erased, and it is this ambiguity that makes friendship a site of both idealization (in which self and other are regarded as one) and demoralization (in which self and other are at odds).

Sometimes we glimpse in the other a world to which we would like to belong or to which we crave access. Through association with the other, we imagine ourselves liberated from our own origins and magically empowered to undergo a sea change in ourselves. This mimetic desire lies at the heart of all sociality. We can no more be sufficient unto ourselves than we can know ourselves through introspection alone. If family is the first context in which we learn this truth, friendship is the second, extending the range of reciprocity to a peer group and potentially to all humans and all living beings.

Anthropologists have argued that social existence is grounded in forms of exchange. But in emphasizing the exchange of wives, words, goods, and services between groups, we sometimes overlook the fact that exchange is, as the Kuranko observe, a recognition that one's personal well-being is conditional on the well-being of significant others. It is an exchange of the wherewithal of life itself and is predicated upon an ability to imagine oneself in the place of another, suspending one's own point of view or one's own immediate gratification to attend to the other's needs.

As an idiom for expressing such ethical and political first principles as altruism, reciprocity, and community, friendship is as ubiquitous as kinship, marriage, and love. Moreover, even when subordinated to the love of God or loyalty to the nation-state, friendship remains as affectively and socially vital to our well-being as any other form of relationship.

Because friendship is such an ambiguous subject, I have organized the chapters of this book into two parts. In Part I, my focus is on friendship as a metaphor for universal forms of association or belonging that transcend boundaries of gender, class, caste, culture, and species. In Part II, my focus is on personal friendships and the dynamics of interpersonal life. A coda explores instances in which principles and persons are in conflict, as when loyalty to a friend overrules loyalty to family, country, or ideology, or vice versa. In closing, I consider what insights can be gleaned from the various case studies, stories, and portraits that I have presented.

Writing Friendship

As previously noted, friendship may be treated both as a subject for intellectual reflection and as a way of recounting a life story. Herein lies the justification for my juxtaposition of discursive and descriptive passages in this book. An anthropological or philosophical thesis becomes a pretext for exploring the life course of a particular friendship. Like dialogue, which Hannah Arendt considered to be the medium of friendship, these explorations resemble Chekhovian slices of life in which the beginning and ending are less important than what transpires in the space between. The art of life is an art of showing as well as telling. Against the grain of inscribed habits of thought and perception, art shares with friendship and love a potential to see the world and ourselves from another point of view.

During a recent visit to Oxford to give a series of lectures, I was invited by a small group of graduate students to take a guided tour of the town. At the Bodleian Library, I bought several of Derrida's "postcards" to send to friends in New Zealand before we went on our way to a seventeenth-century pub called the Eagle and Child, where an Oxford writer's group called the Inklings regularly met starting in late 1933 and throughout the 1940s. Of these writers, C. S. Lewis and J. R. R. Tolkien are the best remembered.

Though Lewis and Tolkien were close friends, they were at loggerheads over the status of myth. A Catholic from early childhood, Tolkien was entranced by our human capacity for creating "myth-woven," "elf-patterned" images and "heroic legend on the brink of fairy-tale and history."[17] While Lewis was also an aspiring poet, who shared Tolkien's enthusiasm for stories that touched on other worlds and recovered lost forms of human consciousness, he was agnostic.

On September 19, 1931, Tolkien, Lewis, and Henry Victor ("Hugo") Dyson were strolling along Addison's Walk in the grounds of Magdalen College, locked in intense conversation. Tolkien and Dyson held the view that, although we are fallen creatures, we nevertheless retain from our divine origin a capacity, as "sub-creators," to create truth. Truth combines historical fact and imaginative insight. This thesis found expression in a long poem that Tolkien wrote to Lewis, who had opined "that myths were lies and therefore worthless, even though breathed through silver."[18]

Within two weeks, Lewis came to believe that God entered the universe he had created, but as a fully human being—in Lewis's words, that "Jesus Christ was the Son of God." This myth was true.[19]

As with all stories, we are consoled by the fictions that darkness is followed by light, time heals all wounds, losses are made good, sins are forgiven, and error is redeemed by truth. Such changes undoubtedly do occur, but they rarely occur instantaneously or are immune to further change. Many influences led to the moment of Lewis's conscious embrace of Christianity, including his brother's "conversion" the previous year; his readings of John Bunyan's confession, *Grace Abounding to the Chief of Sinners* (1666); and the Gospel according to John. Moreover, he had already accepted the existence of

God but was not convinced until his conversations with Tolkien in the spring of 1931 that a direct relationship between humans and God was possible.

One of the striking things about friendship is that the spirit of the gift runs so deep within it that one never knows with any certainty whether oneself or another is the source to which a moment of grace can be traced. This inability to identify an influence or assign a cause makes friendship as mysterious as love. Did Tolkien convert Lewis? As for Derrida, who visited Oxford in June 1977 and chanced to see a postcard in the gift shop at the Bodleian Library—a reproduction of a thirteenth-century image from a book of fortune-telling texts, depicting Socrates and Plato with their roles reversed—he is shocked that Plato, whose beautifully written dialogues are our primary source for Socrates's life and thought, should be dictating to Socrates.

We are in part the creation of our friends, as they are creations of ourselves. We like to think that the books under whose spell we fall, the parents who brought us into the world, the period of history in which we happen to live, or the people who have the greatest influence over our lives, have an identity that is wholly independent of us, and it is this that gives them their power over us. In this view, Plato was simply the mouthpiece of Socrates, translating the master's oracular wisdom into print so that posterity would have the benefit of it. In the same vein, we might conclude that without the poetic arguments of Tolkien, Lewis would not have found his way to Christianity. These perspectives reflect the natural progression of the generations. The past brings the present into being in the same way that parents bring their children into the world. But as Jean-Paul Sartre observed, "What is important is not what people make of us but what we ourselves make of what they have made us."[20]

There is, therefore, a reciprocal movement between the forces that shape our destinies and our responses to those forces. Insofar as we create our own precursors, we are not wholly conditioned by them.[21] They may shape us, but we, in turn, shape them, particularly when they are no longer living and cannot question the meaning we attribute to them. Michael White speaks of this process as "re-membering," whereby we imaginatively reorganize the events and persons that have figured most prominently in our lives, much as we might reorganize the furniture in our homes to create a more convivial living space. By implication, one thinks of oneself not as an autonomous being, with a distinctive internal character and external appearance, but as part of a collectivity, a member of a family, lineage, or circle of friends. Re-membering evokes the image of a person's life and identity as an association or club. The membership of this "association of life" is made up of the significant figures in one's history, as well as the families and friends that constitute one's current world. "Re-membering conversations provide an opportunity for one to engage in a revision of the membership of one's associations of life, affording an opening for the reconstruction of one's identity."[22]

This book is a testimony to the power and importance of re-membering.

PART I

The Politics of Friendship

CHAPTER 1

Oases of Friendship

Hannah Arendt had, in the words of a close friend, "a genius for friendship." Her life was centered on her friends, to whom she dedicated her books, whose birthdays she remembered, whom she supported emotionally and materially, and to whom she wrote constantly.[1] Perhaps the value she placed on friendship reflected the loss of her family, scattered far and wide by the tragic events that overwhelmed mid-century Europe. Perhaps her childlessness accounts for her focus on friends. What is certain is that friendship was not only vitally important to her as a person, it also lay at the core of her political philosophy, exemplifying the trust and openness to dialogue without which human beings cannot hope to create a common world.

That her personal friendships flourished is undeniable, but whether her idea of political friendship could ever be realized is another matter. It raises the question as to whether the binding power of constitutional law, let alone common values and common interests, can hold a modern nation-state together. Even an African village, numbering fewer than a hundred families, may become so socially divided that it will physically split apart. As the Kuranko say, "Neighborliness is not sweet" (*siginyorgonu ma kin*) or "People and their neighbors quarrel" (*morgonu be i siginyorgoye le kela*), as if resigned to the fact that even the intimate relationships of kinship and friendship are often riven by dissension and distrust. And everyone knows that one's closest friends seldom become friends with one another.

With the exception of Mary McCarthy, Hannah Arendt never felt the deep affinity with her American friends that she felt with the friends of her youth and her fellow German émigrés. "Old friends are better than new ones," she quipped. "She clung to her European background and particularly to the German language," her biographer notes, "never really exchanging her mother tongue for English."[2] For these reasons, it is impossible to understand Arendt's intellectual sensibility and her "genius for friendship" without understanding what she meant when she spoke of herself as a "conscious pariah."

In two of the first essays she published after coming to the United States in 1941 as a Jewish-German refugee from Nazi occupied Europe, it is not only the loss of Europe that preoccupies her, but also the resistance of Americans to accepting her as she is and not expecting her to become like them and show gratitude for the opportunity.[3] There were times when she feared the fate that her friend Walter Benjamin had envisaged if he migrated to America. As he confided when they were both living in Paris in 1940, he could not imagine being without his library or his vast collection of quotations, and that America offered no other prospect than of being carted up and down the country and exhibited as the "last European."[4] Three months after Benjamin committed suicide at Portbou, on the border between France and Spain, Arendt passed through the town. She found no trace of where her friend was buried, and she traveled on to Lisbon and thence to New York, and into exile.

In writing about the Jewish people as perennial outsiders, "excluded from society and never quite at home in this world,"[5] Arendt identifies with Bernard Lazare's concept of a "conscious pariah," who in becoming fully aware of one's invidious situation becomes a rebel against it, refusing to accept any orthodoxy, whether political, philosophical, or cultural (including one's own ethnic or social heritage). This was more than a matter of refusing to become a victim of circumstance. It was a decision to make an intellectual virtue out of one's marginal and unassimilated status.[6]

As a refugee or immigrant, one sometimes feels that the natives assume their worldview to be natural and incontestable. Even the stigmatizing label *refugee* is unquestioned. By contrast, the newcomer can take nothing for granted. Even if naturalized, one may feel that one is a citizen in name only, and may hesitate to speak one's mind, and nostalgically remember one's natal country, whether one left it gladly or reluctantly, as a place where one felt self-confident and had every right to exist.

This sense of being an outsider can affect your choice of friends, making it likely that you will gravitate to people who also feel out of place, rather than seek the company of those who speak and act as if their belonging were a divine right. And, here, one thinks of Adolf Eichmann, whose "fetishization" of normality as a rationale for the murder of those who deviated from the "norm" became the subject of Arendt's controversial book on the banality of evil. Yet, as she observed, no one is immune to seeing others through the lens of their own history, and even the humanity that Jews acquired from centuries of insult and injury did not survive "the hour of liberation by so much as a minute."[7]

Her views cost her several friendships, notably with Hans Blumenberg But her bitter experience of fascism fueled an aversion to all forms of collective dogma, whether these were academic agendas, political allegiances, social causes, or mass movements that involved going along with the crowd. As Theodor Adorno would write in 1968, besieged by demands from the left that he declare his support for the student movement, "One does not capitulate to the collective," he wrote. "The uncompromisingly critical thinker, who neither signs over his consciousness nor lets himself be terrorized into action, is in truth the one who does not give in. Thinking is not the intellectual reproduction of what already exists."[8]

In her 1964 interview with Günter Gaus, Arendt confesses that that though she studied philosophy, she did not stay with it. Indeed, she had said "goodbye" to it and did not regard herself as a professional philosopher.[9] One can take this to mean that Arendt's commitment to open-mindedness makes her wary of conversations in which the terms of reference are narrowly predefined or overinflated—as in totalitarian societies. In her arresting phrase "thinking without a banister," she echoes Friedrich Nietzsche's lines in *Thus Spoke Zarathustra* about everything being in flux now, with all "railings and bridges [having] fallen into the water."[10]

Her refusal to blindly align herself with philosophical positions or political parties is not unconnected with the value she placed on friendship. Both reflected her belief in the redemptive power of the particular, "the little things of life . . . in which the secret of reality lies hidden."[11] In these words, Arendt echoes Hugo von Hofmannsthal's celebration of the homely, fugitive, and minor experiences of life that "awaken in us again the old fondness for the world."[12] In her introduction to Walter Benjamin's *Illuminations*, Arendt celebrates her friend's "passion for small, even minute things" and his desire to capture history in the most insignificant moments, "its scraps, as it were." Benjamin was particularly fascinated by two grains of wheat in the Jewish section of the Musée de Cluny "on which a kindred soul had inscribed the complete Shema Israel," and he sought to achieve something similar on the printed page. From the beginning, Arendt notes, he was less attracted to theories and ideas than to specific phenomena. His central concern was for "directly, actually demonstrable concrete facts, with single events and occurrences whose 'significance was manifest'"[13]—phenomena that many academics would dismiss as contingent, ephemeral, and unenlightening.

Arendt's conception of thinking is intimately connected to her conception of friendship, which also consists in small gestures and everyday sharing.
And she compares such actions to going visiting. Thinking is an expression
of what she called "the visiting imagination," in which one puts oneself in the
place of another and sees the world from a displaced standpoint.[14]

But it is humanly impossible to be equally open to everyone, and Arendt
clearly preferred the company of people with whom she felt a connection and
continuity with her past. Perhaps her care in choosing her friends reflected
an awareness of how comradeship (*kameradschaft*) had been exploited by the
Nazis in creating their version of a "common world"—a nightmare of conformity and homogeneity that had earlier led Nietzsche to extol the "jealous"
friendship of solitude, in which a free spirit resists the allure of mass media
and turns a deaf ear to the call of the crowd.[15]

Arendt's relationship with Karl Jaspers (her teacher at Heidelberg) lasted
from 1926 to 1969, and although she revered him as an intellectual mentor
and father figure, he became, after fifteen years, a close friend whom she
addressed as *Liebe Freundin* or *Leibe Verehrtester*. As someone who had
"migrated within" during the Nazi years, Jaspers might also be considered a
conscious pariah who shared Arendt's view that "a decent human existence
today is only possible on the fringes of society, where one then runs the risk
of starving or being stoned to death."[16]

Arendt's relationship to the man she married also evokes the margins.
Heinrich Blücher was born at the turn of the century into an impoverished
working-class family and received only minimal formal education. Blücher
was an autodidact and communist with a distaste for the ivory tower. He
never published anything yet taught successfully at Bard College and the
New School, and Arendt would confide to Jaspers that it was Blücher who
taught her "to think politically and see historically."[17]

There is an uncanny similarity between Blücher and Eric Hoffer, a maverick intellectual and longshoreman whom she met during a teaching stint at
University of California, Berkeley, in 1955. After settling in at the Faculty Club
in February, Arendt wrote a long letter to Jaspers describing her rail journey
out to California and saying how much she was looking forward to her next
trip to Europe and seeing him. In response to her mention of feeling lonely,
Jaspers suggested she might like to meet Leonardo Olschki, a literary scholar
of German-Jewish descent who taught at Berkeley, and Manfred Bukofzer, a
historian of early music who had emigrated from Germany in 1939. Arendt
immediately introduced herself to the Olschkis and sent a postcard to Jaspers

comparing the meeting to finding "an oasis in the desert."[18] Three weeks later, however, she apologized for her dishonesty and explained that the Olschkis "can't be an oasis for me anymore. I can't return to that world of pure culture, which isn't even very pure." Not only was their thinking not anchored in the gritty realities of life, they cultivated a comfortable but alienated simulacrum of the world into which they could escape. She continued: "On the subject of oases: the first real oasis I found appeared in the form of a longshoreman from San Francisco who had read my book." Eric Hoffer was also reading Jaspers and was keen to have Arendt tell him all she could about her old teacher. Though her academic colleagues might have shown her around the campus, Hoffer showed her around the city. "We were friends right off," she wrote to Jaspers,[19] and she read Hoffer's book *The Passionate State of Mind and Other Aphorisms* as one friend might read another's mind.

The resemblances between Blücher and Hoffer are striking. Although many details of Hoffer's early life are difficult to verify, his roots were working-class and German, he received little formal education, and his father died when he was young. After his father's funeral, he received about $300 in insurance money and spent the next ten years wandering across the country, doing odd jobs, spending time on Skid Row, and reading voraciously.

Michel de Montaigne's essays may have been the inspiration for Hoffer's own career as a thinker and writer, and although he left the docks in his early sixties and became an adjunct professor at Berkeley, his world remained the world of the common man. He had no ambition to be known as a scholar or public intellectual, and when he retired from teaching in 1970, he declared, "I'm going to crawl back into my hole where I started. I don't want to be a public person or anybody's spokesman. . . . Any man can ride a train. Only a wise man knows when to get off."[20]

Arendt was not only drawn to him as a kindred spirit who scorned the well-worn tracks of the academy, but she adopted his image of thinking as a "train"—a train that one should learn when to get on and when to get off of. "Surrounded by friends, she rode like a solitary passenger on her train of thought," Mary McCarthy wrote of her friend in 1970, for Arendt's mind was always on the move, always ahead of the game.[21]

A couple of years after Arendt's magnum opus, *The Human Condition* (1958), was published, a second-year undergraduate at the University of Auckland won the university's Anthropology Prize. With his modest prize money, he decided to buy a book and paste the paper plaque celebrating the award on the inside cover. Although this student received a small bursary, which covered his fees, he was obliged to work on the waterfront as a "seagull" (casual laborer) several days a week to meet his living costs. On the day he went to Progressive Books in Darby Street, he was wearing his working clothes—hobnailed boots, dirty jeans, a tartan shirt. He chose this bookshop because it specialized in left-wing publications. It would not be the typical place one would expect to find a copy of *The Human Condition*, but perhaps the fact that it was about labor, work, and action (the *vita activa*) qualified it to appear among the Moscow Publishing House editions of Marx and Engels. The student was first attracted to the title and spent some time skimming the opening chapters before deciding that this was the book he wanted to buy. But almost forty years would pass before he realized that his research on storytelling among Somali and Iraqi refugees in Wellington, New Zealand, would be illuminated by the pages that Arendt devoted to the subject in her book, as well as in her reflections on being a refugee. He had stumbled on a work that engaged his intellectual sympathies, and an author with whom he could identify as an outsider, like Albert Camus and Franz Kafka. "My writing grows out of my life," Hoffer wrote. This student felt the same way, and when he read what Arendt wrote about Hoffer ("my first real oasis"), he felt that in some uncanny way, he was an avatar of this maverick philosopher and that he had found his own oasis in the desert.

CHAPTER 2

A Society of Friends

In my early twenties, I did not give friendship much thought. I longed for love and wrote countless poems about finding it or losing it, but I took friendship for granted. Just as everyone had a family, so everyone had friends.

For my mentor, Brijen Gupta, however, friendship was his raison d'être, even more fundamental perhaps than family or love.

Brijen taught Asian studies at Victoria University of Wellington, where I was completing my bachelor of arts degree. I cannot recall our first meeting, but in 1961, when the student population was relatively small and relations with faculty were often socially, and sometimes sexually, relaxed, I may have been introduced to Brijen by my brother-in-law, who was a student of the radical geographer Keith Buchanan,[1] whom Brijen regarded as a comrade in arms. Among others who regularly congregated in the new student union cafeteria was the soft-spoken historian and poet Bill Oliver, the outspoken German-born Peter Munz (who had studied under Ludwig Wittgenstein at Cambridge and was a close friend of Karl Popper), and several students, including Margaret Clark, Narena Oliver, Gerard Macdonald, and myself. Like many groups of friends, we were not necessarily friends with one another. We were held together by a single charismatic individual, and when he moved on, we parted ways.

I felt so privileged to be included in this coterie, over which Brijen presided like a guru, that I never asked myself why he seemed more devoted to us than to his own family. Perhaps this had something to do with the fact that real family ties involved obligation and duty, whereas friendship was a matter of choice, including the choice of whether to regard one's friends as family. In any event, Brijen assumed the role of paterfamilias, and I became his protégé. "You will go off to war," he once told me, "and imagine returning home a conquering hero. But you will die of the flu without ever firing a shot." On several other occasions, he took me to task for not having a point of view. Although he never complemented me on anything I wrote or did in the almost sixty years I knew him, I always considered myself in his debt, and his approval was never a precondition of my affection. Perhaps I believed, as he did, that friendship transcends such worldly considerations as age, social standing, wealth, and keeping score of what you give and what you receive in return, which may explain why I have never forgotten the lines he recited to me one night as we drove through the streets of Wellington in the rain:

And in the evening of my days
Let me remember and be remembered
by the friends that I have made.

As it was for Aristotle, friendship for Brijen was a virtue, as crucial to politics as to ethics. This was brought home to me in 1965, when Brijen, ruing his decision to leave New Zealand and return to the United States, confided that his energies were being drained by the civil rights movement and the war in Vietnam, both of which he regarded as campaigns against systemic American racism.[2] "I wish I could be nearer to you," he wrote in a letter to me. "I know that we [i.e., kindred spirits from Wellington days], could start a circle of friendship in which sharing and creativity bind us together. But I know now it will not happen. I dreamt of it in India when I was in college, and it was shattered; then I had a vision of success in the sixties, it has now turned into frustration."

Brijen would return to this utopian theme whenever we met, convinced that an intentional community of mutual friends could provide a viable alternative to the hierarchical and discriminatory regimes of national, academic, and corporate life.

*   *   *

As I approach "the evening of my days," my thoughts also return "to the friends I have made" and to the meaning of friendship. But while, for me, friendships were personal, not political, Brijen made friendship a moral basis for *communitas*—something his friend Christopher Lasch called "a haven in a heartless world" and Hannah Arendt spoke of as an oasis in the desert of modern life. From an early age, Brijen believed that friendship fostered a spirit of social solidarity that was conducive to the common good. The question, for me, however, was whether I-Thou relationships, such as love and friendship, were in their very nature exclusive attachments that could not be effectively generalized, even though they articulated ethical ideals, as in friendly societies, kibbutzim, ashrams, social media, age-classes, and forms of political comradeship. Given Arendt's celebration of the binding power of friendship, can we dismiss love as decisively as she does, seeing it as "by its very nature . . . unworldly" and, therefore, "not only apolitical but antipolitical, perhaps the most powerful of all antipolitical human forces"?[3]

∗   ∗   ∗

Brijen was born on September 17, 1929, in Dehradun, India, in the foothills of the Himalayas. His family was, in his words, middle-class, well-to-do, and westernized.

In a series of conversations with me in 2009, Brijen described Dehradun as home to a unit of the British brigade and a host of government agencies and institutions that gave the town an urbane atmosphere and encouraged interracial contacts. Dehradun was also the home of many anglicized schools and a refuge for boys and girls who wanted a "modern" education.

"At my parents' home," Brijen told me, "we had electricity, running water, and a flush toilet. A maid washed the dishes and kept the house clean. A full-time gardener doubled as a watchman. And there was a Brahmin cook. The most remarkable feature of our life was evening meetings when, as a rule, men congregated in one room and women in another. Children were not allowed to attend these discussions but sat on the stairs and listened to the talk, which ranged from the pedestrian to the profound. Moreover, I was enrolled in the American Presbyterian Mission High School from grade four to ten and made friends with my American teachers and matrons. Attending a mission school meant heavy doses of English language and literature and compulsory Bible classes. To balance my religious education, my mother had me study Sanskrit and Hinduism with a private tutor. I graduated from high school in my 14th year, two years earlier than the average. Thanks to my principal, Rhea McCurdy Ewing, a Princeton graduate who was a regular at our home, I had early exposure to Western classics. My parents' expectation was that I would respect and stand in awe of both the literatures of India and the Western canon. This was no easy feat since, after [Thomas Babington] Macaulay, Indian literatures were not considered worthy of study, and the mission of the Empire was to create a class that was brown in color but English in outlook.

"My first moving encounter with the West came, I believe, in 1942. That summer in the hills of Mussoorie, in the company of my matron (and lover to be) and a couple of other boys, I visited a European cemetery. I was touched by the great number of graves of little boys and girls, children of British civilians and military officials, as well as the numerous graves of wives who had died in India. The number of adult males paled in comparison. I grieved that, whatever their motives, thousands of 'innocent' Westerners had given their lives in and to India."

Brijen's mention of the wives of colonial administrators brought back memories of the week I spent with him in London during the winter of 1963–64. He was making daily trips to the British Museum to record on index cards synopses of the many novels written by women who had dutifully followed their husbands from England to India in the nineteenth and early twentieth centuries. My task was to bring these books from the central desk of the reading room to where Brijen was assiduously jotting down details from their dust-jacket blurbs. At the time, this project seemed to have little academic merit, but I now see its connection to his early experience of the psychological damage that colonialism does to both oppressor and oppressed.

"I think I came of age in 1942," Brijen told me. "Gandhi had launched the Quit India movement, and I had entered puberty, though did not know at the time what puberty was. But the crisis I faced was to identify which part of me was Indian (or Hindu), and which part Western. Like [Jawaharlal] Nehru, I had become a curious mixture of East and West, out of place everywhere and at home nowhere, and I did not have any close friends in my own age group."

A potential source of community lay within reach. Some fifty miles from Dehradun was the holy city of Haridwar, and in the hills of the Siwalik range were dozens of ashrams led by followers of Vivekananda and Aurobindo, preaching neo-Hinduism (Shankara's Vedanta) to illiterate but English-speaking Hindus who felt uncomfortable with Hindu religious rites and temple visits. One of the women swamins was Anandamayi to whom Brijen's parents were devoted and who subsequently became famous when Nehru and his daughter, Indira Gandhi, joined a group of her acolytes. From 1942 to 1952, Brijen visited her almost every month, either in Dehradun or Benares, and toyed with the idea of renouncing the world and living in her ashram.

His parents, however, had decided he should become an engineer, and in 1943, he entered a local college to study English literature, physics, chemistry, and mathematics.

"Thanks to the librarian, Daulat Singh Chauhan, whose ramshackle library probably contained fewer than 10,000 books, I embarked on a curriculum of my own," recalled Brijen. "He urged me to go through 'histories'—the history of English literature, the history of Western political thought, the history of economic ideas, the history of religion, and so forth. In one of the junk piles at the library, I found a beat-up but complete set of the *Encyclopaedia Britannica*, and I persuaded my parents to have it bound and placed on the library shelf. Then, one fine day, out of the blue, a bundle of books arrived from my great-uncle, Bhupal Singh, author of *A Survey of Anglo-Indian Fiction*. This bundle included [James] Hastings's *Encyclopaedia of Religion and Ethics*. So 1943–45 became two of my most academically instructive years.

"These were also troubled times. I was being pulled in different directions. The nationalist struggle pulled me one way; my desire to be a hermit pulled me another way, not to mention my desire to read and reflect. I was also confused about my sexuality. Though [I was] relatively short and small, college girls found me attractive, and I had modest sexual encounters almost every week."

In the summer of 1945, Brijen enrolled at Benares Hindu University. Though averse to studying engineering and confused about his future, a fortuitous meeting helped him find his path.

"In early 1946, at the end of my first year of studying at Benares Hindu University, I was delayed at the railroad junction of Laksar because of the derailment of an earlier train. I was obliged to spend thirty-six hours in an overcrowded waiting room. As providence would have it, an ocher-robed swami, Lokeshwaranand of the Ramakrishna Vivekananda Mission, took pity on me and kept me amused, wondering why I, who had such good knowledge of his mission and its founders, had not made any attempt to be active in it.

"These were the final years of British rule in India, and I had excellent political connections with the Congress-left. I now began an active correspondence with Swami Lokeshwaranand. His own story of why he had renounced the world made a deep impact on me, and at his urging I left home to spend three months at the Ramakrishna Vivekananda Mission in Mathura."

Brijen's story reminded me of Leopold Fischer, who was born into an assimilated Jewish family in 1923, became enamored of India from an early age, and was inducted into the Dasnami order as Agehananda Bharati. Bharati was six years older than Brijen and just as intellectually precocious. They became good friends. But while Bharati found himself more at home in India than in Europe, and Brijen rejected the relevance of Hindu philosophies for his personal growth, they shared a cosmopolitan vision that eschewed identification with any one nation, religion, or ethnicity. Thus, Bharati embraced a humanism exemplified by G. E. Moore, M. N. Roy, Bertrand Russell, and Wittgenstein, while Brijen adhered to an ethos of friendship and communitarianism that he had first experienced in an Indian ashram. Moreover, both Brijen and Bharati were fascinated by the tantric tradition, and Bharati's succinct observation that "the theme of harnessing instead of suppressing the senses for the sake of the higher life is one of the most delicate and . . . most important in the religious traditions of Asia"[4] found echoes in Brijen's discomfort with asceticism and his view that the sexual impulse was not inimical to liberation but one way of achieving it.

These preoccupations entered every conversation Brijen and I had over the next few years as our paths crossed in London, New York, Rochester (NY), Bloomington, (IN), and Cambridge (US). In his belief that poetry, stories, myths, and art—like friendship and love—make the emptiness of existence bearable, and that "analysis makes the absurdity of life more than one can bear,"[5] I found consolation for my own attempts to integrate social science with philosophy and literature. In the delight he took in Frank Harris, the Kama Sutra, and literary pornography, my own puritanism was exorcised. But though I spent years in community development and welfare work in Australia, England, and the Congo, committed to ameliorating the lives of the poor, the homeless, and the downtrodden, I would never find in myself the sustained devotion to the needs of others that characterized Brijen's life.

In 1948, abandoning his political and social activities and breaking off his contacts with the Congress Socialist Party, Brijen intensified his reading of religious and philosophical texts—Hindu, Buddhist, and European. To cover his material needs, his parents (at his grandfather's urging) paid Brijen a monthly stipend.

"As I read more and more religio-philosophical tomes, a desire came upon me to go traveling and visit various ashrams. I had the proper letters of introduction to speak directly to the leaders of the ashrams, but the results were mixed. My difficulty lay in my rejection of religious rites, temple worship, and an anthropomorphic God. Under the influence of R. L. Nigam[6] and the radical socialist Ram Manohar Lohia,[7] as well as Marxist and existentialist writings, I had become a humanist in its narrowest formulation. I found Vedanta troubling but could not bring myself to accept Cārvāka's materialism as an alternative.[8] Buddhism fascinated me for its nonmonotheistic outlook, and Nigam helped me discover the Buddhist doctrine of *sunyata* (void), which was only a stone's throw away, I would later discover, from Camus's notion of the absurd. *Sunyavad* (the doctrine of voidness) rejected the absolutism of Vedanta as well as nihilism, and I decided to study it further.

"In addition to Anandamayi and Lokeshwaranand, my memorable visits in 1948 were to Sri Krishnaprem, the Aurobindo ashram, and Ramana Maharshi's ashram.[9] Sri Krishnaprem, born Ronald Nixon,[10] was a Cambridge don who had come to Lucknow University with another don, J. A. Chadwick,[11] to teach English. Both fell under the influence of Vice Chancellor Chakravarti's wife (Monika Devi, later Yashoda Ma). Chadwick left Lucknow to go to Aurobindo at Pondicherry, and Nixon, initiated by Yashoda Ma as Krishnaprem, went to Benares and then Almora in the Himalayan foothills, where he and Yashoda Ma built a temple and ashram called Uttar Brindaban a few miles away from the palatial home of Gertrude Emerson Sen, granddaughter of Ralph Waldo Emerson.[12]

"Sri Krishnaprem was a remarkable man—a scholar and a religious devotee rolled into one. I stayed with him for about a week, found him very amiable, yet was not equal to his intense devotionalism (*bhakti*) and left dissatisfied. My week at Gandhi's ashram at Wardha was also unfulfilling. The devotion of his disciples to Gandhian ethical social action (*karma*) was admirable, but Gandhian ashrams, like most other ashrams in India and elsewhere, rejected libido."[13]

According to George Orwell, Gandhi believed that "for the seeker after goodness there must be no close friendships and no exclusive loves. Close friendships are dangerous, because friends react on one another and through loyalty to a friend one can be led into wrong-doing. . . . Moreover, if one is to love God, or to love humanity as a whole, one cannot give one's preference to any individual person. This again is true, and it marks the point at which the humanistic and the religious attitude cease to be reconcilable."[14]

This struggle to "reconcile" the pleasures of the flesh with spiritual aspirations, like the struggle to cultivate exclusive attachments while remaining responsive to the needs of strangers, led Brijen to become disenchanted with ashrams and to seek answers elsewhere.

Quakerism offered a form of pacifism that Brijen found "more clearheaded than Gandhi's or any Buddhist's. Suddenly, I realized that the tension between agape and eros, which non-Tantric Indian religions had resolved by renouncing libido, was a creative one. Quaker references to God were, moreover, benign, and Christ was seen as neither relevant nor irrelevant. And their relief efforts were more than Boy Scout exercises."

In early 1949, feeling the need to put some distance between himself and India, Brijen sailed to England where Radhakrishnan (a fellow of All Souls College) had arranged a visiting studentship for him at Balliol College.

"Once at sea," Brijen told me, "I saw my voyage as a passage into exile."

He continued: "The ship was almost entirely occupied by English families, returning to the motherland with bittersweet memories of their departure from India. I thought the source of their bitterness came from their knowledge that they would never replicate their Indian lifestyle in their homeland, and many were already talking about packing up again and migrating to Canada, New Zealand, or Australia. Several opined that they would soon be back to India, to govern a country that Indians would find ungovernable."

Of his year in England and Europe, Brijen confided little except that he spent several months as a relief worker in a Quaker center in Darmstadt, Germany, and that, in retrospect, it was a period of withdrawal. I suspect that he had encountered endemic racism in Britain. When I pressed him on this point, he grudgingly admitted as much, referring to "pervasive and subtle" snobberies of class, grafted onto a deep-seated contempt for people of color and colonials who would not accept their lowly place in the allegedly "natural" order of the world.

"I slipped back into India in May 1950," Brijen said, "as quietly as I had slipped out of it. I had made up my mind to resume college and eventually become a teacher. After finding my Dehradun apartment intact and debating whether I should return to Benares or remain in Dehradun, I opted for the latter. Geographically, Dehradun was midway between the political capital Delhi and the ashrams that dotted the Himalayan foothills, and this tension between political and spiritual yearnings still ruled my life. My life was also suddenly and deliriously complicated by love.

"Her name was Beena Banerjee. She came to Dayanand Anglo Vedic College in July 1951. I was then in the final year of my BA, and from the very first moment I laid eyes on her, I was smitten. Whenever I saw her, she would return my glances with a mysterious but mischievous smile. Then, one rainy August afternoon, as I stood half-drenched under one of the classroom verandas, she crept up behind me. 'I am Beena. Can I talk to you?'

"I froze. Though notorious for straight talking, I was speechless. Sensing victory, she smiled. 'You see, I am taking English Literature, and Professor Nigam told me that you have the best notes for the first year. Can I borrow them?'

"It was sheer flattery. She needed my notes like a hole in the head. But the ploy worked. Now, however, I was in command of myself. 'And what do I get in return?' I asked.

"'Friendship,' she said, and without waiting for any response, she darted off to her philosophy class, leaving me to wonder whether she meant merely friendship or love.

"The whole conversation took less than a minute, but it transformed my life. Over the next twenty-two months we exchanged 917 letters. We walked to and from college, read books together, shared private jokes, mused on life, and loved each other intensely. With Beena, my philosophical outlook matured. Following Sartre and Heidegger, I affirmed conflict as the natural relationship between man and man; stressed the absurdity, suffering, and futility of life; and assumed the evanescence of God.

"On the political front, I resumed my contact with Lohia and assisted him in firming up his ideas about the 'Third Camp'—equidistant from the orbits of Washington and Moscow. I had met Harris Wofford and his wife, Clare, who were to become close friends of mine after 1953, and I had become fascinated by their idea of a world government—though I told them it was a pipe dream. As for Lohia's socialism, in which I had a great investment, it was rapidly going down the tube, though he would only realize this several years later. Those whom he considered possible partners in an International that would rival Trotsky's Fourth [International], like Tito, were courting Nehru. And he refused to believe, despite my persistent urging, that nationalism was already on the way to eclipsing socialism. He believed the opposite would be the case. Together with Tito, Mao, and Ho Chi Minh, he envisaged a creative synthesis of humanism, agrarian socialism, and nationalism. As for me, I considered nationalism a cancer that was bound to lead to chauvinism and strengthen totalitarianism."

Disconcerted by these political debates, Brijen refocused on his own inner growth. "New ashrams had sprung up in the Himalayan foothills led by gurus who hailed from what is now Pakistan. I visited a few of them and found them unappealing. With a friend of mine, Balram Khanna, who shared my spiritual yearnings and had become my close confidant, I revisited Sri Krishnaprem in the summer of 1951. He granted me a private audience, only to denounce European philosophies as the devil's handiwork, designed to lead true believers astray. In his public audiences over the next three days, he propounded on Indian and European ideas of consciousness, and I considered him ill informed. On the last day of our visit, I found a note in Hindi pinned to my pillow. Beautifully handwritten, it read: *Find God, peace without Him is not possible.* I never saw him again. But in 1965, at the Abbey of Gethsemani in Kentucky, Father Louis [Thomas Merton] said the same thing to me.

"My break with Hindu worldviews was now almost complete, though I could not rid myself of the Maya postulate that *the world does not exist; it is merely an idea, an idea that wishes to be entertained, and once entertained, forces the mind to accept it as reality.*

"It was in 1953 that I met Agehananda Bharati for the first time. He was an honorary professor of philosophy at Benares Hindu University and came to Dehradun to visit Nigam and Nigam's mentor, M. N. Roy, the ex-Stalinist who mentored Mao, established the Communist Party in Mexico, and was a humanitarian philosopher in his own right. It was great to see Bharati and Nigam get along so well.

"Bharati and I kept in touch thereafter. Ironically, after I had left India, Bharati and Beena became lovers, and he was expelled from Benares Hindu University when caught in a tryst with her. In May 1991, he died in my presence and in the arms of his last lover, Rita Narang. Together, we had nursed him during his last days.

"In 1952, I declined a Rhodes scholarship, mostly at the urging of my mother who was then not well, but partly because of my involvement with Beena. I was not at peace. I was smoking heavily and had begun drinking. Beena disliked both. I proposed to her, but she declined, asserting that one marries to have babies, and she was not ready for that. We also toyed with the idea of setting up an intentional community on the model of the kibbutz, as many of my Gandhian friends had done, but neither Beena nor I were the salt of the earth.

"That same year, Radhakrishnan was elected vice president of India. Since 1946, he had been my mentor and patron, and had castigated me from time to time for my left and pro-Western orientations. But he was pleased that I was aiming to be a teacher, and early in 1953, when asked by Maude Hadden, president of the Institute of World Affairs (Radhakrishnan was on its board), to nominate an Indian student to participate in a six-week-long international affairs seminar, he nominated me. Maude accepted his recommendation. Three weeks of hard bargaining followed before I secured an all-expenses-paid, six-week trip to the States with the added provision that Maude would help me get into an American university for graduate studies.

"In the summer of 1953, I left for the States. My mother was convinced I would never come back. All partings are partings forever. I promised annual

visits and kept my bargain until she and my father died. Lohia was in mourning, but both he and I knew that there was no political future for me in India.
As for Beena, she was angry that I had announced my decision without con-
fiding in or consulting her—which was not entirely true. One day, soaking
our legs in the Sulphur Springs near Dehradun, I had told her of my decision.
She wanted no explanation, and simply said, 'All right.' When I told her that I
would come back to her, and she could later join me in the States, she replied
with a sense of resignation, 'We shall see.'

"In June, I was on a TWA flight to Paris and New York. I had a premoni-
tion that my break with India was now final. In another few weeks, Beena left
for Benares Hindu University to read philosophy. We never met again."

∗   ∗   ∗

In the United States, Brijen was drawn into Quaker circles, as well as to the
left-wing intellectuals and activists associated with the Catholic Worker
movement. But the tension between political engagement and spiritual withdrawal remained unresolved and became central to conversations Brijen had
with Merton, whom he met in 1965. Both men were concerned with the "gap
between thought and action."[15] Like Brijen, Merton pondered the relationship between religious traditions, East and West, only to come up against
their "essential difference." For Merton, the Christian view that Christ is at
the center of all reality, "a source of grace and life," and that God is love, could
not be reconciled with the Hindu view that "God is void," though he would
foster interfaith dialogue with a passion that Brijen could not share.[16] Moreover, both Brijen and Merton were deeply influenced by the Catholic Worker
movement and preoccupied by the systemic racial violence and social injus-
tice in America, as well as the war in Vietnam. How could one bring together
a monastic life on the edge of the polis (*atopos*) and an active life within it?[17]

During a year of reflection at Pendle Hill,[18] with weekly breaks to attend
a seminar on Arnold Toynbee in New York City,[19] Brijen's interest in the relationship of "withdrawal" and "return" was sharpened by Toynbee's ideas, by
conversations with Dorothy Day, and by his reading of Thomas Merton's
recently published *The Sign of Jonas*. Later, he would fall back on Arthur
Koestler's contrast between "change from without" and "change from within,"
and Bernard McGinn's contrast between "flight" and "commitment," to
articulate this struggle to be a "hermit in the water of life."[20]

This struggle also arose from Brijen's relationship with his homeland.

"After Yale, I made a quick trip to India to visit my parents and Radhakrishnan. Radhakrishnan was quite upset at my plans. He called me something of an aimless wanderer, dismissed me uncharacteristically without offering a meal, and I do not think he ever replied to my notes thereafter or agreed to see me again. His son Sarvepalli Gopal, a distinguished historian, also grew quite hostile to me over the years and berated me at two conferences. I have already told you that I had lost Beena's friendship a year earlier, though had gained Bharati's.

"By the summer of 1954, I realized that my ties to India—to family, friends, politics, and philosophy—were attenuating and changing. [A. J.] Muste and Scott Buchanan[21] had replaced Radhakrishnan. The Labor Action crowd of Irving Howe, Lewis Coser, Hal Draper, and Michael Harrington had replaced my socialist friends in India. Likewise, the troubled Bayard Rustin. And in a superficial sense, Dorothy Day and the Catholic Worker, Muste, and Liberal Quakers had taken the place of Mother Anandamayi. Why I hung around Muste and Dorothy Day remains an unexplained mystery to me. Their mysticism was Christ-centered, and their faith in Christianity unshakeable. Yet here I was, totally rejecting Christianity and Christ. Though I had utopian ideals, the Kingdom of Heaven was not one of them.

"September found me settled in a cozy little room at Pendle Hill. Henry Cadbury and Howard Brinton were also in residence; Gilbert Kilpack and Peter Docili ran the 'academic' curriculum. Every morning there was an hour of silent worship. I found these times greatly strengthening. Peter introduced me to Simone Weil and her pamphlet on the *Iliad*, published under the Pendle Hill imprint in 1956. My commitment to peace and pacifism grew even stronger, and I not only extended the frontiers of my knowledge but experienced greater peace with myself. I felt that I was destined to establish a new Pendle Hill—not a transient but a permanent intentional community, without the academic rigors of an Institute for Advanced Study and faithful to Martin Buber's vision."

During his year at Pendle Hill, Brijen had come across Karl Marx's *Economic and Philosophic Manuscripts of 1844* and Ludwig Feuerbach's *The Essence of Christianity*. These books confirmed his view that industrial societies create an alienated man, and unless human beings returned to what Ralph Borsodi called romantic agrarianism, what Gandhi called rural socialism, or what Buber envisaged in the Israeli kibbutz, humanity was doomed to a culture of internecine violence.

*   *   *

My conversations with Brijen brought me to consider two paradoxes, the first pertaining to our relationship, the second arising from his autobiographical reflections. I was struck by the difficulty, if not impossibility, of converting an asymmetrical relationship into a symmetrical one—a mentor, teacher, or parent becoming a friend. Though Brijen and I considered each other close friends, we never became true equals. He treated me like an adopted son, with compassion but condescension, and I looked up to him as a father figure. That is to say, we invoked friendship as others might invoke kinship, not as a synonym for altruism and goodwill but as a metaphor for deep and inextinguishable affection.

As for Brijen's idealization of friendship as a basis for *communitas*, my ethnographic work taught me how difficult it is to organize a community along egalitarian lines, though it is ritually and occasionally possible to create the semblance of unanimity. Social organization requires a division of labor, as well as hierarchies, however transitory, based on competence and skill. Even when inequalities of wealth and power are minimized, differences of talent, attraction, and temperament remain. This partial incompatibility of collective and personal goals may explain Brijen's lifelong vacillation between disenchantment with the world and an engagement with it.

This "dialectic between withdrawal and return, flight and commitment," has always been, as Bernard McGinn observes, "an essential element in the history of the monastic movement,"[22] and I once asked Brijen if he could help me understand why he had been so attracted by ashrams, Quaker retreats, and places of peaceable community, yet had thrown himself so vigorously into the struggle for civil rights and social justice. "Would it be true to say," I asked, "that you often found the polis to be exhausting, corrupt, and disillusioning, and that, despite your commitment to improving the state of the world, you have recoiled at times and sought refuge among close friends or in solitude?"

Brijen's response was to draw my attention to Koestler's famous essay "The Yogi and the Commissar," in which Koestler uses the image of the light spectrum to account for "all possible human attitudes to life." At the infrared end, the figure of the commissar exemplifies a commitment to *change from without*. He is the revolutionary for whom all means, fair and foul, are justified in realizing his vision of a brave new world. At the opposite, ultraviolet end of the spectrum, where the waves are short and of such high frequency that they cannot be seen, crouches the yogi, who believes that little can be accomplished by willful and worldly striving. In seeking *change from within*, he distances himself from the public realm in order to make possible a mergence with "the universal and cosmic all-one." "It is easy to say," writes Koestler, "that all that is wanted is a synthesis—the synthesis between saint and revolutionary—but so far this has never been achieved. What has been achieved are various motley forms of compromise . . . but not synthesis. Apparently, the two elements do not mix, and this may be one of the reasons why we have made such a mess of our History."[23]

A synthesis between personal and political friendship is equally difficult to achieve. Hannah Arendt argued that love tends to be so personal and jealous that it is incompatible with the *amor mundi* (love of the world) that is the essence of the political.[24] Like Aristotle, but unlike Montaigne, she believed that friendship was different from love, even going so far as to say that one can love a person but not a people. But if love cannot overcome differences and build community, can friendship fare any better? Ironically, Arendt seems to have shared with Theodor Adorno (whom she intensely disliked) a commitment to friendship as a medium for intellectual dialogue and for arriving at binding common knowledge, rather than a mode of subjective and sympathetic attunement. In the light of her deep feelings for her friends, one wonders why she developed a theory of friendship that made no reference to them, and why she regarded subjectivity and love so ambivalently.[25]

Just as Arendt was ambivalent about "love" and "friendship,"[26] so, in the discourse of the nation-state, do the familial concepts of care, civility, and compassion become entangled with political ideas of law and order—hence our vacillation between desiring a strong leader and our insistence that said leader must show love, by hugging and comforting the victims of a natural disaster, kissing babies, or calling on citizens to come together in the name of the common good.

The fact is that the semantic ambiguity of "love" and "friendship" reflects the existential complexity of what Arendt called "the human condition." Our very existence is, at once, contingent on exclusive relationships with people we think of as family or friends and on inclusive relations with people we identify collectively as neighbors, fellow citizens, and members of our tribe, our faith, or our ethnic group, not all of whom we necessarily feel emotionally close to or connected with. This paradox of pluralism can never be resolved, as it is neither a political nor logical problem but reflects the inherent ambiguity of being human—possessing traits unique to ourselves and traits we share with others.

Walt Whitman begins his "Song of Myself" by celebrating the life of an author who "dotes" on himself only to propose that "every atom belonging to me as good belongs to you." Whitman avers that his thoughts "are really the thoughts of all men in all ages and lands, they are not original with me." "Do I contradict myself?" he asks. "Very well, then I contradict myself, I am large, I contain multitudes."[27]

Brijen Gupta contained multitudes. The various elements did not always coexist harmoniously within him, but he refused to suppress any one of them. I like to think that when Brijen was honored with the India Community Center of Rochester (NY)'s first award for lifetime achievement in 1997, it was not only for his financial and personal gifts to this community, or even for his efforts as a social activist over many years, but for a humanitarianism that was realized through direct engagement rather than extolled as a set of precepts to which lip service alone was due—a humanism born of a struggle to reconcile spiritual and political passions—the hermit and the water of life made one.

CHAPTER 3

No Man Is an Island

I am in the Kuranko village of Kondembaia, northern Sierra Leone. Night has fallen, and a group of men, women, and children have crowded into the parlor of a mudbrick house, waiting for the storyteller to spin his first tale. The smell of sweat, the sound of a crying baby, and an excited clamor fill the room. A single hurricane lamp illuminates expectant faces but fails to penetrate the shadows. A man behind me orders a small boy to give me more space. He refuses to budge.

Tonight, the indefatigable Keti Ferenke Koroma will recount a story about friendship (*dianye* or *kentiye*). While *dianye* may be translated as "amity," it is used in a variety of contexts to connote fellowship, conviviality, and even a marital alliance between two lineages. *Dian'morgoye* implies trust and transparency between people. As such, it exemplifies personhood (*morgoye*), for unless people are open with one another, sociality risks being subverted by backbiting, malicious gossip, rumormongering, and the nefarious forces of witchcraft and sorcery. To be transparent (*gbe*, literally "white" or "clear") and straight (*telne*) is nowhere more vital than between friends. As Ferenke frequently explained to me, friendships are chosen, by contrast with kinship which is prescribed, and deciding to behave well is more crucial to the viability of a community than passive conformity to custom. Exercising judgment and not being deceived or distracted by appearances are, in Ferenke's opinion, the essence of social and moral intelligence (*hankilimaiye*).

But what if intelligence is as unequally distributed in a community as power and wealth? Ferenke's answer echoes Karl Marx's famous 1875 dictum "From each according to his ability, to each according to his needs." The possession of material or symbolic capital can only be justified if used for the good of all rather than personal advantage. In the same way, one's own intellectual acuity should, ideally, compensate for its absence in others. A friend in need is a friend indeed.

The first story Ferenke tells this night begins, like many Kuranko tales, with a dilemma. A certain woman declared that she would only marry a man who was her intellectual equal. Whenever a suitor came to her village, she would contrive to do something to baffle him, then demand that he explain her action. Several years passed, and numerous suitors sought her hand in marriage, but none passed her test.

A man in a remote village heard of this woman and became fascinated to meet her. Asking his closest friend to accompany him, he journeyed to the woman's village. On the very night that the two friends arrived, the woman instructed her younger sister to take a calabash of rice to the strangers. On top of the rice, the woman placed a red kola nut. The two friends ate the rice.

On the following night, the woman sent another calabash of rice, this time with a white kola nut on top. Though the man's friend was mystified and anxious, the man assured him that he knew what was going on.

The next night, the calabash of rice had three bones on top of it, and the lip of the calabash had been broken. The man's friend was now afraid and did not want to eat the rice, but the man assured him that everything was all right, and he took the bones and put them in his pocket.

The following evening the man told his friend that he was going to sleep with the woman. "But she has not sent word for you to come," the friend said.

The man assured his friend that he knew what he was doing and set off to find the woman's house.

A high fence surrounded the compound, which was guarded by three dogs. The dogs ran at the man, baring their fangs and barking, but he tossed them the bones and they fell quiet. Now he was faced with several houses, all much alike. One, however, had a clay porch that had been eroded by rain and resembled the broken lip of the calabash.

It was dark inside the house, and several people were sleeping there. The man noticed that one woman was covered with a country-cloth blanket. He went and sat beside her. She woke but pretended to be asleep. Only at dawn did the man announce himself and explain how he had interpreted the kola nuts on the rice she had sent for him and his friend every evening. The red kola signified that she was menstruating, the white kola signified that her period had passed, the chipped calabash helped identify her house, and the bones were to quiet the dogs. The woman was impressed and declared that she had finally found a husband worthy of her.

But now the man needed bridewealth, so he and his friend set off in search of it.

They soon arrived in a village where, according to rumor, the chief had sequestered his daughter in a special house with three locked doors that he alone could open. Before presenting himself to the chief, the man put his friend in a hamper and told him not to move or speak until he was inside the girl's house. The man told the chief that the hamper contained kola nuts and he asked the chief to keep it in a safe place while he went in search of more kola.

No sooner had the hamper been stowed in the girl's house than the man's friend called to her to untie him.

Each evening, when the chief brought food for his daughter, the young man hid in the hamper. When the chief had gone, the young couple ate and spent the night together. Five months passed. The girl was now pregnant and the man who had gone in search of kola returned and asked the chief for his hamper. When the chief went to fetch it, his daughter implored him to allow her to walk out into the daylight. Only then did the chief see that she was pregnant. He was now faced with a dilemma, for if people saw her condition, their only conclusion could be that the chief had sequestered his daughter so that she could not see other men and that he had impregnated her. The clever man seized the moment. Addressing the entire village, he said, "Chief, you have done something no other man in the world has ever done. Your grandfather married your grandmother and begat your father. Your father married your mother and begat you. Then you married and bore this child. How can you now say that she can never marry or have children? I have never heard of such a thing. This is the reason I put my friend in the hamper and pretended it contained kola nuts. I entrusted it to you for safekeeping. It was my friend who made your daughter pregnant."

The chief was overjoyed to have escaped disgrace.

So, both men got wives, though without the cleverness of the first man, the second would not have succeeded. That is why, if you are clever and have a friend who is not as clever as you, you should not look down on your friend or laugh at his misfortune but help him in whatever way you can.

Two months after recording this story, I returned to Kondembaia. Ferenke's house was in the middle of the village, overshadowed by an immense cotton tree that had grown from a palisade built to protect the community after the depredations of the Maninka warlord Samori Turé in the 1880s. Samori's scorched-earth policy left the village in ruins, with scores of villagers dead. One hundred years later, in 1998, the village was sacked and burned to the ground by the Revolutionary United Front (RUF). When I visited Kondem-baia a decade later and several years after Ferenke's death, the two great cotton trees that people once spoke of as husband and wife were dying. No trace of Ferenke's house remained, but a commemorative stone marked the grave of the forty men, women, and children murdered by the RUF in a single day.

As I recall the afternoon in 1970 when I recorded Ferenke's second story about friendship, I marvel that, at that time, I discerned no connection between the violent events of the past and the violent events recounted in the tale. Nor did I see the poetic irony that, while the first story—recorded in the dead of night—presented friendship idealistically, the second, which was recorded in the light of day, revealed its shadow side.

In this story, the two protagonists are close friends. They bear the same name—Momori—and conscientiously share the profits from their joint trad-ing ventures. When it comes time for them to marry, however, they discover they have only enough bridewealth for one wife. They, therefore, decide to share the same woman. When this arrangement proves untenable, the first friend, whose name is Gbekeyan ("Pure-hearted") Momori, generously gives the woman to his namesake, declaring that if their trading is successful, they will soon have enough money to pay bridewealth for a second wife. But the second Momori schemes with his wife to kill Pure-hearted Momori and steal the money they have made. One day, traveling far from their village, they ambush Pure-hearted Momori, pin him to the ground, gouge out his eyes, and leave him for dead among some rocks. Despite being blinded, Pure-hearted Momori manages to drag himself into the shade of a great cotton tree where, it so happens, an old hyena and an old vulture meet each evening to share news of what they have seen and done during the day. Pure-hearted Momori overhears their conversation, in which the vulture confides to the hyena that it has laid a sixth egg in its nest, and that whoever breaks any of these eggs will have his wishes fulfilled. In turn, the hyena describes how, earlier that day, a young man was beaten and blinded beneath the tree and left to die. "Too bad that young man is not here now," he says, "because if he was, I could tell him that if he bathed his eyes in the sap of this tree, he would recover his sight."

The following morning, as soon as the hyena and the vulture have gone on their way, Pure-hearted Momori takes a stone, dashes it against the tree, and bathes his eyes with the sap that issues from the cut. He then climbs the tree and takes three of the vulture's eggs. After a long journey into an unfa-miliar land, Pure-hearted Momori breaks one of the eggs and wishes for a large town to appear. He breaks the second egg and wishes to be made chief of the town. Then he breaks the third egg and wishes to become the wealthiest man in that land. In the years that follow, he marries many wives, has many children, and prospers.

As for the other Momori and his wife, they fall on hard times. Their luck runs out and their ventures fail. But one day, hearing of a great chief who rules a distant town and possesses immense wealth, they decide to beg him for help. It takes them two days to reach the town, and two more days before the chief grants them an audience. Despite their ragged clothes and woeful appearance, the chief thinks he recognizes the couple, and he gives them lodgings in the house next to his own and orders that they be fed and given new clothes.

That night, when the town is asleep, the chief goes to the house in which he has lodged his guests. The man and his wife are afraid of the chief, and their fear only increases when he asks them to recount the story of their misfortunes. In telling their story, they pretend that Pure-hearted Momori died of natural causes. The chief then retells their story, describing what really happened. Realizing the identity of the chief, the man falls to the ground in terror. As he and his wife prostrate themselves before the chief and plead for forgiveness, Pure-hearted Momori says, "I never showed you anything but goodwill. That is the nature of friendship. In giving goodwill, you deserve to receive it in return. And so, tomorrow, I will divide my chiefdom into two. I will rule one half, and you the other. We will share everything, just as we did in the past."

No sooner does the chief return to his house than the man and his wife begin wondering how the chief became so wealthy in the first place. As dawn breaks, they go to Pure-hearted Momori's house and ask him how he became so rich and powerful. When the chief tells them about the hyena and the vulture, they waste no time in going to the place where they ambushed and blinded Pure-hearted Momori so many years ago. The man finds the three remaining vulture's eggs and asks his wife what he should wish for. She tells him to use the first egg to get a large town in which to live. With the second egg, she says he should wish for a great river, since one cannot live without water. With the third egg, she says he should wish for her family to become wealthy, as a man with rich in-laws will want for nothing. What happens, however, is that the man's own family becomes impoverished, and the woman's family takes her away from him, and he is left with nothing.

This story of two young men who appear to have each other's best interests at heart suggests that our private and public lives are inextricably connected.

The flaws in our characters will produce fault lines in our lifeworlds, and corruption in the body politic will have destructive repercussions in the lives of individuals. But if, as Ferenke argues, friends complete or complement each other, this will set an example and help build a community in which each person makes good what others lack.

I included these stories in my *Allegories of the Wilderness*, and although the book was not published until 1982, it was written during the 1970s, when I lived in the Manawatu region of Aotearoa New Zealand. At this time, my wife and I were friends with several Dutch, Norwegian, and Hungarian expatriates, and we often spent weekends together at a lodge in the Ruahine ranges. We would go for long bushwalks every day, and one evening, after a meal, we sat around an open fire and told stories. One story struck a chord with me and echoed Ferenke's stories about friendship.

Our friend Joost had survived the Japanese invasion of Java in February 1942. As a paramedic, he knew that everyone's chances of survival depended on a collective understanding that the healthy would care for the sick and, in return, they could expect to receive care when, as was inevitable, they fell ill and could not care for themselves. "It was not a question of putting yourself in the place of another," Joost explained, "or sacrificing yourself for the common good, or even being responsible for your fellow men. It was a practical question of survival. If the healthy took care of the sick, everyone's chance of survival would, in the long run, be enhanced." Several prisoners rejected Joost's counsel and, as he had predicted, those who decided to take their lives into their own hands, confident in their individual stamina and will, were those who perished. Most of those who were prepared to help others in need were helped in their own hour of need, and lived. "But even those who helped others and later died could be said to have lived," Joost said, "because they had retained their humanity to the last."

CHAPTER 4

Friendships in the Field

For many years, I have wanted to write about my friendship with Noah Marah without, whose help I would not have been able to record or transcribe the stories of Keti Ferenke Koroma. Indeed, without Noah, my first fieldwork would have been impossible, and my career as an anthropologist might never have got off the ground. Our relationship spanned more than three decades— from our initial meeting in late 1969 to the days we spent together in Freetown only three weeks before his untimely death in 2003. Our friendship flourished, however, only after he ceased working for me and my trips to West Africa became more focused on spending time with my Sierra Leone peers than pursuing anthropological research.

In Shakespeare's *A Midsummer Night's Dream*, the character of Lysander rues the fact that "the course of true love never did run smooth." The same could be said of friendship, the course of which is interrupted by misunderstandings, fallings-out, and long separations. Few friendships last a lifetime. That my friendship with Noah not only survived for as long as it did but deepened with the passing years suggests that undergoing adversity together may reinforce a friendship as much as, if not more than, sharing a common world. Accordingly, I have to go back to before Noah and I first met—to the Congo in 1964—in order to illuminate the history of our friendship and the colonial epoch that foreshadowed it.

Léopoldville, 1964. The storms come up from the south. By midafternoon, anvil-topped thunderheads tower over the city. The air is charged with electricity. You hear thunder far off. Then the sky is torn apart by lightning, making you cringe. With the first spattering of rain, you smell asphalt and earth. As it pelts down, people run for cover under the mango trees along the Avenue Valcke, and cars slow to a crawl along the flooded Boulevard du Trente Juin.

I buy a copy of *Le Progrès* outside the Café Léopold II. The boy at the news stand has lost most of his fingers to leprosy. A burnt-out case. Luckily for him, the soaring inflation rate has made coins superfluous. He holds a grubby wad of ten-franc notes between the stumps of his fingers and palm, and with the knuckles of his other hand, feeds me my change.

The café smells of sweat and rain. I take a seat by the door, order a Primus beer, and spread the newspaper open on the table so I can scan the headlines. "Rebels Northeast of Léopoldville . . . Bolobo and Mushie Isolated . . . Ranger VII Takes Photographs of the Moon." These events feel equally remote.

The waiter sets down a bottle of beer, capped with an upturned tumbler. He looks perplexed, like *le Premier ministre*, M. Moïse Tshombe.

"C'est vrai ce qu'on dit—qu'il faut que les blancs partent?"

"Only the families of UN personnel," I say. "And only women and children."

"You are not afraid to stay, monsieur?"

"With the National Congolese Army to protect us, how could one possibly be afraid?"

It's the kind of cynical bravado everyone cultivates now. Though I still surprise myself that I go along with it.

*   *   *

I saw Marthe this morning at Le Royal—the apartment building that serves as the United Nations (UN) headquarters in Léopoldville. Marthe has developed several marketing cooperatives throughout the country. How many have survived Pierre Mulele's incursions in Moyen Congo, Gaston Soumialot's invasion of North Katanga, and General François Olenga's rebellion in Kivu is anyone's guess. For more than a month, it has been dangerous to travel outside the provincial cities. Stacks of paper projects collect dust in the Département des Affaires Sociales. Haitian stenographers file their fingernails and stifle yawns as UN heads confer in closed meetings. At midday, the UN-subsidized PX store is packed with UN personnel spending their per diems on packets of Camel cigarettes, sixpacks of Budweiser, and bottles of Glenfiddich. By six o'clock in the evening, when the curfew begins, all have retreated into the hill suburbs, white Peugeots parked behind padlocked gates.

When I see Marthe at the end of the corridor gesturing angrily, my first thought is that she has once again been refused permission to travel to Kivu and check on her community development projects there. But when I get close enough to hear what she is saying to the UNRRA office staff, I learn that she has been ordered to prepare for evacuation.

"I am nobody's wife. I am not a child. I am not a dependent," she rails. "I have been here since sixty-two. I do not need *une petite vacance*! It's an outrage. It's discrimination!" Catching sight of me, she demands, "What do you think?"

If anyone should be flown back to Europe, it should be me. I haven't created a single community development scheme—not even on paper. Nor am I likely to do so, even if the national Congolese army, inspired by the optimistic pronouncements of its high command, succeeds in crushing the rebellion. I spend most of my time in my hotel by the river, reading and translating Blaise Cendrars.

"What can one do?" I say. "*C'est le Congo.*"

Marthe is incensed. "*Ce n'est pas le Congo. C'est New York!*"

*   *   *

In colonial times, Parcembise was Léopoldville's elite neighborhood. The streets are shaded by jacarandas. Villas are enclosed by high walls, topped with broken glass and barbed wire. Behind wrought iron gates, guard dogs bark ferociously at Congolese passing up and down the street. The air is scented with frangipani and bougainvillea.

On the street door to Marthe's apartment building is a sign—*Attention au Chien Méchant!* As I unlock the door, I half expect an Alsatian to leap at my throat. But the lobby is deserted.

It has only been two days since Marthe left, yet already her apartment smells moldy. I drop my duffle bag on the parquet and look around. There are two paintings propped against the bookcase. Touristshop art. Wiry African figures strolling through a forest clearing. A fisherman in a pirogue on the river. Maybe she intended to take the paintings back to Europe as gifts for her family. Then I remember, she doesn't have any family.

On the dining table is a bunch of keys, a note telling me to make myself at home, and a ledger in which I am to keep a record of payments to Albert, her "houseboy." She has also left me a photocopied file of documents that date back to colonial times—official wage rates for domestic servants. It amuses me that despite her hurried departure, Marthe found time to respond to my misgivings about paying Albert the equivalent of twenty dollars a month.

Waiting for him to turn up, I go out onto the balcony. In the square, there is a boulangerie called Le Coq Hardy. All the other shops are boarded up. I am having second thoughts about moving out of my hotel. I am going to miss the river and its floating islands of hyacinth, the OTRACO river boats such as Joseph Conrad may have captained, beached and derelict beside the ferry landing, and the distant roar of the Livingstone rapids in the night. I regret having let Marthe talk me into living in her apartment and taking care of it while she is away. And the prospect of dealing with Albert unnerves me.

Marthe's "boy" is old enough to be my father. In fact, one of the first things he tells me when I ask him about his family and where he lives is that he has two sons about my age in the army. He is worried about them. They are stationed in Kamina, defending the town and airstrip against Soumialot's guerillas.

"*C'est loin, Kamina,*" he says, making Kamina sound like a synonym for loss.

As he moves toward the kitchen, I follow and stand in the doorway while he rummages in a closet for his bucket, mop, and detergent.

"Look, Albert," I say, "I'm not sure I really need a servant. I mean, I can't have you doing all my menial tasks for me. I thought it might suit us both if maybe you came here once or twice a week, just to put in an appearance. . . ."

"But Madame Haedens said I should come every day."

"But why? There's nothing for you to do. If you come every day, we'll get in each other's way and feel uncomfortable.

"And another thing, if I'm going to call you by your first name, you must call me by mine. I can't have you calling me monsieur. My name is Michael."

"*Oui,* Monsieur Michel."

"And there's the question of your wage. I've already told Madame Haedens that I cannot agree to pay you only a thousand francs a month."

Albert stands with his arms by his sides, rigid and startled, as if posing for a photograph. I try to hide my irritation.

"I want to pay you three thousand francs a month. But I want us to keep the arrangement to ourselves. I'll pay you on the 25th of each month, like Madame Haedens, but I'll enter only a thousand francs in the ledger so that everything will be *en règle.* Is that okay?"

Albert picks up the bucket and tilts it under the tap.

"*Oui,* Monsieur Michel," he says, and starts running water into the bucket.

Driving back to the apartment for lunch, I am flagged down by the Belgian driver of a refrigerated meat van. He's had a tire puncture and asks if I can keep an eye on his vehicle while he walks to the Total service station for help.

"No problem," I say, and park my jeep about twenty meters behind him.

No sooner has he disappeared up the road than people converge on the meat van from all directions. They saunter around it, kick at the flat tire, and inspect the padlocks on the back doors.

It is as though I am invisible. One guy breaks open the padlocks with a jimmy. Another positions a jack under the rear axle. Have they been lying in wait all morning, equipped with these tools, expecting such a windfall? Or has all this been carefully planned—sixinch nails strewn on the road and a team of helpers?

The metal doors are flung open. Men, women, and children clamber up and begin handing down carcasses. People hack up the meat with pangas. Everyone is laughing.

Before long, people with headloads of meat are filing away over the open fields, vanishing as quickly as they came. As for the truck, its axles are chocked up on hunks of wood, and a group of men are bowling the tires away down a muddy track.

I switch on the jeep's ignition, jolt back onto the road, and accelerate past the stranded truck.

* * *

"Albert," I announce, "I'm going to make *you* lunch today. Give me your apron." Nonplussed, he unties his apron and hands it to me, then stands aside as I peel and slice potatoes for *frites* and crush garlic and black pepper for the *entrecôte* steaks.

He says, "It isn't right, Monsieur Michel."

I push past him to get the lettuce and tomatoes out of the fridge.

He says, "What is there for me to do?"

"Put a record on."

"Which one, Monsieur Michel?"

"You choose."

Albert puts on a rumba called "Nabanda Kala."

I set two places at the table and open two bottles of beer.

"*Bon appétit!*" I say, ignoring Albert's disgruntled expression.

"*Bon appétit*," Albert mumbles, and sits down.

I ask him if he has always worked as a houseboy.

"Always," he says.

"Always for whites?"

He looks at me guardedly.

"You don't regard such work as beneath a man's dignity, as women's work?" I ask.

"Some people say that."

"Do you like the work? Is it hard to find work like this?"

"One is lucky to have work. Times are hard, Monsieur Michel. Everything costs. Everyone suffers. It is not a question of what one wants to do. It is a question of survival."

"Have things changed much since Independence?"

"What things, Monsieur Michel?"

"The way people treat their servants, for example."

"Sometimes people are kind, sometimes they make life very hard for you."

"And Madame Haedens, is she kind?"

"Madame Haedens, yes, she is very kind."

"In what way?"

"She gives me clothes for my wife. She gives us food. Sometimes she gives me a box of cigars."

Albert sips his beer.

"You're not eating," I say.

"I am sorry, Monsieur Michel, but I am not hungry."

"Does it bother you that I serve you lunch?"

"Yes, monsieur, it bothers me."

"Why?"

"It is not right."

"But you can't *always* be a servant, Albert. Isn't that what independence means—becoming your own master?"

"It is true what you say, but porcupine can't teach pangolin to climb trees."

"I didn't know porcupines could climb trees."

Albert begins to clear the table—his uneaten *entrecôte* and *frites*, his salad, and glass of beer.

"Am I the pangolin or the porcupine?" I ask.

"You confuse me, Monsieur Michel," Albert says, and pads out to the kitchen in his bare feet.

*   *   *

A *carte postale* arrives from Geneva:

> The newspaper headlines here would make you think the entire
> Congo is a bloodbath. I'm still trying to persuade those imbeciles in
> New York that it is perfectly safe for me to return. I hope you are
> enjoying your *petit séjour* in my apartment and that all is well.
>   Say *bonjour* to Albert for me.
>   *Cordialement*,
>   Marthe.

I have bought an alarm clock so I can wake at six and do all the housework
before Albert turns up at seven thirty. When he arrives, I follow him into the
kitchen and wait while he disentangles himself from his string bags and unfolds
the scrap of paper on which he has written the cost of the fresh vegetables.

He gives me my change, then puts the vegetables in the refrigerator. He
appears more subdued than usual.

"Have you heard from your sons?"

"They say the army is regrouping."

Both of us know this really means the army is retreating.

"I received a postcard yesterday from Madame Haedens. She says to
greet you."

"Is she well?"

"Yes, she is well."

"I hope she comes back soon."

Albert unstraps his sandals and pushes them out of the way. He takes his
mauve apron from behind the door and ties it around his waist. I follow him
as he pads around the apartment.

I have waxed the parquet so well that I have to tread carefully. Albert's
bare feet give him a firm grip. He checks the bathroom. It is spotless. He
looks into my bedroom. The window is open, the bed made without a crease.

"Everything is very clean and tidy," Albert observes.

I seize my chance. "You see, Albert, how pointless it is you making
this long journey here every day. Wouldn't you prefer being at home with
your wife?"

"My work is here, Monsieur Michel. I do not want to be at home with
my wife."

*　*　*

A night of torrential rain. I sit at the dining table, working on my translation of Blaise Cendrars's *Moravagine*:

> I don't believe there are any literary subjects, or rather that there is only one: man.
>
> But which man? The man who writes, of course. There is no other subject possible.
>
> Who is he? In any event it's not me, it is the Other. "*I am the Other*," Gérard de Nerval writes under one of the very rare photographs of himself.
>
> But who is this other?
>
> Doesn't much matter. You meet someone by chance and never see him again. One fine day this guy resurfaces in your consciousness and screws you around for ten years. It's not always someone memorable; he can be colorless and without character.
>
> This is what happened to me with Mister X—Moravagine. I wanted to start writing. He had taken my place. He was there, installed deep down in me, as in an armchair. I shook him, struggled with him, he didn't want to trade places.
>
> He seemed to say, "I'm here and here I stay!" It was terrible. I began to notice that this Other was appropriating everything that had happened in my life, assuming character traits I thought of as my own. My thoughts, my favorite studies, my tastes, everything converged on him, belonged to him, nourished him. At great cost to myself, I fed and nurtured a parasite. In the end I no longer knew which of us was copying the other. He took trips in my place. He made love instead of me. But he never possessed any real identity, for each of us was himself, me and the Other. Tragic tête-à-tête.
>
> Which is why one can write but one book, or the same book again and again. It's why all good books are alike.
>
> They are all autobiographical. It's why there is only one literary subject: man.
>
> It's why there is only one literature: that of this man, this Other, the one who writes.

The *portefenêtre* is open. The night smells of decaying foliage and rain. Above the noise of the rain, I hear snatches of a Françoise Hardy song.

Plaintive. Remote. Someone in a nearby apartment has been playing it all evening.

I shove my books and papers aside. Who is playing this record? Why the same song over and over again?

The next morning, Albert doesn't turn up. I wait until midday, then drive to Nyanza.

The *cité indigène* is a labyrinth. Shanties made of mud bricks, beaten sheets of tin, palm fronds and packing cases. The pulse and jangle of highlife. Young men in dark glasses staring. When I ask, "Is this Nyanza?," they smile. A woman sidles up to me and urges me to go back—it is dangerous for me here. I press on, followed by children begging for coins.

Sweat is trickling down my rib cage. I curse the heat, the potholes into which I stumble, the children pursuing me.

"Fiche-moi le camp!"

My voice is cracked and feeble. The crowd of children is not following me now; it is moving ahead of me like a wave.

When I finally locate Albert's house, he is waiting outside, as though word of my coming had already reached him. His face is contorted with anger.

Then I realize he is looking past me, at the children. Brusquely, he raises his arm and shouts something at them in Lingala. They shamble a few yards back and stop.

"White men never come here," Albert says.

"Is this your house?" I ask.

He pushes aside the plastic strips in the doorway and gestures for me to go inside. "It is a poor man's house," he says, "but you are welcome."

The darkness blinds me.

"You have come a long way, Monsieur Michel," Albert says.

"I wanted to see where you live."

I stand nervously in the middle of the room, trying to get accustomed to the gloom.

Albert indicates that I should sit down on the battered sofa against the wall. Then he goes to the backyard and says something to a woman sitting there. The woman immediately picks up a scrap of tin and starts fanning the embers between the hearth stones.

When Albert returns, he sits opposite me on a folding metal chair but keeps glancing toward the back door. I direct my gaze to the photographs on the wall and the glassfronted cabinet containing candles, bunches of native tobacco, plates, and cutlery.

"My wife will bring tea," Albert explains.

She enters the room with her eyes lowered and hands me a thermos of tea. She has pulled her *lapa* over her breasts before entering the room. I put a sugar cube and some evaporated milk in the cup she gives me. She holds the box of sugar cubes in front of me, as if I should take more. I shake my head, and she leaves the room without having spoken a word.

"Where is your cup?" I ask Albert.

"It is all right, Monsieur Michel."

He watches as I pour tea from the thermos.

"Albert," I begin, "I wanted to talk to you. . . ."

"*Ah bon*," he says, as though he has no idea why I have come.

"I missed you this morning. I thought you might be ill."

"There was something monsieur wanted me to do?"

"No, no. . . ."

"You have told me ever since you moved into Madame Haedens's apartment that I was not to come every day. . . ."

His eyes meet mine but betray nothing.

I dig into my pocket and pull out the plastic pouch of aromatic Dutch tobacco I bought in the PX.

"This is for you."

"That's very kind of you, Monsieur Michel."

He opens the pouch, sniffs the tobacco, and begins to fill his pipe.

"Are these your sons?" I ask, glancing at the photos of the somber men in battle dress.

"*Oui*, Monsieur Michel."

"Have you lived here long?" I ask.

"Since two years. I used to live in Kinshasa, but my wife felt that it was unsafe, so we moved here."

"It's safer here?"

He throws up his hands. "I am getting old. In a year or two I'll go back to my village. I'll quit work. I'll let my sons take care of me."

"Where is your village?"

"It is far."

"How far?" Albert lights his pipe but ignores my question. I sit down on the sofa again.

"I'd like to go with you sometime. I'd like to see your village. I'd like to see where you live."

Albert guides me out of the labyrinth of Nyanza to where I left my jeep. It's not there. Albert insists on searching up and down the Avenue Mahamba, but I tell him it is pointless.

I catch a minibus into the city and walk to the Nigerian police headquarters. The sergeant in the skyblue beret tells me I will have to make a written statement. He shows me into an air-conditioned room and gives me a form on which I am to describe the circumstances of the theft. When I have done this, I return the form to him.

He casts his eyes over it and frowns. "You have written your statement in English!"

"What else."

"Your carte d'identité says *Nationalité: Néo Zélandais.*"

"So?"

"So you have to write your statement in French."

"But English is my first language."

"You must write your statement in French. Those are the rules."

It takes me half an hour to complete my translation. The sergeant is satisfied. "We all have to follow the proper procedures," he explains, as he passes my statement to the police translator.

An hour later, the statement—now rendered into unreadable English—is returned to me for my signature.

At the Département des Affaires Sociales, the news is that Marthe is coming back.

I immediately move out of the apartment and return to my hotel. It is several days before I put in an appearance at Le Royal, to collect my mail.

There's a note from Marthe. She wants me to contact her urgently.

The following afternoon she tracks me down at the Café Léopold II.

"Michael!" she cries, and with the back of her hand bats aside the newspaper I'm reading. "What have you done to Albert?"

I open my mouth to say something.

"You've spoiled him completely! He won't do a thing I tell him. He turns up late in the morning. He demands more money. He looks as if I disgust him. What did you do to him while I was away?"

"I didn't *do* anything to him, Marthe. I paid him a little more than you do. I told you I'd probably do that. And I told him he didn't have to come to work every day. There was nothing for him to do."

"Nothing? The place is a pigsty! I knew I couldn't trust you. I knew this would happen if I went away."

"I paid Albert more because he needs the money. I went and saw where he lives. He and his wife don't even have a floor in their house. It's just linoleum over bare earth. . . ."

"Oh! He's actually seen how the natives live, has he?" She glances around as though she wants her sarcasm to reach every corner of the café. "What selfrighteousness! Do you think we can be laws unto ourselves? Is that your idea of a civilized world—everyone doing what they please?"

"This isn't a colonized country anymore, Marthe. You can't exploit peo—"

"Exploit! Don't be so naive! What did you hope to gain by your ridiculous performance? Did you think Albert would become your friend? Do you really think you know what he thinks and feels? Bullying him, blackmailing him, undermining his position. You call that equality!"

Marthe turns and walks away, and the whole café stares at me as if I owe them an apology too.

Chastened, I accept an assignment in Kasai. I drive down deserted roads, through brakes of elephant grass, the bush swathed in mist. I am now convinced that the UN's development program is little more than a new mask for what Joseph Conrad called Europe's "civilizing mission." Like his character Kurtz's vainglorious enterprise, it simply disguises and euphemizes Europe's longstanding desire to control Africa's wealth, and I find it hard to rid my mind of King Leopold II's savage dominion—the amputations and castrations as punishment, the millions enslaved or shot in the course of Belgium's quest for rubber, gum-opal, and ivory.

In Elizabethville, I check into the Hotel Léopold II, with its anachronistic balconies, dingy dining room, and Corinthian columns that recall a regime that has gone for good.

Over the city, heavy blue thunderheads are massing. People drift past me on their way to the market. A group of women move slowly down the center of the road, keening for the dead child they carry on a wooden litter.

As the first heavy drops of rain patter down through the pendulous flowers of the jacaranda trees, the storm light becomes tinged with lilac. I feel strangely free. As if the Congo's bloody struggle for independence has been, obliquely, my own.

But as with any revolution, the new is never ushered in without the old being ruthlessly attacked, cut out, and destroyed. For an individual, rebirth is both an ordeal to be endured and a death. Old ties are cast away; one turns one's back on one's parentage, one's childhood. Bridges are burned. There is no turning back. This is no less true for a country attempting to radically reinvent itself. The old must be erased if the new order is to arise. So declared Christopher Gbenye when he ordered the execution of everyone who was literate or had worked for the Belgians: "We must destroy what existed before, we must start again at zero with an ignorant mass."

This was the backdrop against which I began fieldwork in Sierra Leone five years after leaving the Congo, resolved not to change Africa but to be changed by it. But memories of Albert haunted me, and when I hired Noah to assist me in my research, I had no illusions about the pitfalls that lay ahead. My misadventure with Albert had taught me that hierarchy was incompatible with friendship. It had sensitized me to the trap of imagining that those who do our bidding without protest are not acting out of respect and affection but under duress. Yet there have been anthropologists who have convinced themselves that their servants were their friends, as if the inequality of wealth and power between them was no impediment to congeniality and trust. Hortense Powdermaker, for example, sings the praises of her field assistants, acknowledging that her research would have been impossible without their help, and referring to them as "alter egos" and "friends" whose relationships with her were informed by "a mutual liking, deep affection, and respect." These friendships lasted, she goes on to say, "whether or not we ever saw each other again." Aren't such comments a reflection of the anthropologist's indebtedness and gratitude to key informants? Isn't it a mistake to assume they reflect the informants' perception of the anthropologist?[1]

In the case of Noah and me, this social opacity prevented us from seeing beyond what we imagined to be common goals. When we first met, Noah was teaching at a district council school. After I explained that I was doing doctoral studies in anthropology at Cambridge and was hoping to write a book about the Kuranko, Noah's enthusiasm was immediate and overwhelming. He had often thought of writing something about his own society and was only too happy to assist me. Before the day was out, I found myself sitting on the porch of Noah's house, practicing Kuranko phrases of greeting and learning Kuranko kinship terms. As for actually using these greetings, this would prove as difficult as moving from a formal knowledge of the kinship system to a practical understanding of real-life relationships. In this way, our initial sense of common purpose soon became challenged by the incompatibility between the frenetic pace at which I tended to work (mindful of all I wanted to accomplish within a year) and Noah's laggardly pace (as if we had all the time in the world).

In a friendship, each person affirms a truth about the other. Sometimes this truth contradicts the story one has been telling oneself and may lead to self-understandings that could not have been attained alone. In the relationship of master and servant, by contrast, each gives the other a false impression. The passivity and subservience of the servant makes the master feel that everything he or she does is acceptable simply because it has positive repercussions for the master, whereas the power of the master puts the servant in the unenviable position of having to endure degradation if that servant is going to earn the pittance on which he or she depends to survive. Because neither Noah nor I wished to fall into this trap, my complete dependence on him as an interpreter and go-between and his dependence on me for a salary and help in studying for his general certificate of education became burdens that we found increasingly difficult to bear.

In referring to me as Noah's djinni, villagers may have perceived this double bind, for in return for help rendered, a djinni will take the life of someone you love. Noah's mother had similar misgivings, reminding him of what had happened to his father, who, in working for the colonial administration, became reviled by his own people.

Despite Noah's seeing me as his "hope" (*yugi*) and my academic future being in his hands, we were often at odds. I expected too much from him, and he set his own expectations too high. As the months wore on, Noah stopped studying for his general certificate exams and found excuses for not accompanying me into the field. Despite our liking for one another, I felt I was fast becoming Prospero to his Caliban.[2] Like the history of colonialism itself, which projected an image of itself as a civilizing mission based on paternal care for a benighted son only to degenerate into exploitation and enslavement, Prospero is the master of magical power, while Caliban is a victim of his base instincts.

Although this comparison with my relationship with Noah is exaggerated, we both struggled with the colonial past. Older villagers associated me with their erstwhile masters, and anthropology itself was still informed by the assumption that European epistemologies were superior to African ones. As for Noah, his beloved father had spent his entire life working for the British, which partly explains why he tended to place his hope in others rather than in himself.

The tension between Noah and me was exacerbated by another issue. If, as John 15:15 explains, knowledge is kept for oneself and not shared with others, it perpetuates a relationship of inequality, as between master and servant. Friendship involves sharing knowledge (in the biblical context, knowledge of God). But while my knowledge of the Kuranko would be assimilated to the jargon of anthropology and circulate within the academic world, the proper use of that knowledge was as a "tool for conviviality" and not to be converted into a commodity that profited one person at the expense of others. Yet, as Noah himself would repeatedly tell me, my work *did* benefit the Kuranko, whether in the form of my so-called "*ferensola* book"[3] that helped the Kuranko in their bid for political representation in the 1977 elections, in my archive of oral traditions and folktales, or in the stipend I continued to pay Noah for many years and that I later paid his sons and grandsons, enabling them to receive the university education of which Noah once dreamed.

In friendship, what is good for oneself is supposedly good for the other. But this ideal of mutuality is never wholly achieved. Sometimes, one friend is the beneficiary of the relationship; sometimes, the other, as in Ferenke's story of the two friends (Chapter 3). At any moment in any friendship, one person will have more than the other, and the spirit of amity consists in making good this imbalance. As Ferenke observed, if one lacks something vital to one's own well-being and one's friend possesses it, it behooves the latter to provide what the former lacks.

Clearly, a sense of indebtedness is inherent in friendship—but an indebtedness that is incalculable. Although I have defrayed the costs of Noah's sons' and grandsons' educations in the same spirit that I once helped Noah pursue his educational goals, my moral debt to Noah can never be repaid. It follows, therefore, that equality between friends is always deferred. As with gifts, and by contrast with trade or barter, what is given is neither returned immediately nor returned in kind, and it is this sense of something owing that sustains a friendship over time. Were the debt quantifiable and fully repaid, the friendship would, paradoxically, lose its rationale for continuing.

For Aristotle and Hannah Arendt, friendship was a virtue—a moral foundation for creating a viable political order. But for as long as societies are divided by inequalities of power and wealth, the possibilities of political friendship are compromised. At the same time, if friendship is inextricably connected to a sense of indebtedness, such that we owe others the same opportunities we desire for ourselves, then we are collectively in debt to those whose labor, as slaves, built our national monuments and whose resources were plundered in creating a "common world" that would exclude them from it in the same way that Aristotle's virtue-friendship excluded women, commoners, and slaves.

CHAPTER 5

Man's Best Friend

I am in the lobby of the Angell Memorial Animal Hospital in Boston. It's ten o'clock at night, and most of the clients who approach the desks are picking up cats or dogs that have been admitted for emergency care. Suddenly, a sobbing woman passes me, her hands empty, her partner clutching her shoulder and trying to console her. She has lost a beloved pet. She has said goodbye to it. Its body will be cremated. But she will mourn her pet for a long time. Perhaps she will add a brass plaque to the wall of tributes to hospital staff and sentimental adieus to companion animals that passed away here. Although I am writing a book about friendship, it is only now that I realize that attachment between a person and an animal can be as profound as any—and this raises questions about what kind of mutuality or friendship exists between different species, and whether humans simply project virtue onto animals that gratify their desire for loyalty and love or satisfy their need to be obeyed.

We project images of the world as we wish it to be and become so enamored of these simulacra that we forget the disappointment, duplicity, and inconstancy that punctuate our everyday existence. These idealizations share a common feature. Though they are distant, they retain enough human traits to make them believable.

The process of idealization begins with every death. Not only are we enjoined not to speak ill of the dead, but we quickly overlook the flaws and foibles that marked their lives, transforming them into ancestors that embody moral ideals. Moreover, we create quasi-mythological exemplars, such as the Buddha, Jesus of Nazareth, the Virgin Mary, and various saints, though in many societies people focus on animals to exemplify virtue, possibly because it is easier to anthropomorphize animals than to find absolute virtue in a human being, and this includes the virtue of friendship.

With friendships with persons and friendships with animals, each makes the other thinkable. Through the advice, feedback, criticism, and demeanor of the other, we get to see ourselves from without, not merely from within. But not only do friends provide us with alternative *images* of ourselves, they also sustain our *lives*. This is why a willingness to sacrifice one's own life for a friend is a basic leitmotif in friendship narratives, and why friendship is such a powerful trope for understanding sociality as exchange, in which each person ensures that others have what they need in order to live, even though the giver may risk his or her well-being in the process.

Stories of friendship between persons and animals combine both these aspects of reciprocity—as a way of thinking about our relations with others and as a form of practical, ethical action (*phronesis*). Although Aristotle reserves primary friendship (which is reciprocal) for human beings because it reflects an awareness of reasoned choice (*prohairesis*), thereby excluding animals from primary friendship because their choices are merely utilitarian and opportunistic, it is universally the case that human beings tend to see certain animals as not only potential but exemplary friends.[1]

In *Train Dreams*, the fiction writer Denis Johnson recounts stories from the Idaho panhandle in which dogs behave like persons. One dog goes for help and saves the life of a lone prospector who has injured himself badly while trying to thaw out frozen dynamite on a stove. Another dog shoots his master after getting wind that the man was going to shoot it. "Much that was astonishing was told of dogs in the Panhandle," Johnson writes, "and along the Kootenai River, tales of rescues, tricks, feats of supercanine intelligence and humanlike understanding."[2]

In such stories, a relationship of reciprocity is assumed to exist between animal and human, such that each is said to owe its life to the other. Because each is morally constrained to sustain the life of the other through exchange, it is logically possible that one may physically change into the other or take the place of the other. Thus, a Kuranko man whose clan totem was the elephant ontologized this relationship and became convinced that he could actually change into an elephant at will.[3] Lucien Lévy-Bruhl spoke of such shape-shifting as "participation mystique," and Rane Willerslev speaks of the phenomenon as "mimetic empathy."[4] The terms could just as easily apply to friendship.

Consider the following examples.

*   *   *

Two women from two Kuranko clans (Yaran and Kamara) gave birth in the same house, at the same time, and on the same day. One of the infants was a boy, the other a girl. One day, when the mothers left the village to tend to their gardens, the house caught fire. A dog ran into the house, picked up the infants and carried them to safety under a banana tree. When the mothers returned home, they began to wail and weep, believing their children to be dead. Because of their distress it took them some time to notice the dog running to-and-fro between them and the banana tree. At last, they followed the dog and found their infants safe and sound. But they could not tell them apart. Since the infants were indistinguishable, the mothers made a random choice as to which infants they would take. As a result, the two clans made a rule never to intermarry. They adopted the same totem and became joking-partners.

*   *   *

During my fieldwork in 1970, I recorded the following account of how the leopard became the totem of the Marah clan. Whereas most Kuranko myths concerning the origins of a totemic relationship between a clan and an animal species express this moral bond in terms of kinship, this myth evokes friendship, thereby suggesting that an ethos of mutual care lies at the heart of both forms of relationship.

My informant was Bala Kondé, who lived in a ramshackle wattle-and-daub house behind the market in Kabala. A country-cloth tunic barely covered Bala's bony torso, and as Noah Marah (my research assistant) and I explained the reason for our visit, Bala bade us sit and, after shucking off his plastic sandals, leaned back in his hammock to begin his story.

Long ago, he said, rapidly repeating the word *fiu* to suggest remoteness from present time, the ancestor of the Kondé and the ancestor of the Marah were close friends, though the Kondé were the more powerful. The Marah were anxious that in the event of the Kondé and Marah settling the same country, the descendants of the Kondé would look down on the descendants of the Marah. The Kondé ancestor assured the Marah ancestor that he wished only that their friendship should endure, even if they settled the same country (and the Kondé ruled over the Marah). The

Marah ancestor then proposed that they eat rice flour together to seal their friendship.

In the same year this oath was taken, the Marah ancestor died. But on his death bed, he had requested, in the name of friendship, that the Kondé ancestor take care of his two sons. A few years later, the Kondé ancestor also passed away, though not before asking his sons to honor the bond of friendship that existed with the Marah ancestor. Though they might quarrel, they should never come to blows.

One day, when the Kondé sons and the Marah sons were together clearing and burning underbrush on their farm, the elder of the Kondé brothers, whose name was Fadu, gave his gun to the elder of the Marah brothers and went to a nearby stream to slake his thirst. At the streamside, he came upon a female leopard in labor. As he made to retreat, the leopard beckoned him, and as he approached in trepidation, the leopard said, "I know you are a hunter, but you find me here in labor. If you allow me to give birth to my cub in peace, I will give you a spell that will help you find game." Fadu Kondé spared the life of the leopard, who gave birth to her cub and then told Fadu the magical words that would help him in the hunt. When Fadu asked the leopard why it attacked and killed people, the leopard replied, "Because you people attack and kill us. Had we not struck a bargain just now, you would surely have killed me, or I would have killed you."

The leopard now declared that none of its descendants would ever harm a Kondé, and Fadu Kondé declared that none of his descendants would ever harm a leopard.

When Fadu returned to the farm, the elder Marah brother demanded to know what he had found at the streamside, and what had kept him so long. Fadu refused to speak of what had happened, declaring that it was a secret he was not at liberty to divulge. The two men came to blows. Though Fadu Kondé struck first, he died seven days later from the injuries he had suffered at the hands of the elder Marah brother. But people did not blame the Marah. They blamed Fadu Kondé for breaking the oath of friendship his father had sworn with the Marah ancestor.

The elder Marah brother now went to the streamside and met the leopard. He told the leopard what had happened, and that his "elder brother" (meaning Fadu Kondé) was dead. The leopard now befriended this Marah brother, just as it had befriended Fadu Kondé, and shared the secret words with him that it had earlier shared with Fadu. The leopard thus became the totem of the Marah.

*   *   *

Stories in which animals and human beings give life to each another, either by providing help or succor in a time of peril, or by sacrificing their own lives so that the other may live, are legion. All these stories are predicated on a distributive theory of being. For example, among the Kuranko it is axiomatic that will and consciousness are not limited to human beings, but distributed beyond the world of persons, and potentially found in totemic animals, fetishes, and even plants. The attributes of moral personhood (*morgoye*) may become manifest in the behavior of totemic animals and divinities, while antisocial people may lose their personhood entirely, becoming like broken vessels or ruined houses. In other words, being is not necessarily limited to human being. Indeed, in Kuranko totemic myths, an animal saves the life of the clan ancestor who then decrees that his descendants must respect the animal as if it were a kinsman, for it exemplified the magnanimous qualities of personhood (*morgoye*).

The source of the life of any species, whether animal, plant, or human, is understood to be life itself, which is distributed unequally and unevenly throughout the world. It may, however, be ritually, imaginatively, and magically redistributed, increased, subtracted, or exchanged. Thus, among the Kuranko, while every effort is made to respect and preserve the life of a totemic animal, other bush animals are "fair game" and hunted for meat, and the lives of "village" animals (goats, sheep, cows) are only taken when offering a sacrifice to one's ancestors. Even hunting is highly regulated, however, for a life can only be taken on condition that something equivalent is given in return, which is why hunters offer blood sacrifices to the first hunter, Mande FaBori, just as villagers offer sacrifices to their forebears. Among the Warlpiri of central Australia, the same logic obtains, for the life of the plants and animals on which human life depends requires periodic rituals of increase.

Typically, these ritualized transfers of life across species boundaries imply a reciprocity of perspectives in which *one is thought of in terms of the other or seen as itself in other circumstances.* Even though kinship is commonly used as a metaphor for this bond, the image of friendship carries the same moral weight.

This was vividly brought home to me when observing mimetic performances of mythological events, involving older Warlpiri men who had grown up in the desert as hunters and gatherers and knew the habits of their totemic animals by heart.

*   *   *

During our fieldwork in central Australia, my wife and I visited a Warlpiri Dreaming (ancestral / mythological) site associated with the travels of two mythical kangaroos. We were accompanied by Paddy Nelson Jupurrurla, his brother-in-law, and an elderly kinsman whose hand signals guided us across spinifex and saplings, and around anthills, ghost gum trees, and mulga brakes, to a wide flood plain and sandy creek bed where we left our vehicle and walked the remaining half mile to a broad expanse of red rock and a large pool of still water. There, Paddy showed me the kidney-shaped depressions in the rock where the kangaroos had camped in the Dreaming. The two kangaroos rested at Yirntardamururu for two or three weeks, Paddy said, before traveling south. But he revealed no further details, and I did not press him to do so. All he would say was that this was an important initiation site, and that many people used to camp here when he was a boy.

My imagination was stretched, as much by the lack of detail in Paddy's remarks as by my difficulty in picturing the two kangaroos, who seemed to be simultaneously animals and human beings, kin and companions.

"Were they like kangaroos to look at?" I asked Paddy.

"*Yuwayi* [yes]."

"Were they half men, half kangaroos?"

"No."

"But they acted like *yapa* [Aboriginal people]?"

"*Yuwayi*. They were very powerful."

Later I would learn more about the travels of the two kangaroos, but it was only when Zack Jakamarra *performed* an episode from the myth that I was able to fully appreciate it. As Zack had told me many times, abstract knowledge meant nothing; you had to see things with your own eyes, experiencing them bodily, sensibly, and directly.

The incident took place before the two kangaroos reached Yirntardamururu. Following a cloudburst, the country was flooded, and as the kangaroos searched for higher ground, one became bogged down in the mud and drowned before his companion could rescue him. Though grieving his loss, the surviving kangaroo journeyed on alone, and at a place called Wulyuwulyu ("western chestnut mouse") he discovered a marsupial mouse cowering in the spinifex. He decided to transform the mouse into a kangaroo, "a new mate."

"He bin grab 'im now," said Zack, already animated by the story. "He bin carry 'im along *Mulyu* ["nose" or "snout"], teach 'im there like in school. Big camp there. He make that little one really kangaroo now."

Zack placed his forefingers alongside his ears to show me how the ears got bigger. He pulled at his nose, drawing it out into an imaginary snout. He stretched his legs . . . the long, sinewy hind legs of a kangaroo. He tapped its genitals and tail, giving the kangaroo the features of an initiated male.

I laughed.

Zack narrowed his eyes and cocked his head. He looked paternally upon his protégé as it hopped around, getting accustomed to its new body.

Zack said, "That kangaroo bin ask 'im: 'Can you eat grass?' Go around now, look for tucker, good tucker there. That little rat bin look around. Come back. 'How are you? You all right?' He bin ask 'im, 'Can you scratch?' Teach 'im, you see. Teach 'im about those things . . . lie down, get up, look around country. Learn 'im all that. Really make a kangaroo out of 'im now."

Zack repeated his antics, mimicking the little kangaroo as it took its first tentative steps, nibbling at the grass, venturing out on its own. "Growing 'im up, you know?"

Although the little kangaroo was at once a neophyte and a "mate" (companion, friend), the essential thing was that he was in the elder kangaroo's care, just as I was in Zack's care.

Zack was "growing me up" too, as well as revealing to me, albeit obliquely, that the two-kangaroo Dreaming was intimately connected with initiation, and that ritual acts of subincision and "increase" (life-generation) occurred at almost every place the kangaroos camped in the Dreaming. Zack was also making it clear to me that knowledge was both mimetic and eidetic.[5] He could not have embodied his Dreaming without possessing a keen firsthand knowledge of the behavior of these desert marsupials, and this knowledge had been acquired mimetically in his youth, hunting with older men.

This deep familiarity with the habits of desert fauna gave the Warlpiri a practical edge over the animals they hunted. But there is a subtle and important distinction between mimicking an animal and identifying with it. The hunter may be skilled in reading the spoor of an animal and divining how best to track and hunt it, and this skill may suggest that he knows the animal as well as he knows himself; but at no moment is the line between self and animal so completely erased that the hunter no longer knows himself, and no longer acts as a separate being.

Consider the following commentaries on this phenomenon, by a philosopher and by an ethnographer.

> When I find again the actual world such as it is, under my hands, under my eyes, up against my body, I find much more than an object: a being of which my vision is a part, a visibility older than my operations or my acts. *But this does not mean that there was a fusion or coinciding of me with it*: on the contrary, this occurs because a sort of dehiscence opens my body in two, and because between my body looked at and my body looking, my body touched and my body touching, there is overlapping or encroachment, so that we must say that things pass into us as well as we into things. Our intuition, said [Henri] Bergson, is a reflection, and he was right, though the truth of the matter is that the experience of a coincidence can be, as Bergson often says, only a "partial coincidence."[6]

Rane Willerslev sums up his understanding of Yukaghir hunters in similar terms:

> It is this borderland where self and other are both identical and different, alike yet not the same, that I have tried to capture using phrases such as "analogous identification," "the double perspective," and "not animal, not *not* animal." What I mean to suggest by this is that if we are to take animism seriously, we must abandon the idea of total coincidence (the Heideggerian tradition) or total separation (the Cartesian tradition) and account for the mode of being that puts us into contact with the world and yet separates us from it. And there is, of course, such a mode of being, a mode that is grounded in mimesis.[7]

These commentaries provide crucial insights into the experience of friendship, for while there is a long tradition of speaking of friendship as a fusion of self and other, it is their "partial coincidence" or "analogous identification" that explains why the possibility of estrangement is present in even the most intense moments of fellowship. This was vividly illustrated in Keti Ferenke Koroma's two friendship stories discussed in Chapter 3 where the possibility of friendship as identity entails the possibility of friendship as difference.

Another way of making this point is to remind ourselves that persons and animals lack stable identities, despite the ways in which we sometimes represent them. Friends can become enemies, just as dogs can be friends in one context and "mere animals" in another.

Among the Runa of Ecuador's upper Amazonia, hunters and their dogs "partake in a shared constellation of attributes and dispositions" that Eduardo Kohn calls a "transspecies ecology of selves."[8] Yet, though dogs and humans possess souls and share the same subjectivity, dogs and people *live* in independent worlds. "Dogs are often ignored and are not even always fed, and dogs seem to largely ignore people." This is reminiscent of the way that Warlpiri (and other Aboriginal people) give skin names to their dogs, thereby assimilating dogs into their social world, yet treat dogs with an indifference and harshness that stands in complete contrast to how they treat their kinsmen. Among the Yarralin, a distinction is made between camp dogs, which are dependent, like children, and dingos that are independent of humans and wild. To be fully human "is to be neither totally dependent nor totally wild," which is why socialization involves learning how to live and forage as an autonomous person in the bush.[9]

What is true of human relations with animals is equally true of relations between friends. Though sameness *and* difference are *potentialities* of all these relationships, we must be careful to describe the contexts and interests that determine which one of these potentialities is realized. This leads me to one of my favorite anecdotes—from Steven Feld's ethnography of the Bosavi in the highlands of Papua New Guinea. Here, it is not the fusion of dogs and men that is at stake, but the impossibility of this fusion, and in recognizing this, a friendship between two men is spontaneously affirmed.

Feld and several Bosavi men are watching as a pig is slaughtered and the meat divided. Blood is running freely, and the village dogs are running up and down hoping for a share of the meat.

> Seyaka, a close friend and the younger son of Yubi, my first mentor in things Kaluli, is actively assisting by shooing dogs away from the butchering area. Challenging the dogs with menacing gestures, taunts, and hissing sounds as they dart in to lick at the blood, Seyaka suddenly lets out a whoop. And then, idling up to me, he starts to say the words I know he will. As he begins, I overlap and echo: "enowo: enendo: a:dababo:!!" (they repeatedly lick their own things!!). Immediately we are laughing uncontrollably, and Seyaka grabs onto my

biceps with both his hands, as if breaking a fall to the ground, but practically dragging me down instead. Mutually off balance, yet somehow
holding each other up, we catch ourselves alternately glancing at the
dogs in ridicule and disgust, and at each other in fondness and deep
play. We are pressed together in the moment, in a particular space of
male intimacy created by a collision of overlapping biographies.[10]

PART II

Personal Friendship

CHAPTER 6

Elective Affinities

Johann Wolfgang von Goethe borrowed a term from chemistry (*Wahlver-wandtschaft*) and made it a metaphor for the mystery of human bonds. Of such "elective affinities," in which attraction transcends indifference, the captain in the fourth chapter of Goethe's novel remarks: "Those natures which, when they meet, quickly lay hold on and mutually affect one another we call affined. This affinity is sufficiently striking in the case of alkalis and acids which, although they are mutually antithetical, and perhaps precisely because they are so, most decidedly seek and embrace one another, modify one another, and together form a new substance." In response to the captain, Charlotte observes that "it is in just this way that truly meaningful friendships can arise among human beings: for antithetical qualities make possible a closer and more intimate union."[1]

The concept of "elective affinities" may be extended to encompass all our relations with others—singular or collective, human or extrahuman—for in all such encounters, we stand to lose *and* find ourselves; some aspects eclipsed, others thrown into relief. And since *something* transpires in the course of every encounter, leaving us slightly changed, human existence is always, to some extent, a living beyond ourselves. This is why emotions of anxiety *and* exhilaration arise in every interaction, and why face-to-face relations may be thought of as border situations par excellence, for here, more than anywhere, we risk confirmation or nullification and are made or unmade. We are thus, in a sense, all migrants. Every day and in every encounter, we cross the dark sea that lies between the known and the unknown, embarking on journeys in which we hazard all that we are and from which we return transformed. This is not primarily a struggle to find God or to come home, but a struggle for being itself, in which we are sustained by the faith that life will either be found or will find us. When tragedy befalls us, we sometimes say we are "undone" or "shattered," and "fall apart." We stretch our bodies, minds, or senses to the limit, so that we may escape the confines of ourselves. We still the mind and steady the body, altering our sense of who we are. We enter into relationships that change us utterly. We travel and see ourselves as if from afar.

CHAPTER 7

Where Is the Friend's House?

In life, as in literature, a recurring leitmotif identifies friendships with self-sacrifice. In John 15:13, we read, "Greater love hath no man than this, that a man lay down his life for his friends." Although there is no reason why such altruism should be ascribed to men rather than women, or that fraternal love should be considered more exemplary than maternal love, history is biased toward patriarchy. As for friendship among children, examples are few and far between in the historical record. It is as if the eclipse of self in the service of another is, by definition, an adult virtue. As the great Iranian filmmaker Abbas Kiarostami observed, we find immense difficulty in seeing what lies outside the frame, whether the frame is determined by ideology, habit, or prejudice.

The first film in Kiarostami's *Koker Trilogy*, titled *Where Is the Friend's House?* (1987), is at once a celebration of childhood friendship and a commentary on the tension between egalitarian and hierarchical forms of sociality.

The story unfolds in a remote Iranian village of mud-brick houses, narrow lanes, and impoverished families. The opening scene is a classroom. The teacher enters the room, closes a window, and moves from desk to desk, inspecting the boys' homework. From time to time, he demands that the class be quiet and lectures the boys on the need for discipline. "There are rules for everything," he says.

When he comes to Namatzadeh Mohammad Reza, he scolds the boy for having done his homework on a sheet of paper rather than in his notebook. Mohammad's best friend, Ahmadpour, is sitting beside him. It is clear from the expression on Ahmad's face how deeply he is experiencing his friend's distress.

When the teacher suddenly rips up the notepaper, Mohammad bursts into tears and buries his head in his hands. The teacher demands that he look up. He asks the boy to say how many times he has been told to do his homework in his notebook. Mohammad says, "three times," and under pressure from the teacher says, untruthfully, that he visited his cousin the previous evening and left his notebook there. The teacher then holds up Ahmad's notebook as an example of how homework should be done, but Ahmad's sympathy for his friend outweighs any pleasure he might feel in being singled out as a model student. As the teacher threatens to expel Mohammad if he again fails to do his homework in his notebook, Ahmad is clearly experiencing the dismay and distress of his friend.

As the two friends run home together after school, Mohammad trips and falls. Ahmad helps him to his feet. "Did you hurt yourself?" he asks, and palms water from a street faucet onto Mohammad's grazed leg. On reaching home, Ahmad's mother and grandmother ask him to do several chores and some boys come by, begging him to come out and play, but Ahmad's homework is on his mind. When he finally sits down, opens his satchel, and takes out his notebook to do his homework, he finds that he has inadvertently picked up his friend's notebook. Though Ahmad is preoccupied by the urgency of returning the notebook to Mohammad, his mother ignores him and insists he do his own homework. Ahmad continues to plead with his mother, saying it is imperative he get Mohammad's notebook to him. "I have to go," he says, as his mother repeatedly demands he do his homework.

Crouching on the floor, Ahmad hurriedly tries to complete his homework but is interrupted by his mother asking him to rock the baby or fetch things for her. Again, Ahmad implores his mother to understand his dilemma. He holds up the two identical notebooks and explains how his friend will be expelled from school if he fails to do his homework today, not tomorrow. His mother becomes angry. With no hope of making her understand, Ahmad finally slips out of the house with his friend's notebook tucked under his jersey.

It is easy enough to follow the track to Mohammad's village, but Poshteh is a labyrinth of narrow defiles, stone steps, and cul-de-sacs, and no one he asks can give Ahmad clear instructions on how to find his friend's house.

As we watch this eight-year-old boy following false leads or being rebuffed by villagers who simply ignore his pleas for help, we bear witness to a world in which a child cannot hope to negotiate the obstacles, the indifference, and the demands that face him or her at every turn. The daylight begins to fade. Poshteh begins to feel more and more ominous. The alleyways are feebly lit by occasional streetlights or lost in shadow. In the gloom, a flock of sheep clatters past, bleating. Ahmad hears the jangle of a donkey harness and eerie sounds behind shuttered windows.

Significantly (considering Kiarostami's comments about framing), an elderly door-and-window maker with failing eyesight who happened to have made the door to Mohammad's house offers Ahmad a glimmer of hope. The old man complains that nobody wants to buy the traditional wooden doors and lattice windows, preferring iron shutters that will last a lifetime, but despite tiredness and shortness of breath, he leads Ahmad through the darkness to Mohammad's house, where (though we do not see this moment on screen) Ahmad delivers the notebook to his friend.

Impatient to get home, Ahmad arrives back in his village of Koker to find his parents getting ready for bed. Curiously enough, he is not asked where he has been or why he failed to buy bread, and he is not reprimanded for being late. Kneeling on the floor, he finally gets to complete his homework. But a gust of wind blows the door open. Curtains flail. The wind flips over the pages of his notebook. He sees his mother outside in the darkness, taking washing from the line. A dog howls in the distance.

The final scene echoes the first. Again, we are in the classroom, but by contrast with the opening scene in which the teacher closed a window, this morning he opens one. Ahmad is late for class, and Mohammad, already at his desk, is obviously dreading the moment his teacher examines his homework. The teacher lectures the class on the value of education, telling the boys that their schoolwork must always come first. Ahmad turns up and takes his seat next to his friend. He tells Mohammad that he did his homework for him. The teacher examines Mohammad's work. "Good," he says, and moves on.

*   *   *

It is tempting to see this film as a commentary on a changing world in which the innocent mutuality of friendship is undermined by the iron fist of autocratic power, and even education becomes another marker of inequality. This is a world in which Ahmad is continually being told what to do. "Be quiet," the teacher barks. "Do your homework," his mother says mechanically, when her son attempts to explain his friend's plight to her. "Go buy me cigarettes," his grandfather demands. "Don't wear your shoes on the stars," his grandmother says. His friendship with Mohammad, however, is his choice and his alone. When he goes to Poshteh to return his friend's notebook to him, this is a personal decision, not the result of a moral command. It cannot be explained as an internalization of a social norm, since the norm is clearly one that demands that children obey their elders without question. Ahmad's conscience, if we must use this word, has its source not in the external world but in an intimate identification with someone that he sees as himself in other circumstances. As such, friendship, unlike family, is a matter of choice, not obligation, an elective affinity rather than an inflexible rule.

For the philosophical ethicist K. E. Løgstrup, this is an example of "the sovereign expressions of life"—spontaneous and unconditional acts of compassion toward others that eclipse any consideration of the cost to oneself. Such actions are both free and ethical, Løgstrup argues, because they are not wholly determined by social prescriptions. Nor can they be instrumentalized and generalized after the fact as moral norms.[1] Though Løgstrup does not mention friendship explicitly, it is synonymous with freedom, for whereas moral and legal codes are dictated by ancestors, Gods, parents, and politicians, ethics is "responsive to the surprises that regularly punctuate life."[2] Such minor and accidental events as Mohammad's misplacing his notebook or Ahmad's spontaneous act of pretending to go out to buy bread but going to Poshteh instead are instances of Løgstrup's "sovereign expressions of life."

It is this challenge—to address this primitive recognition that oneself and the other are of a kind, namely humankind, regardless of any specific morality, law, or convention—that defines the field of ethics, whose quintessential expression is love and friendship, which is one's capacity to place oneself in parentheses and thereby enter into the situation of someone else, to see the world as they see it. There is a parallel here between Løgstrup's notion of the sovereign expressions of life and Edmund Husserl's notion of the phenomenological standpoint. If the "natural standpoint" implies a world of facticity and presence, "in which I find myself and which is also my world-about-me,"[3] the "phenomenological standpoint" implies a world of pure consciousness, in which my presuppositions about fact and fiction, or truth and falsity, are bracketed out.[4] Rather than emphasize "pure consciousness," I find it more interesting to explore the ways in which the *epoché* entails a movement toward the consciousness of the other—a suspension not only of one's own taken-for-granted *ideas* about the world *but of one's own sense of self.* The *epoché* thus embraces what we call empathy. Husserl's intentional "consciousness of something"[5] becomes "consciousness of another,"[6] though this "other" is *a suppressed dimension of one's own many-sided self*, occluded or held *in potentia*, since one inevitably inhabits a social milieu that privileges one mode of being at the expense of all other possible modes of being.

CHAPTER 8

Childhood Friendships

When I was an eleven-year-old boy living in Moabite, New Zealand, a new boy joined our class. Our teacher introduced him and invited us to welcome him into our midst. I was the only one who did so. Though chronically shy, I walked up to him at recess, introduced myself, and asked where he had come from and what had brought him to Moabite. Did I see him as another incarnation of myself or recognize him as a kindred spirit? Certainly, he was unlike any other boy I knew. Quietly confident and not averse to using "big words" or being accused of having "swallowed a dictionary," David Derbyshire accepted my offer of friendship, either because he recognized in me a fellow outsider or was simply grateful to find acceptance in a foreign environment. We quickly discovered a shared passion for building model airplanes, and this led to my visiting his home, where he showed me several balsa-wood gliders he had designed himself, introduced me to books by Arthur Ransome, and played me some Spike Jones and Stan Freberg records. His inventiveness, intelligence, and zany sense of humor left a deep impression on me. I wanted to be like him. I envied his initials, *DKD*, which he emblazoned on his comics and drawings, and I envied his self-assurance.

In one's choice of a childhood friend, one may hope to find oneself. Not a mirror image of who one already is, but a glimpse of whom one might become. Through friendships, we venture beyond the narrow confines of kinship and begin to explore the world, not as a place where we will be overwhelmed but where we will be free. Journeys that would otherwise daunt us were we to embark on them alone, become adventures in companionship. And so, with DKD, I expanded my horizons, cycling to the mountain from where we could look back at our town, a handful of dice scattered insignificantly on the plain, or make out the sea in the distance. With Ransome's *Swallows and Amazons* in hand, we trekked for miles along the streams that flowed from the mountain, charting and naming places of interest, and seeing how many loop-the-loops our balsa airplanes could achieve.

Though I was raised in a loving family, this did not prevent me from imagining that my friend's family was more interesting. I wished that my father drove a grader, like Mr. Derbyshire did, rather than work in a bank. Mrs. Derbyshire's meals were tastier than the meals my mother made. And why didn't my parents own a car like the Derbyshires'—a Bradford estate wagon that David nicknamed "Brick" after one of our favorite comic superheroes? Such fantasizing is as fundamental to friendship as it is to love, for in both instances, we transcendent ourselves.

Among the most memorable times I spent with David were Saturday matinees at the Moabite Town Hall where we would be entranced by yet another episode of *Flash Gordon*. As I write these lines, I am back in the semidarkness, pinholes in the tar-paper screens over the windows, like stars in the night sky, and the silver screen illuminating our rapt faces. Passages of dialogue also come to mind, along with the irreverent humor we delighted in.

Flash Gordon has just crash-landed on the planet Mongo and is brought before the tyrant, Ming the Merciless.

"How did you enter my kingdom?" Ming demands.

"In a rocket ship of my own design," Flash answers.

"Good, we can use him. Take him to the laboratory and give him everything he needs *except toilet paper* [these three words added by us]."

Two years after arriving in Moabite, the Derbyshires moved on. I visited David in Wellsford once, and his parents drove us to the coast in "Brick Bradford," where I took photographs of Mrs. Derbyshire nursing an abandoned dotterel on a white-sand beach. I regret not having a photo of my friend, for despite exchanging letters for a year or two, we lost touch.

This, too, is a mystery. Why should friendship, which so many writers have regarded as the highest good, be allowed to atrophy and die so easily? Ironically, we sometimes cling to the image of friendship more tenaciously than we cling to our friends. If I keep alive my memories of DKD, it is not because our childhood friendship lasted into adulthood, but because these memories sustain the illusion of continuity and constancy over time, redeeming my losses, recovering that sense of imperishability that is the natural possession of every child.

I take one other thing from this childhood friendship—the gift of being able to play, not with toys but with words, concepts, and images. To pretend. To imagine other worlds and lives, and even imagine other friends.

CHAPTER 9

Imaginary Friends

In his seminal study of transitional objects and transitional phenomena, the psychoanalyst D. W. Winnicott describes the actions of a troubled seven-year-old boy whose parents had sought his professional help. The boy's mother suffered from depression and was frequently hospitalized. During her absences, the little boy stayed with his maternal aunt. Increasingly, however, his parents had become concerned by his compulsion to lick things and people, a habit of making compulsive throat noises, threats to cut his little sister into pieces, and overcontrolling or losing control of his bowel movements. In his first interview with Winnicott, the boy revealed an intense preoccupation with string, and subsequently his parents told Winnicott that this "obsession" worried them, for their son had gotten into the habit of tying up tables and chairs and had recently tied a piece of string around his elder sister's throat. Winnicott suggested to the mother that her son was dealing with his fear of separation, using the string in an attempt to deny it, much "as one would deny separation from a friend by using the telephone."[1] With this insight, the mother talked to her son about the times she had gone away from him, and about his fear of losing touch with her. Six months after the first interview, the mother told Winnicott that her son had stopped playing obsessively with string—though the string play temporarily reappeared, once when the mother had to return to hospital and another time when she again suffered a bout of depression.

Winnicott observes that we form affective bonds with persons, objects, and ideas, and that separation from a loving caregiver, the loss of a familiar environment, or the death of a loved one may lead us to form surrogate attachments or fall back on our inner thoughts and feelings as substitutes for whatever or whomever we feel has abandoned us. "Transitional objects," such as soft toys, teddy bears, blankets, or imaginary friends, may serve as emotional stopgaps when the people on whom we depend for our well-being disappear from our lives.

Consider the poignant account by the writer Aleksandar Hemon of his family's struggle to cope with their infant daughter's life-threatening illness. Their elder daughter, Ella, imagines she has a brother with whom she can share experiences or who will follow her orders. In this way, Ella recovers a sense of agency in the face of circumstances she can barely comprehend or control. Her father recognizes that Ella is doing what he has always done—creating fictional characters who will do his bidding, creating a narrative space into which he can extend himself. "I'd cooked up those avatars in the soup of my ever-changing self, but they were not me—they did what I wouldn't or couldn't do. I understood that the need to tell stories was deeply embedded in our minds and that the narrative imagination was a basic evolutionary tool of survival."[2] The psychological affinity between the "work" of storytelling and friendship is striking.

Separation and Loss

Merleau-Ponty writes that a small child "lives in a world which he unhesitatingly believes [is] accessible to all around him. He has no awareness of himself or of others as private subjectivities, nor does he suspect that all of us, himself included, are limited to one certain point of view of the world. That is why he subjects neither his thoughts, in which he believes as they present themselves, without attempting to link them to each other, nor his words, to any sort of criticism. He has no knowledge of points of view."[3] What, then, happens to a child when someone who is familiar, beloved, and integral to that child's world suddenly disappears? With no way of taking up a point of view on this experience, how does the child process it?

*   *   *

My son, who just turned four, has a soft heart. At the pool today, despite the 90-degree heat, he said he did not want to swim or play on the waterslide. Instead, he spent the morning rescuing june bugs from the pool. When we headed home for lunch, I steadied him on his brand-new bicycle as he told me how he was going to put the half-drowned june bugs in the bug house that his friend Harry had given him as a birthday gift.

Josh also likes to collect action figures. They have scary names, these figures his parents buy him from Kmart, Target, or Service Merchandise—names like Tremor, Venom, Violator, and Overtkill. Josh has explained to me, however, that some are "naughty ones," but others are "good ones." Hence his innocent query at Kmart yesterday: "Is this a good one or a naughty one?" he asked the store clerk. We bought Spawn—a "naughty one," made in China.

I could not understand the link between Josh's compassion for june bugs and his liking for these gothic and mutant superheroes, until he got his bug house. He filled the bug house with wood lice, spiders, ants, and various insects from the garden, then watched in fascination as they fought and killed each other, vying for space.

Josh has not only got an impressive collection of action figures, he also imagines himself to be one of them. He calls himself Creepy One. Adopting a karate stance, he frowns at me and throws up his bladelike hands.

"Looking good," I say.

The other day at Josh's school, one of his friends pointed me out to his father. "That's Creepy One's father," the little boy said.

*   *   *

"Big butthead!" Josh says. "That's what Roger said to Doug." *Doug* is an animated television program on Nickelodeon that Josh and I sometimes watch together.

"Perhaps we should have a 'doug house' as well as a bug house," I say.

"Doug's not in this land," Josh rejoins seriously. "That's on TV."

"What are some other things that are not in this land?" I ask, curious to know what he considers imaginary, versus what is real.

"*Rugrats*. Nickelodeon. *Beetlejuice*. It not in this land. *Beetlejuice* doesn't keep me awake."

That night, writing up this dialogue in my journal, I note that, unlike people, transitional objects cannot hurt us.

*   *   *

Yesterday evening, Josh and I were fooling around on the sitting-room floor when the telephone rang. "Can you get it?" I called to my wife. As I tried to shush Josh yet still respond to his desire to continue our roughhousing, I noticed that Katherine was not saying much to whomever was on the phone. But her face was grave, as though the caller was unburdening himself or herself of a matter of life and death. Every now and then Katherine said, "Oh my God," and I tried to guess what had happened. Had someone been hurt in an accident? Someone in her family? "Yes," she said to the caller, "Yes I will," and then "yes" again.

When she hung up, she did not say anything.

"What's happened?" I asked. "Is someone hurt?"

"Baba is dead," she said. "She must have had a stroke or heart attack while she was splitting firewood. Lois found her this morning."

I thought it odd that she should refer to her mother as "Baba"—the word Josh used. I got up and went to comfort her, but she said she was all right. So calm. So detached.

We went for a walk in Bloomington's Bryan Park, and under the big chestnut tree by the tennis courts we sat Josh down and told him that his beloved grandmother, his Baba, was dead.

After taking this in for a while, he said very simply and emphatically, "I'm angry. I'm not sad, I'm angry."

The following day we made the flight from Indiana to New Zealand. Baba had lived on the coast. Her living-room windows overlooked an estuary and dark green hills. It was unnerving to enter her house and find, on the dining table, a list she had written of things to do before she traveled to the United States in ten days' time to visit us—air tickets to be collected at Campus Travel, potatoes to plant—and then, beside the list, a sweater she had knitted for Katherine, ready to have the buttons sewn on, and two knitted teddy bears she had made for her grandchildren.

One of the first things Katherine did was telephone the mortuary in Hamilton. She wanted her mother back home. And so, for two days and nights, Baba lay in a casket in her bedroom. Josh went in to see her from time to time, to touch her face, to hug her. We cautioned him from trying to pry her eyes open, from kissing the dead body. It was not healthy.

I gazed out the window at the mudflats along the estuary where Baba and Josh would go to gather periwinkles, the two of them out there for hours in their wellies, even when rain swept in from the hills. A fishing boat chugged down the estuary as I watched, its wake spreading from one side of the estuary to the other. I called Josh to come to the window. "Come here," I said, "it's the fishing boat you used to watch out for with Baba." He did not respond.

After the funeral, there was a lot of legal business to take care of, not to mention the sale of Baba's car and house. The work of cleaning the house and sorting through Baba's possessions was interrupted by numerous visits. Members of the family, their faces sorrowful, their voices lowered, commiserating.

Ten days later, we returned to the United States, still in the shadow of Baba's death. We all, in our different ways, felt abandoned and lost. Katherine had lost her mother, her confidant, her mainstay in troubled times. I had lost, with Baba, my last point of anchorage in my homeland. As for Josh, it seemed at times that he had lost his reason.

Late one autumn afternoon, I guided him down to Bryan Park on his bicycle, negotiating the broken sidewalk, looking out for traffic at the intersections.

"You know my *old* Baba," Josh said, out of the blue. "Not Emily or Baba," he explained, mentioning his other grandmother, who died two years earlier and whom he did not remember. "Well, she was eaten by a crocodile."

I tried to take this in, the past split off from the present, and death as a predator. But Josh was hurrying on:

"My old father," he said, "not you. You're not my real father. My old father was eaten by a crocodile too. And my old mother."

That night, as I tucked Josh into bed after reading to him from his *Book of Fabulous Beasts*, he said: "I want you to die. I want to be ayone [alone]. I don't want to be with you. I want to be naughty. I want to stay up all night yong [long]."

Indeed, at 9:15 p.m., as I recorded his comments in my journal, he was still awake, reading his *Book of Fabulous Beasts*, entranced by the Phoenix that is consumed by fire, yet every morning is reborn from its own ashes.

He feels that the rug has been pulled out from under him, I wrote. Through no rhyme or reason known to him, by dint of things beyond his comprehension and control, a vital element in his world has been cruelly and unjustly snatched away. Desperate not to be a victim, not to suffer this outrage in silence, and to feel that the world recognizes and responds to his needs, he inverts his relationship to everything and everyone around him. He speaks of Creepy One, his alter ego, who has no mother or father, who exists alone, a law unto himself. His anger at Baba, or the forces that conspired to take her from him, is turned against his parents. At preschool, he is incontinent. In a place where routines and rules provide no room for emotional outbursts, he has recourse to his own body, his own inwardness. Relinquishing sphincter control gives him a perverse sense that he is, in fact, in control of his own situation. Maybe this is why he fears passivity. He dislikes recess at school. He wants to stay up at night. He does not want to go to sleep. If he slept, death would come. We would disappear. The world would ring terrible changes in his absence, and the morning would be unlike the morning he last awoke to.

He keeps telling me how much he would like to fly.

The truths we live by are not always the same as the truths we swear by.

*   *   *

A friend and I take Josh with us to Dunn Woods in search of edible fungi. We find a box turtle, which Josh grasps, kisses, and says he will care for. He is convinced it is the same turtle we found in the woods behind Mary-Helen's house, miles away, not long before we heard of Baba's death. It has returned from nothingness, and now he can take charge of it, and make it his own.

Back home I make a cage for Josh's turtle. Josh packs the cage with sphagnum moss, places a dish of water under the turtle's nose, and tries to feed it some leaves. He says he wants to take it to school for show-and-tell.

The box turtle seems to make a difference. Josh appears calmer, more in control, more his old affectionate, trusting self.

*   *   *

Josh's feelings are easily hurt. When I ask him not to hammer his bicycle with the wrench, he dissolves immediately into tears.

*   *   *

On the way to Bryan Park, Josh tells me, "I don't want you to die." For a split second, I felt the beginning of a rush of great relief. Then he adds, "I want tyrannosaurus to eat you."

*   *   *

First thing in the morning, Josh climbs into bed with us and hugs his mum. "I really love you, Storm," he says. Storm is one of his X-Men mutants.

That evening, I am late home on account of a student exam. Josh is elated to see me and eager to show me the hairy caterpillars he has found. "I really love you, Wolverine," he says.

The X-Men are safe, I tell myself. He feels he can control them, these miniature figures he keeps in a box in his room. These he can trust. But not his parents. Not yet. And so we have to take on the identities of the plastic figures.

As if to drive this home, he once more asks me: "You know my old Baba? Not Emily. Not Baba. My parents who lived before, in Africa?"

The parents who were real and reliable, and did not let him down, I think.

That night, after Josh has gone to sleep, Katherine and I talk things over. She recounts how she took Josh to Bryan Park, and he poked her with a metal rod of some sort. When she asked him not to, because it was hurting her, he retorted, "I want to do it. I want you to die."

"But it won't make me die," Katherine said.

"What if I make you bleed?"

"It won't make me die, it'll just hurt me."

"What if I cut off your arm?"

"I still won't die. It's pretty hard to make someone die, you know, if you're healthy."

"What if I cut off your head?"

"I still won't die."

"I want you to be dead. Pretend to be dead."

My wife pretended, but without lying down.

"Lie down on the ground!"

"No, I'm holding Freya [Josh's baby sister], I'll just have to be a ghost."

Josh's shoe came off. He wouldn't let his mother tie it back on. He ran off.

Katherine said to me: "He's so sweet with living things, so sad if he hurts a butterfly." And she described how he had found one bruised and battered by the creek. "Look," he told her, "it's still alive. I want it to fly away."

*   *   *

Josh leads his mother outdoors. "I want to show you something," he says. "It's *very* interesting. Come with me, I'll show you."

On the lawn, all his action figures are in a bucket. "They are dead now," he explains. "We are burying them up. Don't touch them."

He transfers the action figures to an old barrel, then shreds tufts of grass, and empties ash and dirt on top of them. He then upends the bucket over the buried figures in the barrel. "They got to stay warm. If they stay here, they going to die."

As he performs the funeral, he asks Katherine and me to say something good about each of the buried figures. "Creepy One Supersaver," he prompts us. "Wonder Woman. Boo-in-Bub."

"In staging this funeral, replaying the tragic events over which he had no say, he vicariously brings his feelings until control." At least this is the explanation I spell out in my journal. "In creating a miniaturized simulacrum of the world—substituting plastic action figures for real persons—he is able to play out as theater what befell him in life, re-empowering himself, regaining a sense that he too can make things happen in this world, rather than be at the mercy of things happening to him. But whatever truth there is in this theorizing, the fact is that his parents are at their wits' end, coping with his accident-proneness, his throwing things at us, his declarations of his need to be alone, to be elsewhere, for us to die, his anger, his vulnerability when reprimanded (bursting into tears and protesting that we should not be angry at him)."

*   *   *

In the late evening we stroll along South Woodlawn Avenue. "I'm going to Africa," Joshua announces, apropos of nothing. "That is my land. I have to go there or I will die."

Is it the fall? The colder air? Or is it human warmth he wants? I remember how drawn he is to Salamander and Phoenix in his *Book of Fabulous Beasts*. But how can I guess at his need, except to compare it to my own, when I was his age, feeling the same abandonment, desperate to be elsewhere?

He rambles on about the father and mother and grandmother he had "before," and how they all lived in Africa. Presumably before Baba's death. When the world was warm, and safe, and secure.

*   *   *

I drive to Barnes and Noble and ask the assistant if she can help me locate anything on children's bereavement. She fetches the two titles they have in stock. One promises the reader that his or her loved one is in heaven, safe with God. The other is a secular equivalent, giving assurances that trees and flowers spring up anew from the remains of the dead, brightening the world over which darkness has momentarily fallen. Life goes on. Loss is an illusion.

When I compare these glib consolations, these saccharine evasions, with Josh's complex and heartrending fantasies, I am outraged. How easily adults insult the intelligence of a child. I tell myself that Josh does not need explanations. He does not want assurances. He does not want to be distracted, to be bought off. He wants an arm around him. He wants his parents to be close. He wants them to listen to his nightmares. Just listen, so that in his own way, in his own good time, he can see this thing through.

*   *   *

Another day verging on chaos. Josh brings home a cheap box that belonged to one of his friends. He says he found it in his locker at school and supposed it was his. He cannot be persuaded to take it back, to return it to Harry. He clings to things now with the same tenacity that he clung to Baba, to his parents, to this world of human subjects that has let him down.

Fortunately, Katherine finds an identical box at Kmart. Chaos is averted.

At bedtime, I speak to Josh about his sadness and anger.

"Where do your feelings come from?" I ask.

Again, he tells me about his "other grandmother"—not Emily, not Baba, "who was eaten by a crocodile."

"Did this happen in New Zealand?"

"Yes."

I tell him we are not going to be eaten. No crocodile is going to get us. He has nothing to fear.

"I want to be ayone [alone]," he says. "I want to grow up and be an adult."

I tell him that he does not have to grow up for a long time yet. He should let himself be four, be himself. He does not have to be alone. We will be here with him, loving him, looking after him, making meals for him, always. "I will be here, Mummy will be here, Heidi [his eldest sister] will be here. And Freya."

He tells me we are all going to die. He has to get another Mummy and Daddy.

I try to explain that Baba had been old. Old people die. We are young and healthy. "You don't have to think of dying," I tell him. "Old people sometimes worry about that. But not children, not young healthy people like us. Tell me that you will not worry about that anymore."

"I won't," he says. "I understand."

*   *   *

It is now almost three weeks since we arrived home. Things are becoming resolved. At breakfast this morning, Josh said, "I had a dream about Baba alive."

"That's good," I said. "I'm happy you had a dream about Baba alive and happy."

Josh said that Baba had been taking him to the ice cream shop.

That night, after I had read him his bedtime story, he said he loved me, and he hugged me spontaneously for the first time in four weeks.

*   *   *

Jerry and Betty Mintz live three doors from us along University Avenue. Jerry is a colleague and a friend, the first person in the Indiana University anthropology department to go out of his way to make me feel at home in Bloomington when I first arrived. He walked me around the campus, showing me how to find my way to the library, to the Kinsey Institute, and the gym. Then he invited me to a screening of one of his ethnographic films.

These days I do not see a lot of Jerry. He has leukemia. He is off work, and if he goes out, it is always with Betty and a respirator. One turn around Bryan Park, then home.

Today I spot him standing on the sidewalk in his bathrobe, watching Betty weed the garden. I walk along the street, and we talk about the weather. Then he asks me how Josh is getting on, and I tell him how Josh used his action figures to get a hold on his confused and painful feelings after his grandmother died.

Jerry tells me a story about a friend of his in Brooklyn. His friend is an obsessive collector. "Street signs, stamps, coins—you name it, he collects them all. Even insulators."

"Like the insulators on telegraph poles?"

"Yeah," Jerry says. "He steals them. Only he hasn't got a red one yet. The only color insulators don't come in is red. And this bothers him."

"Why would anyone want to collect insulators?"

"He got started collecting things when his father killed his mother when he was a kid."

*   *   *

A year passes. I show Josh a photo of himself painted as Creepy One, a photo that dated back to just before Baba died.

"I hate Creepy One now," Josh says, "because he's not a real superhero."

*   *   *

In my journal, I noted that, "There is always an arbitrariness about the strategies or objects we use in our efforts to grasp the world. Many children, dealing with traumatic events, draw or paint pictures of homes destroyed by bombing or an earthquake, or buried under a mudslide. Children after the Skopje [Macedonia] earthquake in 1963 played games that involved burying things. And most children create imaginary friends. Friendship remains a possibility when family has proved impossible."

I would now add that friendship is a metaphor for our deepest attachments in life and, as such, it can find expression in our relationships with things, animals, dead authors, divinities, and landscapes as much as with people. But if a friend is whatever or whoever we think of as a friend,[4] when are our friendships mere figments of the narcissistic imagination and when are they true reflections of fellow feeling and common accord?

CHAPTER 10

_____

The Saronic Gulf

Although Christopher Lasch published *The Culture of Narcissism* several years before Facebook, Twitter, and Instagram transformed our lives, his book anticipates the question of what becomes of friendship in the age of social media.[1] Do other people become mere means for our personal gratification? Does our fascination with self-image and celebrity make us see others as potential fans or followers rather than as friends we deeply care about? Like many of my generation, I have a somewhat old-fashioned image of friendship as a relationship between equals in which alter is never subjugated to ego.

Despite these misgivings about virtual friendships, I am a conscientious letter writer who had no qualms about abandoning his typewriter for a word processor in 1990, and I conscientiously keep in touch with far-flung friends. What fascinates me, however, is not the power of digital technology to overcome the tyranny of distance, but the potential of distance to make possible a form of friendship whose intimacy might not be sustainable in everyday face-to-face settings.

*   *   *

Menton, France, May 1983. I hesitate at the top of the stone steps while my eyes grow accustomed to the gloom that is descending over the garden. Gnarled wisteria holds the portico in its grip. Cypresses along the driveway impale the sky. Minutes ago, I was deep in conversation with a young woman, Sofka, who is studying anthropology at Cambridge. She has been staying with a family friend who inherited, when still quite young, a palatial house on Cape Martin, where he shelters Madagascar lemurs and a colony of other exotic animals. When Sofka asks what brought me to Menton, I explain that I am on a writing fellowship and working on my first novel.

We do not talk for long. My wife is unwell, and I need to get back to her. After locating my daughter Heidi, who has become attached to one of our host's fox terriers, we set off down the drive. Sofka runs after us, scribbles her name and Cambridge address on a scrap of paper, and invites me to continue our conversation by letter.

*　*　*

I doubt I would have written Sofka had my wife not died later that year, not long after our return to New Zealand from France, and I was in desperate need of new friends, new music, new books, and new departures.

Sofka and I exchanged letters regularly over the next few years. In retrospect, these letters (mine typed, hers handwritten) resemble a journal in which we chronicled and reflected on key events in our lives—my move to Australia, further fieldwork in Sierra Leone, the vicissitudes of life on the dole; Sofka's doctoral fieldwork in Greece, her unexpected inheritance of an estate in Oxfordshire, her marriage—but it wasn't until 1990 that we met again. We happened to be in New York City at the same time, and after strolling around Greenwich Village for a couple of hours, we had lunch together. We went our separate ways without having closed the gap between the intimacy of our letters and the awkwardness we felt in each other's company. That our correspondence continued was, I suspect, less a matter of wanting to see more of each other than a question of having a trusted stranger with whom confidences could be shared and uncertainties confided without the risk of real-life repercussions. An epistolary friendship can provide a safe place in which two people can more clearly take stock of themselves than in a personal diary.

In my childhood friendship with David Derbyshire (Chapter 8) and my student friendships with Harry St. Rain and Fletcher Knight (about whom I write later), I was driven by a mimetic desire to become a part of their worlds. If I took little interest in their well-being, it was because I assumed they wanted for nothing and that I was the one in need. In being with them, their talents and personalities would somehow rub off on me. I would be completed through them.

The trouble with such neediness is that it can blind you to the needs of others, as I would discover to my chagrin.

With Sofka, I felt no compulsion to belong to her world, much as I marveled at it and realized how different it was from mine. Besides, she was

perfectly capable of describing her world for herself. With literary flair, scholarly acumen, and an ethnographic eye for detail, her 2004 book *Eurydice
Street* recounts the highs and lows of settling in Athens with her husband,
Vassilis, and their two small daughters and coming to feel at home in Greece.
Three years later, her memoir of her paternal grandmother, after whom she
was named, was published in England. The daughter of White Russian aristocrats who fled the October Revolution in 1919, Sophy Dolgorousky was
eleven years old when she came to England. Ten years later, moved by the
suffering caused by the Great Depression, Sophy became an active member
of the British Communist Party.

The story of Sofka's maternal grandfather is no less astonishing. In *The
Mad Boy, Lord Berners, My Grandmother, and Me*, Sofka relates how she
came to inherit Faringdon House in 1987. Made legendary by its eccentric
owner (the Lord Berners of the title) and the glitterati who attended his
weekend parties—Gertrude Stein, Nancy Mitford, Igor Stravinsky, and Salva-
dor Dalí—Faringdon offered decadence and wit in equal measure. To Sofka,
however, who sold the house shortly after she moved to Greece, Faringdon
was not a place to live but a story to be told.

*   *   *

Like falling in love, the inception of a friendship often defies analysis, though
an analogy might be drawn with writing fiction. The seed of a story comes
to mind unbidden. If given time to germinate, and if watered, pruned, and
protected, this seed becomes a plant that one day flowers. I admired Sofka's
ability to patiently nurture life rather than bend it to her will. The most surprising things seemed to fall into her lap, including friendships and stories.
Sophy gave her granddaughter her diary when Sofka was sixteen years old.
Sofka inherited Faringdon when she was twenty-five. She found a new life for
herself in Greece when she was forty. Perhaps this is what we had in common:
we had learned from an early age to make the most of what we were given,
like the sculptures Sofka made from driftwood gathered on a local beach.

In the early summer of 2009, having promised my youngest daughter,
Freya, a trip to a country of her choosing when she graduated from middle
school, I found myself on my way to Greece. When I had told Sofka of my
plans to take Freya on a tour of the Peloponnese, she insisted we stay a couple
of days with her and her family in Athens. It would give us a chance to get
to know each other, a litmus test that might finally determine whether our

long correspondence was born of a real or illusory affinity. As I later discovered, Sofka felt as much trepidation about our meeting as I did. For, if we found ourselves indifferent to each other, or in deep disagreement, this would surely spell the end of our friendship and we would part, disenchanted and deeply embarrassed to have spent so many years in an epistolary folie à deux, assuming an empathy that had no basis in fact.

At Athens airport, my doubts were instantly dispelled by the warmth of Sofka's welcome, her attentiveness to Freya, and her lighthearted attitude toward the strange experiment to which we had decided to subject our friendship.

Initially, we kept to the safety of small talk. How was our flight? Did we get any sleep? How long had we had to wait in Madrid for our connecting flight to Athens? Freya wanted to know about Sofka's daughters, Anna and Lara, and how old they were and whether they lived near the sea. As for me, I found it hard to believe that a mere ten hours had passed since leaving Boston—the offshore islands swallowed up by mist and cloud as our plane ascended . . . sleeping through the night . . . waking to the new day breaking over the sun-baked, biscuit-colored landscape of central Spain, smudged with slate-gray pools of cloud shadow. But what was most astonishing was the sense that I had passed, like Alice, through a looking glass and entered a world where what had been imagined was suddenly there before my eyes, and that what had been so vivid yesterday now seemed vague and remote.

Sofka served a late lunch on the terrace. The artistry that came through in her writing, paintings, and driftwood mobiles was evident in the dishes she placed on the table—an oval platter of feta, sprinkled with oregano and interspersed with glistening black Kalamata olives; ceramic bowls of fried eggplant and zucchini; juicy tomatoes stuffed with savory rice and pine nuts; snap peas drenched in olive oil; slices of country bread; and tumblers of clear water. How strange to be sitting under the pergola she had described in her letters, with the rosemary, sage and thyme she had planted among the rocks; the olive, fig, loquat, and orange trees; and the jasmine climbing a drystone wall. Listening to Sofka's husband, Vassilis, talk about the recent European Union elections, or to Sofka negotiating with her daughters over household chores, music practice, and how long they could stay out that evening, the uncanny similarity between this household and mine began to sink in, and I felt at home.

That evening, with the sun setting over the Saronic Gulf, Sofka and I finally found time to talk. She asked me what I was writing. It was, perhaps, too early to say. But I already sensed that my visit to Greece would form part of the mosaic and speak to the theme I had in mind. I explained this theme as the struggle to strike a balance between one's relationships with others and one's relationship with oneself—of how one may become so absorbed in the lives of others that one's own identity is eclipsed, or so preoccupied by one's own work that one grows negligent of others. "Perhaps you sometimes felt this about our correspondence," I said. "I know I did. Wondering whether, without any face-to-face contact, we risked lapsing into solipsism, each of us construing the other solely from our own perspective."

"But the amazing thing," Sofka said, "is that we *are* face to face, and I have absolutely no sense that you are anyone other than the person I have been writing to for all these years."

I confessed to Sofka that one reason I had always felt anxious about meeting her was our class difference. Her paternal forebears were Russian aristocrats; mine were English working-class emigrants.

Sofka was both irked and amused. "Isn't this an example of what you were just saying? Making me a figment of your imagination, rather than seeing me as I am? Whether or not I was born into a family with relative material wealth, I find that element so much less relevant to my identity than dozens of other factors that affected my childhood. The fact that both my parents battled with depression and alcoholism, for example, and split up when I was a child. In any case, I refuse to think that who we are is decided by our family backgrounds or income. I hate it when people assume that the rich are somehow less human than the poor, and the poor possess moral virtue simply because they are materially impoverished. Why can't we see one another as individuals, as human beings, and not reduce people to abstractions like class, culture, or nationality. These labels only ever seem to apply to the other, and never to oneself! If only people actually met, they would see the artificiality of their constructions. But they don't meet, or won't, and so the constructions are never tested, and become more and more out of touch with reality."

I had to admit that the problem was mine. As a child, I had felt gauche and inferior. I had a dread of appearing foolish, of not measuring up, of being rejected. In writing, I felt in control of my situation. Though I might not be accepted as a person, perhaps my literary work would be. I could hide behind it. It would circulate in the world, but I would not have to. I could remain apart, unchallenged and unscathed.

Sofka found this hard to believe.

"But what of your fieldwork, your travels. You're always venturing out into the world. No one could be less reclusive than you."

"I have pushed myself hard. I still do. But, at heart, there is always this small boy, shaking in his shoes, not sure whether or for how long he's going to be able to sustain the conversation, continue the lecture, or go on returning to the field."

"But everyone's like this, deep down. Everyone gets cold feet. Stage fright. Writer's block. Just look at me!"

Sofka asked if I had read Patrick Leigh Fermor. I knew the name but had not read his books.

He was an old friend of Sofka's family. When Sofka's first book was launched in Athens, Leigh Fermor attended, fortified with whisky, and fulminating against the dying of the light.

In 1933, at the age of eighteen and with only a few pounds in his pocket, he had walked from the Hook of Holland to Istanbul. Having completed this remarkable journey, he settled in Greece, became fluent in the language, and mastered several of its dialects. But before he gained fame as a travel writer, he was known for his exploits on Crete as a Special Operations Executive officer during the war. Disguised as a shepherd, he lived for two years with a band of Cretan guerillas, holed up in the mountains and leading raids against the occupying Germans. He was awarded the Distinguished Service Order for his role in capturing the commander of German forces on Crete, General Heinrich Kreipe, in 1944. Leigh Fermor's longtime friend and correspondent Lady Deborah Devonshire (née Mitford) recalls the event with admiration and affection:

> Their prize was bundled into the back of the German official car: Moss[2] drove them through a town in the blackout, Paddy sitting on the front seat wearing the general's cap in case anyone should glance at the occupants. After a four-hour climb on foot to the comparative safety of a cave in the mountains, they spent eighteen days together, moving from one hiding place to another and sharing the only blanket during the freezing nights. When the sun rose on the first morning and lit up the snow on the summit of Mount Ida, the general gazed at the scene and quoted a verse of an ode by Horace. His captor [Leigh Fermor] completed the next six stanzas.[3]

"It was very strange," Leigh Fermor would write years later, "as though, for a long moment the war had ceased to exist. We had both drunk at the same fountains long before; and things were different between us for the rest of our time together."[4]

Could one say that a friendship was born between Leigh Fermor and the German general at that moment. That enmity became amity?

More telling, perhaps, is that this man of the world—this bon vivant and formidable raconteur, fluent in so many languages, fearless and gregarious—was also a man who would periodically retreat to his study "for unusually long and uninterrupted spells"[5] and chose to build his house on the isolated southern coast of the Peloponnese. Sofka spoke of his "time of silence," when Leigh Fermor retreated from the world—to the Abbey of Saint Wandrille, to the monasteries at Solesmes, La Grande Trappe, and Cappadocia. "In the seclusion of a cell—an existence whose quietness is only varied by the silent meals, the solemnity of ritual and long solitary walks in the woods—the troubled waters of the mind grow still and clear, and much that is hidden away and all that clouds it floats to the surface and can be skimmed away; and after a time one reaches a state of peace that is unthought of in the ordinary world."[6]

I told Sofka that Leigh Fermor reminded me strongly of my old friend Brijen Gupta and of the writer Blaise Cendrars, both of whom embraced worldliness but valued solitude.

"How hard it is, though," Sofka said, "to find the right balance between time to oneself and time for others."

"Perhaps that's what's special about letter writing," I said. "We write in solitude, undistracted by the physical presence of others, yet at the same time we are deeply in touch with the person we are writing to."

*   *   *

The next morning, Sofka took us to see the Parthenon. I told her that when I lived briefly in Athens in 1965, I formed a romantic attachment to one of the caryatids on the Erechtheion. Sofka wanted me to show her which one. Though it was only a copy of the original figure (which had been moved to the Acropolis Museum), the caryatid was still as beautiful to me as when I first set eyes on her. Her arms and feet had been amputated, perhaps when a Turkish shell almost destroyed the building in 1827. Her face was ruined. But the erosion that had scarred her nose and upper lip had imparted to her a beauty more compelling than had she remained perfectly unblemished—her supple shoulders, her languid stance, the left knee slightly bent, breasts and belly sensuous beneath the folds of an Ionian tunic. Years later, I discovered that my experience at the Erechtheion had a literary precedent in Virginia Woolf's *Jacob's Room*:

Jacob strolled over to the Erechtheum and looked rather furtively at the goddess on the left-hand side holding the roof on her head. She reminded him of Sandra Wentworth Williams. He looked at her, then looked away. He was extraordinarily moved, and with the battered Greek nose in his head, off he started to walk right up to the top of Mount Hymettus, alone, in the heat.

I told Sofka that I had often wondered whether Woolf was writing about something that had really happened or something she had imagined. This, in turn, had made me wonder whether it is art that imitates life, or life that aspires ineptly to the example of art. Love and friendship are so often celebrated as moral and even political ideals that we become blind to their empirical reality. Was the marmoreal beauty of that caryatid born of my loneliness?

I suppose I was obliquely confessing that my letters to Sofka had, at times, been idealistic and written out of loneliness, but that meeting each other had brought us down to earth, affirming a true affinity.

As we walked away from the Erechtheion, I was tempted to look back.

I did not.

CHAPTER 11

A Soldier's Story

That my friend Les Cleveland should die without an obituary may be read as a sign of how he chose to live—as a man of few words, self-effacing, uncomplaining, pragmatic, and staunchly egalitarian. In personality, he was a man of his generation, for whom the communitarian ethos of the common man made it unseemly to draw attention to oneself, neither bragging about one's abilities[1] or properties, nor putting others down. Friendship between men of this generation found expression in the camaraderie of the pub, where ribald yarns were exchanged and the ritual of "shouting" created a semblance of reciprocity. As for sharing deep feelings or thoughts, this was dismissed as pretentious or effeminate.

Though Les was almost twenty years older than I was, we were brought together by our wives, who were contemporaries and close friends. I knew that Les had fought in the Second World War, but he never spoke of his wartime experience, and I felt it was inappropriate to ask about it. Once, when the Clevelands were staying with my wife and me in the Manawatu, I cooked spaghetti Bolognese for dinner. Les could not eat it. The garlic was overpowering. Later, Mary, Les's wife, told my wife that when Les was fighting in Italy, the troops were often obliged to steal food at gunpoint from the tables of peasants or ransack chapels for firewood to keep them warm in winter. The taste of garlic and the sight of pasta brought these traumatic memories flooding back. Nevertheless, I learned a lot about Les's many postwar incarnations—bushman, journalist, broadcaster, welder, folk singer, political scientist, photographer, poet, researcher, and writer—and admired him as much for his multiple talents as for the insights he gave me into a New Zealand that was rapidly changing.

When, in the late 1990s, I suggested to Les that I write his biography, he demurred. Although he consented to be interviewed and talked at length about his four and a half years as an infantry soldier in various formations of the Second New Zealand Expeditionary Force (2NZEF), he avoided both the jingoism and graphic realism that inform many war narratives. This avoidance of heroic bombast and morbid reflection allowed him to document in extraordinary detail the everyday experience and popular culture of military life.[2] It also yielded insights into the bonds of friendship that are forged in situations of shared danger and adversity and come to figure in soldiers' songs and stories. This hitherto undocumented culture that Les finally got to write about bore little or no resemblance to the accounts of self-sacrifice and valor that are the stuff of patriotic histories and national propaganda. In fact, they are told in spite of, and often to spite, the official versions of what the war was ostensibly about.

During a visit with Les and Mary in 2011, Les opened up to me about these matters in a way he had never done before.

I had just driven off the Interislander ferry, and at Havelock Street in the Wellington suburb of Brooklyn, I parked by the same flax bush where I had parked so often in the past.

I walked into their house as Les and Mary were finishing a late lunch. The room had not changed. Les's photographs—of ghost towns in Arizona, abandoned diggings in Nevada and Westland (New Zealand), and derelict buildings whose original use could only be guessed at—were still in their place, as were the postcards from Las Vegas and the potbellied stove. Almost the first thing I said was that no time seemed to have passed since I was last there.

As levelheaded as ever, Les said that none of us was getting any younger, and he described how, a couple of months ago, he had been lugging an armful of logs up from below the house when he lost his footing and fell. "It's a fifteen-foot flight of concrete steps," Les said. "On the top step, I forgot to shift my weight forward enough and began falling backward. Something in me took over, as it invariably does in a crisis, so that I somehow turned completely, before landing face down with one arm clutching at the wall for support. I did not do this; my instincts did. Unfortunately, it wasn't enough to save me from a broken wrist and skull fracture."

"I thought he was dead," Mary said. "That's what my instincts told me." And she related how Les was hospitalized only to discharge himself two days later, preferring to take care of himself and recover at home.

"It was a reprieve," Les said. "We both thought: this is it. But there was no magic moment, with my life replayed in a split second. No tunnel of light, any of that stuff. But in the days that followed, I kept thinking of a bizarre incident during the war when I almost lost my life.

"We were dug in around, as well as occupying, a large house. Under cover of darkness, the Germans brought up a fixed gun, and its first shell scored a direct hit on the house. I would normally have been with Podge Hoskins at a machine-gun post at an upper-floor window, but I'd been detailed to the kitchen and was frying up tinned bacon and egg powder when the shell hit. There was an earsplitting explosion, splinters of wood, debris, dust. But in the midst of this maelstrom and the screams from the front room, I covered the frying pan with a tea towel and placed it carefully under the table. Only then did I go to the aid of the men in the other room. I had to kick down the door to get in. Almost everyone had been torn apart. Some were dead, others dying. The scene was as gruesome as any I had witnessed. Podge upstairs had been killed instantly. Yet I survived. And afterwards, what I could not get over was that moment with the frying pan. How I could go on as though nothing had happened. Was it denial of a reality I could not deal with? Was it my military training?"

Mary suggested we move to the front room, where the rain-streaked windows overlooked a sodden sports field and the distant Orongorongos.

I felt a little like the main character in John Mulgan's *Man Alone*,[3] who encounters Johnson in a Breton fishing village and repairs with him to a local café where they eat prawns, drink cheap red wine, and get to talking about the war.

This Johnson, if I might describe him, had just come out of Spain. This was a year or two ago now, it belonged to a different time. He was on leave and was going back again when his leave was over. He was a medium-sized man, very brown, almost black from the sun, with a round, ordinary-looking face and a large mouth and strong teeth stained yellow with tobacco. He had fair hair and no hat, and eyes that were either grey or green. Now I was interested in this war and, indeed, in any war, and I tried to get him to talk about it, but he wouldn't talk much. He said:

"There's a hell of a lot too much talk about war."

I waited a while. The noise in the café got worse if anything. They took away our prawns and brought veal and another bottle of wine.

"You can see war any time you want to," Johnson said. "There's a lot of war about in the world today. A few years ago now, it was different. Then it was an old man's story. It was the sort of thing you'd sit around the fire and tell stories about."

"You were in the Great War," I said. "Tell me about that."

"I've been in all the wars," Johnson said, "but I couldn't tell you anything about it."

"You won't talk about it?"

"I couldn't tell you anything even if I did. It wasn't anything. You wouldn't understand it unless you saw it. If you did see it, you wouldn't understand it."

It was very hot and stifling in the café, though as we sat there it began to grow quieter, and the smell of fish and cooking-oil was mixed with tobacco smoke.

"I couldn't tell you about the war," Johnson said. "It wasn't a lot different from anything else. I could tell you worse things about the peace."

"What was the peace?"

"That was the bit in between."

"Worse things?"

"Truer things."

And so I said to him, not wanting to move and quite ready to listen: "Tell me about the peace then."[4]

In his introduction to *The Iron Hand*, a compilation of New Zealand soldiers' poems from the Second World War, Les mentions a close friend, Ted Scherer, who died of shrapnel wounds during the last offensive of the Italian campaign. Scherer was only inches away from Les when he was hit.

Shrapnel-ripped and lifeless on the Santerno
Helmet tilted back into the lacerated earth,
Face twisted up for one last
Regretful look at the murderous sky[5]

It was April 10, 1945. That morning, Scherer had looked north and said, "When it's over we'll celebrate—we'll climb the highest point in the Alps."

After recovering in hospital from his own wounds, Les went into training in the Dolomites by doing some rock climbing. "But I could not persuade anyone in the battalion to accompany me on an expedition to Mt Blanc. By this time we were in bivouacs at Lake Trasimeno, near Rome. I set out from there on a goods train which took me to Milan, and I traveled by a variety of means through the mountains to Courmayeur where I was able to persuade a young Italian refugee to join me in the ascent. It was late in the season and the climb was arduous, particularly as our equipment was improvised and we suffered a good deal from inadequate food as well as from cold, exposure and exhaustion." Every step of the way, Les was thinking of his friend and all the mountains they might have climbed together, "and all the other friends of friends, shuffling, legions of them, in long, suffering lines across the mortuary of Europe. What good being alive, when those who meant the world to you were dead? Kaput, said the young refugee, who had found sympathy and courage enough to march in a dead man's steps. *Guerra kaput! Jawohl,* the survivor mumbled, *Guerra kaput!*"[6]

Six hours up an icefall on the south face, Les and his companion encountered a line of fresh tracks that drew them across the mountain's shoulder to a high-altitude, unlined, metal hut. Inside, they found a party of German-speaking Swiss, laughing and talking over their experiences on the tourist route from Chamonix. "The amiable vacationers were casually helping themselves to food from their rucksacks, innocent of the terror gnawing at their frontiers."[7] In broken German, Les enlightened them.

> We are climbers, British soldiers.
> They look disbelievingly at our improvised gear—
> Wehrmacht rucksacks, Alpini boots, Kaiapoi woolen
> Jerseys, caps comforter, and old army socks for gloves.
> What sort of army is this? Probably deserters
> Or escaped prisoners; maybe dangerous too.
> Offer them nothing.
> So I pull the Luger on the fattest of the bunch—
> No Alpine-fucking-club outing this,
> *Ich haben grossen hunger*!
> We grab a loaf of their bread and some fruit
> And drain a bottle of wine.
> Nobody speaks: only the autumn wind
> Snickers and squirms in the doorway.
> Before trying the peak I pick over their parkas
> And trade the best one for my military gas cape,
> Then we buckle on crampons, adjust the rope
> And start up the summit ridge.[8]

After the war, the Scherer family got in touch with Les, and he had recently received a letter from Ted's daughter asking if he would write down for her everything he could remember of her father. "It's a bit of a struggle," Les said. "It isn't easy to write about war without including the gory details, the sort of things no one would want to hear about or read about if they were going to have a positive memory of their loved one."

I was thinking: Les is nearly ninety. He has been returning to the war for sixty-six years, mostly to the experiences of others, including now a translation of the notebook of Helmut Metzner, an obscure soldier in Erwin Rommel's Afrika Korps, that contains occasional critiques of the Nazi regime and a crude poem in which he imagines himself having sex with Lili Marleen. When he mentioned this project to me, Les said, "I would very much like a chat with Helmut but we know for certain he is very kaput, kaput, kaput! Still, he lives on in my files along with Charles Smith and others." It was this remark that made me wonder whether the vital difference between Les's forays into the past and the obsessive-compulsive replaying of harrowing experience that we call post-traumatic stress disorder was Les's ability to make his own experiences secondary to those of others, putting them first, sacrificing his story in order that theirs be told.

When I first got to know Les in 1964, I often wanted to press him for details of his war experiences. This was before I realized the oblique and very private way in which he had come to terms with that period in his life. After the war, Les writes, he would "make many more difficult and dangerous journeys in our own mountains, but never under such emotionally disturbed and isolated circumstances. The Mont Blanc affair was a therapeutic venture into self-recovery and a wild leap into a new world of changed personal relationships; it also meant that a sense of bereavement and brooding anxiety could be thrown off in the exuberance of physical achievement."[9]

I had always been impressed by Les's sense of proportion and practicality, and in talking with Sierra Leoneans in the aftermath of their war, it was constantly brought home to me that recovery depends more on one's ability to throw oneself into the tasks of everyday life—caring for a child, making a farm, putting food on the table, sharing with those in greater need—than in one's success in seeking revenge or compensation, or wringing some meaning out of the arbitrary events that changed your life forever. Intellectual reflection has a place in our lives, to be sure, but unless it is connected to the exigencies of life in the here and now, it risks becoming morbid and dissociated. Perhaps this was why Les had steadfastly refused to participate in the writing of official history or to attend postwar ceremonies that extolled the heroic sacrifice of the fallen. Certainly, his healthy pragmatism underlay everything he had written on soldier's songs, poems, and popular culture. "If I were to attempt an epic of our military experiences that tried faithfully to evoke the consciousness of the ordinary soldier, I would probably relegate the formal

historical details to a chronology at the back of the work in order to concentrate on things that really matter, like a concern with food, cookhouses,
liquor, sex, clothing, the weather, rates of pay, equipment, loot, amusements,
recreation, morale, the techniques of deviancy, how to maintain one's precious individuality and, above all, how to avoid becoming a grim statistic on
one of our grisly war memorials."[10]

In Les's view, combat soldiers share with civilian workers in hazardous
occupations a sense of powerlessness that can only be countermanded by
organizing collectively, fostering a sense of solidarity, and having recourse
to gallows humor and dark laughter.[11] You may not be able to buck authority,
disobey orders, go on strike, or escape the nightmare of knowing that an
organized army is bent on killing you, but you can preserve your sense of
connectedness to a world where your individuality has some value and your
actions matter by writing letters home, keeping a diary, or joining forces with
your mates in ridiculing the situation in which you find yourself. Mutiny or
deserting are out of the question, but mocking the powers that be, protesting
one's lot, turning to sexual fantasy, and venting one's frustrations in obscene
songs can sometimes transform one's sense of being a victim into a sense of
being able in some small measure to experience one's situation on one's own
terms. To dwell on a tragedy is to risk drowning in it. To turn it into farce is
to remain afloat, treading water as it were, even though you may simply be
deferring the moment when, exhausted, you sink beneath the waves.

This was what happened to many men, Les said—the psychological casualties who returned home, haunted by what they had seen and done, hoping
that silence, time, and compulsive routines would heal the hidden wounds.
"It is simply not possible to come home as if nothing has happened and step
back into the role of Mr. Normal from Ashburton. There remains a part of
you that is continuously preoccupied with questions like, How can I stop
thinking about the bloke that got killed instead of me? Where is tomorrow's
food coming from? Such sinister, unrelenting calculations. I visited a bloke
on a farm in Taumarunui once. He had about a year's supply of baked beans,
tinned vegetable stew, and other stuff under the floorboards of his house, not
to mention a vast quantity of wine. He had been a prisoner of war and was
determined he would never run out of food again. I looked on in amazement
when he said, 'I'll just get a couple of bottles of wine,' and proceeded to pull up
the floorboards. He had cases of the stuff down there. But he was still living
inside that cocoon of deprivation and fear, and had to come to terms with

it by doing things around the farm. He was always supplying. He had some troubles with the local hardware people, so he bought a sawmill and set it up on the property and milled his own timber. Instead of bringing in a contractor to root up tree stumps and do a bit of earth moving, he bought two bulldozers and had them sitting there in the shed. He was prepared for a siege. That's an extreme example of the prisoner-of-war mentality, but I think he had successfully coped with his experiences, even if his behavior was a bit odd."

Some might consider Les's eclectic range of talents a bit odd. A self-taught builder, welder, motor mechanic, and electrician. A poet, songwriter and singer, journalist and political scientist. A mountaineer, master photographer, and self-styled literary blacksmith. Like the classical bricoleur, everything was grist to his mill, and the past was the raw material with which he hammered out prose that spoke to our present lives. This implies a compassionate attitude toward our ancestry. "I've always tended to look back; I've always been interested in leftovers and survivals."[12]

Of all the soldiers' poems Les collected in the postwar years, perhaps the most moving is by Charles Smith, who was among the New Zealanders ordered to hold a pass near Katerini, Greece, northwest of Mount Olympus, in order to gain time for the rest of the 2NZEF, who were retreating from the rapidly advancing Germans. Smith's poem first appeared in the *NZEF Times* in August 1942. It is simply called "Greece." It is about the bonds that were formed between the New Zealanders and Greek villagers during the tragic campaign of April and May 1941, in which the New Zealand force sustained 2,504 casualties before withdrawing to Crete, where, in the course of its continuing retreat, 3,853 out of a total strength of 7,702 were killed.

Out of the soil comes greatness of soul . . .

These, shaped by old knowledge of their jealous sod
Take on unswerving courage. They belong
To trees and fields, and mountains; so to God.

So first we saw: and never bread so sweet
Nor gift so free, nor welcome waking so;
Kindness so laughing, quick and garlanded,
Nor carnival of fortitude so gay
As heart of Greece in spring, on Freedom's day.

So near the shadow!
Yet in dark retreat
Came dusty envy that they still could cry
"Kalimera, English!" and "Goodbye!"
Hold fleeting friendship past the threat of death,
Give food and shelter: even understand
Our last desertion.
Do they know
How heart-remembered all their faces go?

These things are deathless, memory's cornerstone,
That rivulet that feeds the golden stream . . .

Is Ag Demetrios still a mountain dream?
Storks on the roof and cobbles on the street,
White from Olympus faerying the pines
Where bitter snow and spring of promise meet
Thyme and wild daphne.

Does Kathrina wear
A soldier's badge still braided in her hair?

Some years ago, Les read this poem during a radio interview He mentioned that, despite his best efforts, he had been unable to trace the author
and presumed him dead. Within a week, Les received an indignant letter
from Charles Smith saying he was not dead. He was a farmer near Whanga-
rei, with a family, and was very much alive.

So, we are surprised by what survives from the past, and what does not.
And how something we carry forward into the present can become so transformed that it ceases to possess what drew us to it in the first place, what
persuaded us it was worth keeping.

When Les recounted his visit to the Taumarunui farmer, he went on to
tell me that there were many such men who could not tolerate confinement
or bear to be shut up in a small space. "Who get out on their farms and go
for long walks and talk to dead companions or to God. Some carry a lot of
grievances, but they keep these to themselves."

I could not help but think of Les's own retreat in south Westland, as remote
from the madding crowd as one could wish, and close to the mountains and

bush that have been his *very present help in trouble*. But why do earth, stone, trees, and the sea have this power to bring us calm in troubled times?

In Chapter 16 of the *Tao-te Ching*, stillness is identified with one's roots, one's infancy, and with the nothingness from which the teeming and myriad forms of both life and thought emerge and to which, in time, they return. This original nature may be compared to a rough and unpolished stone. To contemplate it is to be returned to the prephenomenal ground of all being. But the manifold and changing forms of things are also worthy of contemplation, and I find it difficult to accept the fetishization of firstness or the idea that foundations are necessarily more real than anything we build on them. This is why stone implies, for me, not absolute constancy, but an *image* of constancy that helps one endure the vicissitudes of life, in which everything is sooner or later shattered, worn away, or reshaped by the elements with which we have to contend. From this observation arises the question of art, and of what we make of life, for while it is important to remember one's beginnings, to bear in mind from whence one came and to whom one owes one's life, it is, I think, foolish to do so at the expense of recognizing the importance of new departures, in which the original material is refashioned, as it were, in one's mind's eye or in one's own hands.

On the wooden terrace of his Wellington home, Les kept, for many years, numerous river stones and boulders that he had found on his excursions into the wilds of Westland. These stones not only caught his eye; they had, in a sense, possessed him—some because of a curious blemish that he could not reconcile with processes of natural erosion; some, like greenstone, because of their geological rarity; some because of their uncanny similarity to the contours of the human body. Les would lug these boulders down mountain gorges and through heavy bush, sometimes for days on end and often in a rucksack emptied of his personal supplies, before bringing his booty home to be burnished by rain, commented on by friends, or made the occasion for a story. When I left Wellington to pursue my doctoral studies at Cambridge, I would often think of Les's collection of stones, and it was with considerable dismay that I discovered, on my return to New Zealand after four years abroad, that Les had enlarged the living room of his house and built, in the middle of it, a massive fireplace whose chimney consisted of these beautiful stones cemented together into something resembling a cairn.

But now, having known Les for fifty years and having sat in front of his fireplace countless times, deep in conversation about our various travels or current projects, I no longer think that the stones properly belong to the contexts from whence they came. They belong where they are. And at Harvard University, I would discover in the course of long talks on early Chinese traditions with my friend Michael Puett that my thinking was not inconsistent with a Taoist view that sees the world as essentially (and demonically) chaotic, so that our human endeavors to create spaces of order are always transitory, and Les's river stones are destined to be, once again, a natural shambles on a hillside where no vestiges of his house or handiwork remain.

CHAPTER 12

The Other in Oneself

My friendship with Keith Ridler, like my friendship with Sofka Zinovieff (Chapter 10), began in the wake of my first wife's death. Pauline had fallen ill in France and after several months of unsuccessful medical treatment in the UK, we returned to New Zealand with our daughter Heidi. Pauline died a few weeks later. Not only did Keith and his girlfriend, Judith, offer my daughter Heidi and me the hospitality of their house, they insisted we stay until we had figured out our future. Keith's and Judith's love and care, at a time when they were embarking on their own life together, sustained me during a period of complete eclipse, and to this day I have only to play Leo Kottke's "Death by Reputation" or the Talking Head's "Once in a Lifetime" to be carried back to that house on Elmira Avenue where Keith served espresso, cooked Italian seafood meals, and was happy to rap about anthropology and literature at any hour of the day or night.

Heidi and I eventually moved to Australia, to forge a new beginning, but returned to New Zealand over the next few years to keep in touch with our homeland and visit Keith and Judith, now happily ensconced in an old farmhouse in the Pohangina Valley, balancing the demands of university teaching and three small children. When I remarried and moved to the United States in 1989, visits home became fewer, though I kept up a voluminous correspondence with both Keith and Judith, and they spent several weeks with us in Bloomington, Indiana, during their sabbatical year in the early 1990s.

* * *

When I traveled to New Zealand in 2008 to research a book on the theme of natality, I considered it a miracle that Keith was alive and well, for when I had last seen him, eighteen months earlier, his marriage was on the rocks, his father had recently died, his university job gave him little satisfaction, and he was depressed and drinking a quarter of a bottle of whiskey a day, as well as wine with meals, and smoking a lot of dope. I had felt powerless to reach him, let alone help him get back on his feet, and had resigned myself to watching another dear friend dig himself an early grave. Now, as we embraced on the threshold of his Thorndon cottage, I marveled at the transformation I saw in him.

Keith led me through the hallway and kitchen to a table in his brick-paved backyard where he had laid out bowls of arugula salad, olives, pickled onions, avocados, capsicums, fresh French bread, and a saucer of New Zealand olive oil from Kapiti Island.

"I have an Italian red for you," Keith said, uncorking a wine called Menhir from Manduria. Keith, however, was on the wagon. "No alcohol, no meat, no joints. I've returned to Buddhism," he said. "I meditate every day and try to take care of myself." He then uncapped a bottle of nonalcoholic French beer called *La force c'est la goût.*

"Then may the force be with you," I said, drinking to my friend's good health, though not without a pang of disappointment that he and Judith were no longer together.

"There's a Zen parable," Keith said, "about an adept who retires to a tower determined to find enlightenment. He makes himself indifferent to the outside world, sits in zazen for hours on end, deprives himself of sleep, eats only enough to keep himself alive, yet enlightenment evades him. He begins to sink into despair, convinced that his goal is unattainable. There seems nothing left to live for. Climbing the parapet, he is about to leap to his death when he sees clearly for the first time."

"So we have to sink to the bottom before we start to swim?" I asked, and for a split second I was recalling the winter afternoon when I was three . . . falling into a liquid manure sump on a Taranaki farm . . . sinking fourteen feet through acrid and cloying cow shit until I hit bottom . . . pushing instinctively with my feet . . . surfacing, flailing . . . finding the concrete edge of the pit and pulling myself out.

As we ate the good food, I asked Keith if he had any plans.

"I have come back to myself," Keith said. "I've returned to my guitar. To tramping in the Tararuas. To food. To books. To life."

It sometimes happens that when things fall apart, we revert to an earlier time, imagining ourselves starting out again, though on a different path. Just as Keith seemed to have returned to his student years in Wellington, so, when

Pauline died, I regressed to the time before we met. And it was Keith and Judith who helped me see, in that dark time, that there were pleasures and possibilities yet in store.

After lunch, Keith suggested a walk in the nearby botanical gardens.

It was a windless day, and as we negotiated a narrow track above the playground, I told Keith about a conversation I had had with Les Cleveland (Chapter 11) the day before, and how I was still going over in my mind a single phrase he had used when speaking of the trauma of surviving a war in which so many comrades died: *There remains a part of you that is continuously preoccupied with questions like, How can I stop thinking about the bloke that got killed instead of me?* I was convinced that the "bloke" in this case was Les's friend Ted Scherer. I also told Keith that Les had described how, not long after Ted's death and the end of hostilities, in Italy, the New Zealand troops were shown American film footage of the liberation of Buchenwald. "Bodies piled like logs," as Les put it. "Bewildered, skeletal survivors." The film changed him. He felt then, and still felt, that more should have been done to prevent the Holocaust. After seeing the film, none of the soldiers knew what to say or do. As Les put it, "They didn't have the vocabulary for such experiences."

"Even if you had a language for such experiences," Keith said, "it might not ease the moral pain it leaves you with." He paused before reminding me that his father fought with the British Special Air Service (SAS) regiment in the Second World War.

On April 15, 1945, Duncan Ridler was driving along a sandy track through a dense pine forest northeast of Hanover, Germany, when his unit came upon some figures dressed in strange orange-brown uniforms. They were lined up on either side of the road as far as the eye could see. Dunc asked them who they were and what they were doing. They were Hungarians. There had been an outbreak of typhus or typhoid in the camp, and their job was to prevent anyone from leaving. The convoy drove on to a road junction in the forest. Dunc was impressed by the whitewashed concrete curbs, the raked gravel, the military signposts. But there was something else, a stench that was almost overpowering in its awfulness. Instead of finding a camp where they might liberate some British prisoners of war, they had come upon Belsen. It was deathly quiet, with shuttered huts and no sound from the watchtowers. At first, the few German guards seemed unperturbed by the British jeeps, but then Dunc spotted a pile of rotten potato peelings, about six feet high, with what looked like filthy, animated skeletons feasting on the putrid leftovers. At that moment, a German leaned out of the cookhouse window and shot one of the emaciated figures.

Though hardened by combat, the SAS men gagged at what they saw—creatures who were once human, now starved, utterly filthy, their eyes staring out of slate-gray faces, their wounds vilely infected, the stench insufferable. Then the soldiers came upon the pit. One took photos so that the world would know what had happened there. Another stumbled away from the discarded, unburied corpses, grabbed the nearest guard, and beat him to death. The SAS did not stay long in Belsen, but Dunc remained as interpreter for the officer in command of the 63rd Anti-Tank Regiment, Royal Artillery, who took over the camp and accepted the formal surrender of Josef Kramer, Belsen's commandant.[1]

I had recently read a biography of war correspondent Martha Gellhorn and remembered the shame and disenchantment that overcame her at the camp at Dachau and, soon after, at Belsen. She wrote: "It is as if I walked into Dachau and there fell over a cliff, and suffered a lifelong concussion, without recognizing it."[2] Twenty-five years after the war, she confessed: "Looking back, I know I have never again felt that lovely, easy, lively hope in life which I knew before, not in life, not in our species, not in our future on earth."[3]

Perhaps Dunc felt something very similar, I thought. *Perhaps his restiveness was passed on to his son.*[4] In fact, Keith had often mentioned to me that, after the war, his father was looking to make a fresh start, though several years were lost before this happened.

Keith was born in Italy. He was seven years old when his parents separated. Dunc migrated to New Zealand with his "staggeringly beautiful, twenty-year-old housekeeper, Grec." Keith remembers the glaring light (caused by the high levels of ultraviolet radiation in the southern atmosphere), the treeless landscapes, the absence of substantial buildings, and the gorse-infested hill where Dunc rented a bungalow. Dunc and Grec were in love. No longer did they have to pretend they were married. It was Dunc's new lease of life. As for Keith, he was happy with his wild and windswept surroundings, though even at seven he still felt Italy was home.

As we sauntered through a grove of *pōhutukawas*, looking for the great Mediterranean pines that surrounded the children's play area, Keith said that he retained, from his earliest years in Rome, an affinity for all things Italian. A love of food, books, wine, and adventure. "New Zealanders still strike me as strange," he said.

"Yet I've always thought of you as the consummate Kiwi," I said. "Climbing mountains, white-water rafting, striking out into the wilderness."

"I mean the Anglo heritage. The repressed and cautious side of us. The tendency to share resentments rather than show compassion. Point the finger rather than cultivate conviviality. Despite embracing ethnic food, espresso coffee, European fashions, we remain awkward in our skins, preoccupied by tidiness, boundaries, and security."

"This may be true," I said. "I also abhor that uptightness you speak of, but I feel at home here in a way I don't elsewhere. This is where I have a right to be, even if I don't always feel like exercising that right."

"I feel like that in Italy," Keith said.

"Not here?"

"My thoughts wander between the two. One minute I can be thinking ahead to a weekend trip to the Tararuas with Pablo [Keith's son], the next I am thinking of that other green valley, eight thousand miles away, at the foot of the Brenta massif."

Keith had been returning to the Trentino in northern Italy for twenty-five years, doing anthropological fieldwork in an alpine village. His descriptions of his friends in Caderzone and their everyday lives are among the most ethnographically luminous I know: Pier Paolo the salami maker, and the smell of his *salumeria*—a pungent mixture of salted meat, garlic, spilled wine, and the damp pine sawdust on the stone floor; Augusto, who owned the land where Keith stayed, sharing with the young ethnographer details of village history, the workings of the transhumant system, and life in the high Alps. "[Augusto's] sense of continuity was powerful," Keith said, "rooted in his own daily work as a *contadino* (peasant), a word he used with pride. He told me once, as we were haymaking together, that he had used the same scythe for more than sixty summers: 'The blades have changed, but it's always been the same handle.'"[5]

"Isn't this what every expatriate feels?" I asked Keith. "That the blades have changed, but not the handle?"

When I said goodbye to Keith that afternoon, I urged him to publish more of his Caderzone material, to write about the *professore* who cut his own firewood with a chainsaw and had the same appreciation of practical know-how and traditional food as the locals. But perhaps the moment had passed, and Keith would find something very different to devote his energies to. Perhaps, too, I was simply giving my friend the advice I would give myself, who could not imagine life without writing.

As I crossed the city to visit Judith, it occurred to me how remote now was the Pohangina Valley where she and Keith had lived, where their three children had come into the world, and where I had so often enjoyed the bounty of their table, long walks into the hills, and exhilarating conversations about books and writing. How distant, too, seemed the summer night when I brought Katherine to meet Keith and Judith for the first time. After a lavish meal of seafood, washed down by chilled white wine, we walked arm in arm along a moonlit road with the dark furled poplars on either side, and I realized how misguided people had been to tell me that Katherine looked exactly like Pauline, as though I had to be awoken from a spell that could only bring me disappointment.

*   *   *

Over the next two years, Keith's news was upbeat. Now retired from teaching, he described "a quiet life meditating and studying Buddhist philosophy and psychology," occasionally taking his sons on a road trip in New Zealand, traveling alone in Malaysia, spending five weeks in Tonga with his son Pablo. But by 2012, his travels had brought him back to Europe.

*   *   *

I've come to roost in Portugal and have been living here since November of last year. I've settled down with my partner Gui in a former fishing village on the Sintra coast, about 50 minutes' drive north of Lisboa. She has made it her life's mission to treat me with all the care and kindness a Lusitanian male deserves and expects and is educating me in all things Portuguese. It is a sublime part of the world, the westernmost part of Europe, a UNESCO World Heritage area, with an amazing range of natural habitats, castles and palaces, fantastic food and wine and, most important, amiable and courteous people who tolerate my abysmal Portuguese with grace and encouragement. Last, but not least, the cost of living is the lowest in western Europe, so a man with my vices lives very comfortably on what would be a very modest income in New Zealand. I'm still puzzling over what I did to get so lucky.

*   *   *

Keith went on to describe his experiments with abstract painting and photography, and journeys with Gui to Spain, France, and the United Kingdom. They had recently spent two weeks on a canalboat on England's Warwickshire ring, and he was now in the process of buying a canalboat and planned to spend his summers in England and his winters with Gui in Portugal.

Keith bought his boat. But without a computer and struggling with ill health, his emails to me became infrequent. When news of his death reached me, I found it difficult to find out what kind of life he had been leading or how he had died. Although his children visited him from time to time, I did not want to intrude on their grief by plying them with questions. And so I read and reread his emails in search of clues. One phrase struck me as singularly poignant, partly because it resonated with my own sense of estrangement from my homeland. Keith had read my book about traveling through New Zealand in 2008 and exploring the themes of beginnings and belonging. "It moved and provoked me in the most positive way," Keith wrote. "*You wrestle so courageously with the issues that preoccupy us displaced ones and give us all—at the very least—the sense that we are not alone.*" For some reason I had never thought of Keith as "displaced." For all his restiveness, and the fact that his life ended on a canalboat in his father's homeland, far from the places and people he held most dear, I had always seen him as a true cosmopolite— someone who felt at home everywhere.

That we shared a deep sense of not feeling at home in the world per- haps explains why, in the days and weeks following Keith's death, I felt as if a part of myself had been torn from me and cast away. I was mourning my friend's unfinished life, to be sure, but I was also mourning a part of myself that would not exist had I not known him. I needed no other proof that this missing aspect of myself was connected to my friendships and my homeland than the arresting line with which Keith concluded his reflections: *In your writing, I could smell New Zealand, feel the wind from the sea, and hear the voices of people I have known and have cared for, or been cared for by.*

CHAPTER 13

A Plaited Rope, Entire from Source to Mouth

To say that every friendship reflects personal and cultural compatibilities is to state the obvious. But friendship, like love, calls for description before it calls for explanation, and in the final analysis we are often surprised by what we cannot entirely account for. It is this residue of mystery that may be our best hope in a divided world, for it suggests that we are never reducible to the stereotypes to which we so often reduce one another.

I first met Te Pakaka Tawhai in 1967, when we were junior lecturers in the recently inaugurated Department of Anthropology and Māori Studies at Victoria University of Wellington. The uncomfortable relationship between these disciplines echoed the ambivalent relationship between Pākehā (New Zealanders of European descent) and indigenous Māori in the country at large, and since Paka tended to hang out with his Ngāti Porou colleagues, Koro Dewes and Apirana ("Api") Mahuika, I saw less of him than I would have liked. Because I was writing about Māori myth and carved art and completing a master's dissertation on the impact of literacy in early nineteenth-century Aotearoa New Zealand, it would have made sense for me to actively engage with these colleagues. That I hesitated to do so speaks volumes about the simmering tensions and social grievances that afflicted the nation at that time.

When I went to Cambridge University in 1968 for doctoral study, I continued my research on the carved *pare* (lintel), superb specimens of which were in storage at the British Museum. Four years later, I published this research in a Dutch journal, and when I returned to New Zealand the following year to take up a position in the Department of Anthropology and Māori Studies at Massey University, I was elated to discover that Api and Paka were colleagues, and that Paka had read my essay on the *pare* and approved of it.

We became close friends. While Paka helped me acquire a deeper understanding of Te Ao Māori (Māori worldviews), I helped him bridge the gap

between the discursive conventions of the Western academy and the protocols (*tikanga*) of traditional Māori ways of knowing (*matauranga*). Hardly a
weekend passed that I did not drive to Paka's house to find him in the garden
or sitting on the living-room floor, surrounded by sheafs of paper on which
he was writing and rewriting expositions of Māori cosmology. In sharing his
work with me, he helped me appreciate not only the relational and dynamic
character of the Māori worldview but also its relevance to kinship and friendship, both of which are informed by a spirit of *aroha*. One's life is a strand or
moment in the life of one's lineage. It is never wholly one's own, any more than
the land on which one was born. To invoke another metaphor, one's lifetime
is but one layer in the sedimentary beds of genealogical time (*whakapapa*).

*   *   *

During my years in the Manawatu, my family spent two memorable summers on Paka's family's east coast farm, crutching sheep all day and returning
in the evenings to hearty meals prepared by Paka's mother (Pi) and his sisters, and afterward being entertained with stories by Paka's brother Joe. Some
days, Paka would take us on excursions to some of the great carved houses
(*whare whakairo*) of Ngāti Porou.

    One afternoon, Paka and Joe drove me north to the isolated settlement of
Reporoa. We stopped for a while on a high ridge. The hills were bare except
for stands of cabbage trees and an occasional dark grove of karaka trees.
Cloud shadow and wind combed the long grass. Far below the shoulder of
the hill, breakers, like braided ropes, unraveled on a long white beach.

    The road wound down into a hollow in the hills, where the meeting
house, Te Auau, was cradled as in the palm of an upturned hand.

    Unlike most meeting houses, Te Auau had not been conceived as the body
of an ancestor. Carved figures with outthrust tongues and glaring eyes do not
defy the visitor. The spirit of Te Auau is one of welcoming and warmth.

    We spent no more than an hour there, among photos of men who had
gone away to war and not returned, among tukutuku panels whose pastel
tones reminded Paka of "a fading rainbow." In Te Auau, you feel the integrity
and mana of those who put their energy and genius into its construction, the
living presence of those who have gone before. And it was part and parcel of
the landscape around us, whose every knoll and hollow Paka and Joe knew
by name, whose every ngaio and peach grove brought alive, for them, the
mythic past.

*   *   *

When Paka died, I was living in the United States, but from mutual friends I learned that Paka's family had insisted he be buried at the *urupa* (cemetery) on his own marae, tradition demanding that the dead be brought home and buried among their forebears, so that they might be remembered and mourned together. But Paka's widow, who was not Māori, had wanted him buried in the town where they had lived and raised their children. The bitter argument came to a head at the funeral. Paka's sister harangued the congregation, demanding that Paka be returned to his proper resting place. Paka's widow remained unmoved. In the end, a compromise was proposed by Mason Durie, one of Paka's Māori colleagues: let Te Pakaka be buried on Mason's marae, Aorangi. Though Aorangi was neither Paka's birthplace nor the place he had lived and worked for the last sixteen years of his life, it was a place he knew, a marae on which he had often stood and spoken. So that is where he was laid to rest, unlike the arguments among the bereaved. His Ngāti Porou kin went back to the east coast, disowning Paka's mixed-blood children and threatening the widow with dire consequences should she ever remarry.

I felt their distress and recalled how Paka had once pointed out to me that there was something deeply amiss when one observes seagulls far inland, scavenging on trash, for every species and every person has its own appointed place in the scheme of things, a place where it properly belongs. To transgress those boundaries was like mingling the water from different catchment areas or moving genetic material from one species into another—a disruption of their respective *whakapapa* (genealogical identity) and *mauri* (vital essence), a loss of the primordial balance between Ranginui (the male sky) and Papatūānuku (the female earth), an infringement of *tapu*, and thus an invitation to disaster.

It was several months after Paka's death before I was able to make a pilgrimage to his family home in Tuparoa. After renting a car in Auckland, I drove south. Overnight there had been electrical storms and heavy rain, but the air was now fresh and clear, and the sun was glinting on the backs of the offshore waves as I headed toward the Bay of Plenty.

I stopped my car once, between Ōpōtiki and Te Kaha, to look at some flax kits that were for sale. When I inquired about one named *Patikitiki* (bones of people—from war), asking if the pink hue was from *whinau* bark, the Māori woman looked at me suspiciously. The dyes were secret, she said, then added,

"Don't I know you? What's your name?" I told her my first name. "Your sur-name," she said. She was disappointed. "No, you're not the one. For a moment I thought you were that man who wrote the book about our *kete*" (woven flax baskets).

I understood her concern—the age-old tension between the notion of knowledge as a life-bringing gift and the notion of knowledge as a commod-ity, to be invested, traded, and exchanged outside the community to which it belonged. In diverting the gift of knowledge toward the marketplace, books betray its social value, and those whose existence depend upon it may become weakened or ill. It was a problem Paka had wrestled with for as long as I knew him—trying to keep faith with traditional protocols while produc-ing work for academic consumption.

As if reading my mind, the women told me that her son was about to leave for Brisbane, where he was enrolled in a course at a polytechnic school. She thought of Brisbane and of the outside world as places of profiteering, selfishness, and loss. "I just hope he doesn't forget the things he learned here at home," she said.

I reached Ruatoria at the end of a scorching afternoon and turned down the gravel road toward Tuparoa.

When I stopped the car and switched off the ignition, the shrilling of cicadas instantly filled the air.

Paka's home was exactly as I remembered it: the driveway lined with blue hydrangeas and agapanthus, hens pecking and scuffing in the dirt by the back door.

I rapped loudly on the door and waited. There was a radio playing inside. I peered through the dining room window but could see no sign of life. I shuddered at how dark and shabby the room had become, as though I'd expected it to be the same as it had been on New Year's Eve fifteen years ear-lier, with Paka's sisters busy in the kitchen, children racing about, and Paka's father preparing to serve the now-marinated cabbage tree hearts (*tī kōuka*) we had gathered the previous afternoon on a hill above the sea, and telling us how the *tī* symbolizes the power of life to overcome all hardships and rise anew from barren or devastated ground—hence the healing and regenerative power of the *kōuka*.

I went up to the orchard, thinking Paka's sister might be there. The peach and nectarine trees were shaggy with lichen. There was no one in sight.

Walking back to the house, I saw how truly ramshackle it had become and remembered Paka's distress in the winter of 1985 when his father's arthritis made it impossible for the old man to maintain the place. Jim had wanted Paka to come home and repile it and replace the roof and rusty guttering. "A time of change," Paka had said to me, touching his hand to his heart. "Time for me to go home. I *want* to go home now."

I climbed the fence into the neighbor's paddock and walked through lank grass toward the cattle yard. The neighbor and his sons were sitting on a rail fence in the yard. They had just killed and skinned a cattle beast. The flayed carcass hung from the lower branch of a big macrocarpa. Flies buzzed above the blood-soaked earth.

No one showed any interest in me as I approached.

The neighbor was wearing a black woolen undershirt and held a cigarette between his fingers. As I began to speak, one of his boys began dragging the greasy hide up a dirt track toward the house.

"I'm looking for Faith," I said. Faith was Paka's sister.

The big man drew on his cigarette and squinted through the smoke.

"I was a friend of Paka's," I explained. "I've just driven down from Auckland."

"She not there?" the man asked.

"The radio's on in the dining room, but I knocked on the door and no one answered."

"Might have gone to town," the man said.

There seemed little point in asking any more questions. I walked away from the killing yard and climbed through the fence again, feeling the big man's eyes on me all the way.

By the time I got back to the car, he and his sons had mounted their horses and were going down the road in single file, followed by three black dogs. They had haunches of meat wrapped in sacking across their pommels. The air pulsed with the shrilling of cicadas. I was in half a mind to drive to Reporoa, but in the end I went back the way I'd come, churning through the dust toward Ruatoria.

I parked my car outside the post office and wandered down the main street, looking into the local stores to see if I could find Faith. Then I walked back to the post office and asked the woman at the counter if she knew Faith Tawhai. I explained that I was looking for her, that she wasn't at home, and a neighbor had told me she might be in town.

"I'm Faith's cousin," the woman said. "Where you from?"

"Auckland," I said.

"You don't sound like a Kiwi," she said.

"I live in the United States," I said.

"Come over for the [Commonwealth] Games?"

"No," I said, "I'm just looking up a few old friends."

"Oh," she said, as if I had disappointed her, and I asked her again if she knew where I might find Faith. She told me I might try down at "the rec." Seeing my puzzlement, she told me I should go back along the Tuparoa road a little way until I came to Whakarua Park. "She could be there," she said, "at the hall."

Uepohatu Hall was named for one of the renowned chiefs of Ngāti Porou, a direct descendant of Maui, the mythical discoverer of Aotearoa. The hall was the inspiration of Sir Apirana Ngata, who supervised its construction in 1942—a time when the Māori Battalion was suffering calamitous reversals in the North African desert. No family in Ngāti Porou was spared the anguish of loss. To help share the grief and reaffirm the value of life, Ngata brought people together in night schools to receive instruction in *whakapapa* and to recover the waning arts of carving, weaving, and poetry. To give material form to this cultural renaissance, Ngata proposed that a great hall be built as a permanent memorial to all who had fought for freedom in the two world wars. But for succeeding generations, Uepohatu Hall would become not only a memorial to warrior ancestors but also a place pervaded by the spirit of those who built it. As Paka once remarked, Uepohatu was "a memorial not so much to those for whom they wept but to the fact that they wept."[1]

For Paka, Uepohatu had other memories as well. In the summer of 1945, he and other boys from Manutahi Primary School were sent to help work on the hall. Paka stoked fires for cooking *paua* (New Zealand abalone), helped the tukutuku frame makers, and fetched and carried for Ngata himself. Sometimes Ngata would summon Paka to work with him on the tukutuku. Paka would take a seat on the reverse side of the tukutuku frame, pulling the dyed flax threads through the slats while the great man regaled the awestruck boy with stories of his artistic forebears or instructed him in waiata (traditional songs). Paka was aware that he was involved in something momentous, and he would never forget a single detail of that long, hot summer: the stipend he was paid that enabled him to shoe his horse, Dan; the breathless trips to the local shop for Ngata's tobacco; the way the great man ate half slices of bread heaped with marmalade at tea breaks and afterward smoked his bent and foul-smelling pipe before laying it aside and returning to work on his translation of the Bible.

For Paka, Uepohatu was one of the few places that brought Māori and European traditions together without compromising either. The interior of the hall is carved and decorated in the style of other Māori meeting houses, but the outside is unembellished and resembles an ordinary European community hall. Within the body of the hall, biblical motifs are juxtaposed with images of the rivers, mountains, and shoreline that sustained the soldiers far from home. And in its dedication to Uepohatu, associated with Maui who, using his grandmother's lower jaw as a fishhook and clotted blood from his own nose as bait, hauled up the North Island (Te Ika a Maui) from the sea, with Mount Hikurangi emerging first from the waters—a place of salvation and new life.

Paka once wrote that Uepohatu embraces to itself the mana of all the peoples of Aotearoa New Zealand, its purpose being "to concentrate the mana of all New Zealanders under the one roof."[2] Paka's hope echoed the thoughts of Ngata, his mentor, who once inscribed a spontaneous poem in the autograph book of a young Māori child: "Turn your hand to the tools of the Pākeha for the wellbeing of your body / Turn your heart to the treasures of your ancestors as a crown for your head."[3] Rather than treat tradition and modernity as mutually inimical, Ngata saw them as different strands that could be interwoven to strengthen the vitality of all.

During my years in the Manawatu, Paka and I spent long hours in conversation about the conditions under which knowledge becomes alienated from life, its sole value lying in advancing an academic career rather than in its vital power (*mauri*) to bring and bind people together in a common world. As Paka drew on my support in working out a way of honoring traditional protocols in writing his thesis (rather than conforming to academic conventions that assumed that knowledge transcended life), I drew on his support in my own struggles to make anthropology speak to life-as-lived. Vitality was our common concern—the generative potential of language, knowledge, and, dare I say, friendship to serve the common weal.

Paka helped me see how one can steer a course between two or more traditions without sacrificing the integrity of either. As a young man, he had mastered the taiaha (a long fighting staff); as an adult, he worked toward a black belt in karate. He accepted my efforts to understand the spirit of *maatauranga* (traditional knowledge), even when those efforts suggested that a Pākeha could never fully understand Te Ao Māori.

One afternoon, after hours of backbreaking work in a shearing shed in the Waiapu River valley, Paka told me the story of a pregnant woman who, craving *kai moana* (seafood), ignored a *tapu* and, night after night, crept down to the coast to gather shellfish. One morning, as she retraced her steps upriver to her own kainga (village), the sunrise found her out and she was turned to stone. There she is today in the middle of the river, arrested forever, her kits filled with the illicit seafood. The story inspired a poem, which I showed Paka. He smiled. I had got the story a bit wrong, but I had made something compelling of what I had heard, something that was mine, and that was all right. What mattered was life—life that produced life.

Toward the end of his life, Te Pakaka embraced the Baha'i faith and its emphasis on the worth of all religions and the unity and equality of all people, searching like Ngata for the common humanity that might make coexistence possible. Perhaps it was appropriate that Paka should be buried at Aorangi, halfway between his birthplace and the place where his children were born. His vision was always of the common ground that makes conversation and coexistence possible.

I did not find Faith. I walked back from "the rec," got into my car, and headed south.

It was late afternoon. The distant peak of Hikurangi lay inland among the shadows of the range.

And then I heard the voice. At first, I did not think it strange that it was so familiar and so close. I was aware only of my difficulty in understanding *te reo* (the Māori language). But I knew, even before I knew that this was no ordinary voice, that the one reiterated word, *wairua*, meant that I was being assured that Te Pakaka was there in spirit, returned to his people, to that place, and that he had come home.

CHAPTER 14

Friends and Familiars

In the provincial world in which I came of age, male friendships tended to be centered on beer drinking, telling tall stories, and rugby. Love and marriage may have been sources of deep personal fulfillment, but in the pub they were often demeaned as threats to the male bond, and a lot of banter was sexist and scatological. A one-night stand could be bragged about, but dating signaled the beginning of a long decline into domestic servitude. As for the male bonds that were forged in this seamy atmosphere, they were seldom, if ever, subject to reflection. As J. M. Coetzee observes in a letter to his friend Paul Auster, "Friends, or at least male friends in the West, don't talk about how they feel toward each other."[1]

I used to think these prejudices were unique to the working-class, antipodean culture of mateship, but variations of them occur in societies throughout the world and seem to spring from men's ambivalence toward women's generative power, which they envy, and the fact that in bringing a child into the world the continuity of the male line is secured at the expense of the father, who is suddenly faced with the inevitability of his own demise. In Māori thought, women bring children into "the world of light" (*te ao marama*), yet the vagina is also the source of misfortune and death (*te whare o aitua*), for it was the goddess Hine-nui-te-Po who crushed the culture hero Maui between her thighs as he sought immortality by reentering her womb. Male ambivalence toward women extends to the land, *te whenua* (which also denotes the lining of the womb and the placenta that nourishes the fetus). Hence the saying, *He wahine, he whenua, ka ngaro te tangata*—by women and land, men are destroyed. The ambiguity of birth is also a central preoccupation in West Africa. The Bambara say that although fire gives birth to fire (that is, men and women reproduce their kind, and society itself is reproduced through the birth of children), fire also gives birth to ash (a metaphor for barrenness and social death). Nevertheless, ash is ambiguous, which is why one can blow on seemingly dead embers and a live flame will start (the dead live on as ancestors; infants that die before weaning may be reincarnated). It is also true that although birth, like any gift, brings life to another, it may spell a compromise or sacrifice in the life of the giver, as when a mother dies during childbirth or a wayward child brings misfortune upon its home. Among the Tallensi of northern Ghana, begetting (bearing) is said to be hard—a view that is charged with deep emotion and elucidated by women in terms of the pain of childbirth, the distress of losing a child, and the difficulties of raising a family. By contrast, men cite the exhausting work, heavy responsibilities, and irksome taboos that begin with a woman's pregnancy, though their tribulations really begin, they say, with the sex act itself, since ejaculation "is a giving up of something vital that is a source of strength and youth."[2] This assumption finds universal expression in the view that semen loss diminishes vigor and shortens life, as in the widely espoused Hindu view that semen is "closely associated with the idea of the soul that survives after death,"[3] and that "the retention of sperm makes a man a hero and a god; its loss makes him low and animal-like."[4]

*   *   *

No one was more preoccupied by the pitfalls of marriage than George Bowen, with whom I shared an apartment when we were undergraduates at the University of Auckland. George wore purple corduroys, flamboyant shirts, and had a habit of hiding his beer at parties; and though we never became close friends, his story provides a poignant glimpse into the psychology of mateship.

Long after most of our peers were married, George clung to his old routine—drinking in the pub every evening, attending student parties, and keeping his distance from women. When I returned to New Zealand in 1965 after several years abroad, I was astonished to walk into the Duke of Edinburgh Hotel one evening and find him still there. I was even more surprised to discover that he was still in the process of completing his undergraduate degree.

Ironically, when the pub closed at six o'clock and we trudged uphill to the university, where he was scheduled to chair a meeting of the literary society, I would meet and fall in love with Pauline Harris, whom I married two years later.

Whether this event inspired George to change his ways, I do not know, but he too got married in 1968, only to divorce Sarah a few months after the birth of their son the following year, by which time I was in Sierra Leone, embarking on my doctoral research.

Although George and I exchanged letters from time to time, almost thirty years passed before I saw him again. Our meeting was revelatory, for I now understood why I had kept in touch with him. *He was myself as I might have been.* He embodied the shadow side of myself and my deep-seated fear of becoming like one of the dossers I had worked with in London in the winter of 1963–64.

I had flown into Auckland from Singapore, and after passing through immigration and customs, I took a taxi to my sister's address in Mount Eden. Following her emailed instructions, I found the front door key in a hebe bush near the mailbox and let myself into the house. A day and a night ago, I had been in the dank winter-dark of Copenhagen, but in Auckland sunlight filled the living room, and I could see as far as the Waitakere ranges, white cumulus clouds above them like puppets in a Balinese shadow play. All night on the plane, I had slept fitfully, my mind clogged with a sargasso of floating memories and disconnected images—from when I lived in New Zealand or first went to Sierra Leone. Now, walking out into the new morning, I was once again swept back into the past, experiencing the agoraphobia that Auckland's single-storied suburbs always induces in me, the weatherboard houses and mown lawns overwhelmed by an isthmus sky. In the suburban streets, *pōhutukawa* trees, jacarandas, cabbage trees, and privet hedges were in flower. The air was heavy with the peppery, spermy odor of pollen, and shrill with the brouhaha of birds piping, whistling, and warbling around me. All this intensified the oppressive familiarity of the neighborhood from which I nevertheless felt quite estranged. This feeling deepened as I approached the house where my parents had lived until their deaths almost ten years earlier—the trees they had planted now felled, the lot returned to concrete paths and bare lawns, and the now characterless house sitting in the middle of this desolate space like a dog kennel. Occasionally, someone would drive down the street in a car or emerge from a driveway, or an elderly person would pass me without a glance, lugging a shopping bag. But mostly, the place was deserted, its life confined behind curtained windows and locked doors.

For several days, I felt weighed down by the past yet haunted by its unreality. Though stirred to scribble poems about the harsh marine light, the smells that assailed my nostrils, the deafening birdsong, the white clouds, or the old photographs and family letters that my sister kindly copied for me, I found myself struggling like a diver in the depths, desperate to surface and

breathe fresh air, to embrace something new. Auckland belonged to another
life, a previous reincarnation, or to someone else. And I marveled at times,
walking along Dominion Road, at how confused and lost this other "me" had
felt forty-five years ago, riding home on the last bus, his head full of poems of
unrequited love and the longing to get away. Back then, I had my whole life
ahead of me. Now I was entering my *troisième âge*. In another twenty years,
perhaps, I could well be like my mother, who, in her early eighties, began a
journal in which she set down reminiscences of her childhood and youth in
the Taranaki town where she was raised. She told me at the time, "At my age
you don't have a lot to look forward to, so you look back." At what age, I asked
myself, does one cease to have a future? At what age is rebirth no longer possible? I suppose a lot depends on what the world offers you. In Sierra Leone,
I had met young men who felt that the world offered them very little. Some
of my contemporaries, recently retired, found themselves at a loose end and
complained about the things they had dreamed of doing and not done, while
others, following in the footsteps of John Milton's "uncouth swain," were
moving on to fresh fields and pastures new. The repercussions of being born
to particular parents, in a particular place, at a particular time, and what it
means to be born to oneself, elsewhere, and with others, perplexed and preoccupied me throughout my sojourn in Auckland.

*   *   *

The morning after I arrived in Auckland, George Bowen rang to say that he
had heard I was in town and would like to see me. Given the passage of so
many years, I quailed at the prospect of being once more dragged back into
a time I found oppressive to even think about, but I was curious. So, we met
one morning, at George's suggestion, outside one of our old watering holes—
the Queen's Ferry Hotel on Vulcan Lane.

I arrived early and was nervously walking up and down the lane, wondering if I would recognize him. When he finally appeared, shambling up the
street toward me, I was aghast. This once fresh-faced young man was now old
beyond his years—stiff-necked, hunched, unkempt, wearing an unpressed
rust-colored suit, and holding a smoldering roll-your-own cigarette between
his nicotine-stained fingers.

Traits that we shrug off as endearing quirks in a young man are all
too readily read as signs of decrepitude in the old. And so, as I struggled
to come to terms with George's physical decline, I began to realize that his

disconcerting pedantry and self-absorption were not symptoms of aging but simply exaggerated aspects of the person he had always been. The hotel was closed, but George explained that there was now a second Queen's Ferry on Queen Street, so we crossed the road, found a table overlooking the street, and bought ourselves glasses of beer. Then, without further ado, George proceeded to unburden himself of the story of his life. "A series of missed opportunities," as he put it, "and dead ends," his "options now fast diminishing." Two failed marriages. . . . His son, whom he had never really gotten to know, drowned at eleven years old. . . . An unrewarding job in a government department that he had held for thirty years before being unceremoniously laid off. . . . "These days they don't even give you a watch for your pains." Now, his daily routine seemed to consist of reading the morning paper, spending many hours in the pub, and in the evenings reading library books and writing letters to the editors of various newspapers, chiefly about the decline of values in New Zealand political life. And he hinted darkly at a conspiracy he had uncovered and a letter he was intending to deliver to the prime minister's residence in Mount Albert later that day, alerting her to this hidden menace. "But things aren't too bad," he added. "Even though some evenings are rather tedious, I have plenty of time to think, and I have never been afraid of my own company. Indeed, I sometimes think that folk who have ill-considered opinions, or none at all, may not be incurious by nature, but simply have too many calls on their time from family and work to think things through carefully and logically."

Inevitably, our conversation (though the word suggests a degree of mutuality that did not exist) turned to reminiscences. "What ever happened to Harry St. Rain?" "Do you ever run into Fletcher Knight?" I could hardly tell him that I had continued to be close to these friends from student days; it would have been unkind to suggest that George did not share their place in my affections. But George's interest lay less in the whereabouts or accomplishments of our peers and more in the fate of his favorite pubs and old haunts, and he even ventured to suggest that we go on a tour of them. With a memory for banal detail that astonished me, he described how "Auckland had changed for the worse." He seemed to take it as a personal slight that so many of the buildings in which he had lived as a student had been demolished, though he was happy to tell me that "Pembridge"—the state-owned apartment block in Symonds Street where he found an apartment for four pounds a week after our flat at 23 Fairview Road, Mount Eden, fell apart—was still standing. But sadly, the Kiwi Hotel had been razed and a marae built on the site. The Grand no longer existed, nor the Central, nor the Globe. And George recalled the precise dates on which these calamities had occurred.

I felt guilty at my lack of interest in George's stories, my lack of sympathy for his fixation on the past, and my unwillingness to allow him to take my photograph. (He had wanted to do this within minutes of our meeting, explaining that if he didn't do it then and there, he would undoubtedly forget, his resolution now being "Don't put off until tomorrow what you can do today."). But like the Wedding Guest detained by the Ancient Mariner, I was desperate to get away, to get shut of this depressing history in which George was mired, and so I announced that I had another appointment at midday (though it was in fact at two o'clock), and I made to go.

It was then that he met my eyes for the first time and asked after me. He particularly wanted to know about my daughter Heidi. I told him she was thirty-four, lived in Sydney, was a practicing artist, and taught art at a secondary school. I also mentioned that I had two younger children from my second marriage.

"I regret not having grandchildren," George said.

I told George about a Danish man who, finding himself in his late sixties without children or grandchildren, advertised in the papers, offering his services as a granddad. He received hundreds of responses. "Maybe you could do the same," I said.

＊　＊　＊

As I trudged up Victoria Street toward Albert Park, where the red filigree of flowering *pōhutukawas* littered the path, I wondered whether we all, sooner or later, feel the need to render some kind of account of ourselves, divine some pattern in our lives, and imagine that everything somehow "adds up." As if, in that poignant line of Joyce Johnson's, "time were like a passage of music [that] you could keep going back to it till you got it right."[5] But in George's case, his recollections seemed pointless, pervaded by a sense of contingency, with George cast as a baffled drifter who only realizes what is happening after the event. One of his anecdotes preoccupied me, and when I had found a quiet place under the trees, I took out my notebook and wrote it down before I forgot it.

When Sarah and I split up on November 7, 1970, I moved into a squat in Freeman's Bay. I lived there for fifteen years. It was an old warehouse. It cost me nothing. My room was on the top floor. The rain came in, but to repair the roof

I would have had to climb out onto it, which was quite dangerous. So I lived with the rain. After I'd been there for a few years and people had come and gone on the lower floors, I began to suspect that no one knew I was there. Indeed, I was seldom home. After work each day, I went to the pub. I had fish and chips for dinner. Got home late. Left early in the morning. On Census Night the other squatters forgot clean about me, so when I tried to vote in the next election, I found to my dismay that I had not been registered. Officially, I did not exist.

It struck me that, where most people's imaginative lives are oriented toward the future—the prospect of a fortunate meeting, a lucky break, a win on the lottery, a vacation, a better job, or even a favorite television show—George's mind was consumed by the past, which he had suffered in complete passivity, a labyrinth in which his mind wandered endlessly, without finding an exit. He appeared to me as someone who had never given birth to himself, someone to whom life had simply happened. When I had asked if he had any friends, George spoke of an "aging hippie" he had met in the pub one time. A heavy dope smoker. They met regularly in the pub for many months, and then the guy suddenly disappeared. All of George's stories were like this. Nothing added up or made much sense. Life was a series of arbitrary subtractions—a pub demolished "for no good reason," our old flat at 23 Fairview Road redesignated number 35 "for some reason," his prostate cancer "a bolt from the blue," his first wife leaving him "without an explanation, without a word."

I closed my notebook and walked on through the park, past the Moreton Bay fig trees with their buttressed roots, past the fountain, and on through the campus to Symonds Street, where suddenly the thought occurred to me that while George and I had never become close friends, we were nonetheless bound together, and that this bond came from my recognition in him of a possibility that I glimpsed for myself from an early age. Do we not sometimes encounter in another person a hidden side of ourselves and develop a secret relationship with this other that allows us to periodically take stock of ourselves and redouble our efforts not to becomes this person who, but for the grace of God, we might have been?

CHAPTER 15

Objects in the Rearview Mirror
(Are Closer Than They Appear)

In 1999, the anthropologist Galina Lindquist returned to Moscow after ten years away. She strolled through its streets as a revenant, finding them familiar yet strange. This was not only because she had changed; Russia itself was no longer the country she had known during the years of perestroika. The late 1980s had been a time of jubilant expectation—the despised Soviet *sistema* had collapsed; you could buy books in subway kiosks that until recently could have caused you to be sent to the Gulag for possessing them; and you were ostensibly free. Ten years later, this mood of abundant possibility had given way to a sense of anarchic limitlessness (*bespredel*) that called to mind the savage ruthlessness of the jungle. "Faith in the new institutions of the market and banking were crushed; people lost the money they had been saving for decades, the numerous businesses that had sprung up in the preceding years went to the wall, and the tokens of plenty that started to appear on the store shelves after the emptiness of the early 1990s became unaffordable for most of the people."[1] The prevailing mood of disillusionment and despair deepened as evidence emerged with every passing day of corruption at all levels of government, criminality in business, growing unemployment, and the atrophy of state welfare for the old, the sick, and the disabled. Reflecting on this time, Galina would write, "'*Szhivat*' is a derivative from the verb '*zhit*,' to live. There are two verbs with this root that connote gradual retreat from life, the stealthy approach of 'non-life.' One 'can be squeezed out of the living space of one's apartment or one's workplace,' but one can also be gradually edged out of life itself."[2]

Galina became fascinated by the strategies people adopted to cope with the dire predicament in which they found themselves. She observed, both in her old friends and in herself, a longing for a lost time, a kind of aphasia in which one lacked a language to articulate one's sense of a vanishing life, and with it the demise of one's own sense of self. At the same time, Galina noticed how this space of dissolution and absence was being filled with pornography, pulp fiction, escapist videos, and cheap magazines, as well as New Age paraphernalia that offered magical, paranormal, and occult possibilities of healing and renewal. Working closely with an occult practitioner (magus) and one of her clients, Galina began to see that magic was a way in which people sought to regain a sense of control over their own lives in circumstances where normal socioeconomic avenues had been blocked.

In her first account of her Moscow fieldwork, Galina emphasizes the complementarity of markets and magic.[3] When the market (or banking system) becomes a place of danger that one can no longer trust, "business magic" becomes an alternative strategy for making money, obtaining a loan, succeeding in business, or keeping a job. This switch from the material to the ethereal—from market to magic—is predicated on a Western New Age cosmology that imagines the physical body to be surrounded by a "biofield" that holds information about a person's past, present, and future life, and connects a human being to higher realms of astral power and divine influence. When one's physical or financial situation seems hopeless, channeling this mysterious biofield may bring a windfall or initiate a flow of regenerative power.

Six years later, in her monograph, *Conjuring Hope*, Galina's emphasis is less on business magic per se than on the occult search for the "lost sense of tomorrow," and for increased hope.[4] Objective transformations are less significant than subjective transformations, in which a person's confidence is bolstered, despair is assuaged, and hope restored. Rather than being stuck, one can feel that one is getting somewhere. This emphasis on magical action as a transformation in the way the world *appears* to a person echoes Jean-Paul Sartre's famous essay on the emotions and suggests to me that friendship, including my friendship with Galina, possesses this magical capacity to make us feel differently about ourselves, *even when our objective circumstances cannot be changed.*

Galina's determination to do justice to the mysteries of subjectivity and intersubjectivity helps us understand why, in *Conjuring Hope*, she often suspends the question of diagnostic or analytical meaning in order to explore an "indexical mode of transformation" in which a person is changed, or healed, through direct sensory experience rather than objective knowledge, and through ritual rather than political action.[5]

Friendship can be understood in two very different ways—as a sympathetic relationship between two individuals and as a metaphor for one's relationship with the world. Is there any connection between the power of a friend to bolster one's spirits and the charismatic power and caring presence of a healer?

Just as the presence of a friend can reinforce one's self-belief, so a healer's presence can be as meaningful as that healer's ritual manipulations. What is at stake is not so much a cure—for we cannot be cured of being-in-the-world—but an uplifting of the spirit, a replenishment of the will, a resuscitation of hope. "For the people I talked to," Galina writes, "hope was an existential doorway out of the deadliest of deadlocks, the light at the end of the longest of tunnels; a tool for expanding the horizons of the life-world, for intentionality to unfold, for will to return: the will to life, no matter what."[6]

*   *   *

A few months before *Conjuring Hope* was published in 2006, I attended a conference in Oxford on the anthropology and psychology of fieldwork experience. Galina was also there, and we spent time together over lunch and in breaks between sessions, catching up. But Galina was under a cloud, waiting for the results of medical tests and fearing the worst. Although she had little appetite for food, she talked passionately about a recent stint of fieldwork in Tuva, southern Siberia, where she had been working closely with Tuvan healers, studying the shifting balance of religious power between Tibetan Buddhism and traditional shamanism. During her fieldwork in Moscow, Galina had become very close to her key informants. This involvement seemed to me even more intense with her Tuvan collaborators. Drawn deeply into their religious life, she had become unsettled, like many ethnographers before her, by the impossibility of drawing a line between participation and observation. But Galina's ability to dwell in the ambiguity of the ethnographic moment reflected a personal disposition as well as an intellectual commitment to joining "objective analysis to lived experience." Indeed, she shared Maurice Merleau-Ponty's view that this process was "the most proper task of anthropology, the one which distinguishes it from other social sciences."[7] It was her refusal to assimilate immediate experience to abstract knowledge that made her skeptical of institutional religion, biomedicine, and academic fashions. Perhaps this was why, when she first fell ill, she relied on homeopathy and acupuncture, and traveled to Tuva in the summer of 2006 not only for further fieldwork but for healing.

Upon her return home to Sweden, she submitted to chemotherapy, and for a while it appeared to be working. Then the blow fell. "I am ill again," she wrote to me in November 2007. "It all came very quickly and in a month developed into an inoperable tumor. They are now giving me more chemotherapy, hoping it will shrink, but i can neither eat nor move, almost. I'm not sure what will happen to me; the optimistic prognosis is that i'll remain chronically ill, for whatever length of time, living on chemos. Whatever else it means, one thing is that i can no longer make any plans and can't have people depending on me. My teaching this and next semester was cancelled, a conference on 'institutional transformations of suffering' that i have been working on organizing for three years is now going on without me."

Galina had persuaded me to help in organizing a workshop at the European Association of Social Anthropologists conference at Ljubljana, scheduled for the summer of 2008. It was a way of addressing some of the personal issues of fieldwork that we had discussed at length during our meetings. One of our concerns was to broach the question of putting other peoples' epistemologies on a par with our own, of breaking the historical habit of privileging European worldviews. In our draft proposal, we wrote:

Despite the fact that ethnographers often spend many years in societies other than their own, acquiring conversancy in local languages, becoming familiar with very different ways of understanding the world, sometimes advocating politically on behalf of their host society and espousing friendship with individual collaborators, it is rare that an anthropologist adopts a non-Western epistemology in his or her work or even places such an epistemology on the same footing as theories derived from their own intellectual traditions. Invidious distinctions between "scientific" and "folk" models or reason and faith continue to hold sway over our thinking, so that while we may venture to speak, say, of African "philosophy" or "religion," these Eurocentric and logocentric rubrics determine which phenomenon we will include under or exclude from such headings and how we will approach the subject we define in these ways. Assumptions drawn from classical Greek thought, or Judeo-Christian teleology and soteriology, or from Euro-American preoccupations with politico-economic power and instrumental rationality continue to constitute the dominant paradigms whereby we decide meaning, assign cause, and explain human behavior. But if we are going to critique the power inequalities between West and East, North and South, we must also critique the discursive inequalities associated with these geopolitical divisions, and this means taking other worldviews seriously, and seeing our own epistemologies from the vantage point of the other. This does not mean, however, that we cease to be skeptical of the epistemological claims and pretensions of the worldviews that various people espouse. It simply means abandoning the notion that the veracity of any worldview lies in its correspondence to objective reality or its logical coherence, and exploring, instead, the practical entailments of any worldview for human lives. A corollary of this pragmatist turn is that we see beliefs and worldviews not as scripts that actors faithfully follow or principles that guide their actions, but as ways that people give legitimacy to their actions or rationalize, after the event, the often unforeseen and unintended consequences of what they have done. *Moreover, in a reflexive vein, we want to explore our own familiar experience of physical and social reality from the standpoint of unfamiliar philosophies, to see what aspects of our social existence they might illuminate, and what alternative solutions to our existential quandaries and political dilemmas they might offer.*

In italicizing the last sentence, I remind myself how deeply Galina's experiences in Siberia, and her own consultations with shamans, influenced her attitude toward her cancer, delaying her reliance on orthodox medical treatment.[8] And in retaining her quirky use of the lower case letter *i* in her emails, I remind myself of how her personal world shrank as her tumor grew, and how the hope she ascribed to her Swedish doctors was something she could not share.

Three months passed before I found the time and means to travel to Sweden, and as I waited at our agreed rendezvous point in the concourse of Stockholm Arlanda Airport, I felt nervous and fearful, expecting to face a diminished and unrecognizable version of my friend. But Galina looked her old self and confident enough to drive to a nearby lake where we strolled for an hour before finding a lakeside restaurant for lunch. It was like old times, though we now talked of mortality rather than anthropology. I remember Galina commenting on the unseasonal thaw, the unpredictability of our times, and her own experience of reaching a point where there is no future. "One lives from day to day, not knowing whether there will be two more weeks, two more months, two more years," she said. "But I no longer cling to life, and therefore I do not suffer. Suffering is resistance, not wanting to die, not wanting the pain. But I have let go, and in yielding I have found peace."

Paradoxically, it is more often the living than the dying who cannot bear the thought of death. And I had to tread carefully, as I pressed Galina for details of her treatment, lest I appear unsympathetic to the course of action she had decided upon. There was an alternative therapy, Galina said, but because of the lack of communication between hospitals and laboratories, she had had to do all the hard work liaising with the lab and working with the doctors who could administer the experimental drugs. It was too much to ask of a patient, and she had reached the point where the effort was costing her what little energy she had. Besides, she was feeling better than she had in many months, miraculously so.

I confessed surprise at how well she looked. But Galina set no store by appearances. Nor did she hold out any hope of a medical breakthrough or divine intervention. "Unfortunately, none of my family or friends can accept this," she said. "Nobility lies in fighting the cancer, not giving in to it. My mother tells me not to be selfish. My Swedish friends urge me to seek treat-ment abroad. My ex-husband, who is devoutly Russian Orthodox, implores me to embrace the faith. But God is indifferent to me, and I will live without God, though still believing God exists, His ways beyond our understanding."

In Galina's reckoning with life, I was reminded of the philosopher Gillian Rose's memoir, written during her dying days,[9] in which she describes the copresence of a profound vulnerability and an extraordinary strength.

"I am dying," Galina said. Her voice quavered for a second, and then she recovered. And I saw that she had attained a state of grace where death and life canceled each other out, and the ego has been transcended.

I went to Uppsala for a few days, then returned to Stockholm to see Galina one last time. There were no goodbyes, though we both knew we would not see each other again.

*   *   *

To face the prospect of life in a world abruptly bereft of someone whose pres-ence sustained the very reality of that world is also to be confronted by the question as to whether one really *knew* the person whose absence one now mourns. Clearly, our knowledge of our friends and those we love is unlike our knowledge of things. It cannot be fully fathomed, for this "cloude of unknowyng" encompasses senses, sympathies, emotions, and intuitions that lie on the outskirts of consciousness. One may readily list a person's deeds or describe their appearance. One may recount the story of their life, dating critical events, naming places where they lived and worked, mentioning significant others. But their aura and influence slip away from the substantives with which one compiles a resume, writes an obituary, or charts a career. A death sharpens, often unbearably, one's sense of being deeply a part of a friend's existence while remaining a stranger to it. And one is left with the mystery of what it was that made their presence essential to oneself in the first place.

It is also common at such times that one doubts one can know others at all and concludes that one's own life runs parallel to theirs with only the illusion of overlap or empathy. What one thinks one knows of the other seems as unstable as memory, a mere approximation, or a single arrested moment, like a snapshot, that one wishfully believes to have captured the whole.

D. W. Winnicott coined the term *potential space* to describe a hypothetical area between the infant and the mother at a stage when the infant is exploring the existential difference between being apart from and being a part of another's world.[10] In bereavement, one's sense of separateness is not chosen but traumatically forced upon one. To lose someone you love is to pass from a space in which you and the other *coexisted* to one in which you exist in relation to a memory, an after-image, a shadow, a simulacrum. In so far as being-*in-potentia* implies a reaching out for another that is reciprocated by the other's openness and responsiveness, the experience of bereavement is one of unrequited and unconsummated longing—analogous to the phantom limb phenomenon of the amputee.

Curiously enough, the experience of separation and loss may also shock one into realizing the deep intersubjectivity of human existence—the being of the other comprehended through one's own being and one's own being brought to light through theirs. "In reality," writes Merleau-Ponty, "the other is not shut up inside my perspective of the world, because this perspective itself has no definite limits, because it slips spontaneously into the other's, and because both are brought together in the one single world in which we all participate as anonymous subjects of perception."[11] Accordingly, solitude and sociality are not the two horns of a dilemma, "but two 'moments' of one phenomenon,"[12] in which self and other are always copresent, even though the other is sometimes reduced to an object, or momentarily disappears from sight and mind.

CHAPTER 16

The Rock and Pillar Range

Of certain friends, we often say, "We go back a long way," as if the source and strength of the relationship were a shared place and time as much as a personal affinity.

Vincent O'Sullivan was a year or two ahead of me at the University of Auckland, and we did not meet until after I'd published a poem in a student magazine, whereupon Vincent reached out to me and generously invited me to show him some of my work in progress. *Il miglior fabbro*, he not only provided me with meticulous critiques, pointing out an image that did not ring true, muddled syntax, and slipshod prosody; he also gave me the kind of encouragement that makes all the difference when one is writing blind. What satisfaction did Vincent get out of helping me? I suppose it was the same sense of relief that we all feel when we discover that we are not laboring alone in what Dylan Thomas called our "craft and sullen art." Slowly, we warmed to each other as persons, not just poets, and became friends. I was a fool for his mordant wit and envied his literary wisecracks culled from Oscar Wilde, Sydney "the Smith of Smiths" Smith, and his run-ins with bullshit artists. Here was a man with the gift of the gab, who could talk his way out of a paper bag and bring a smile to the face of a clock.

The same year that my first poem appeared in print, I went south to a University of New Zealand arts festival in Dunedin. Among the many bohemians, beatniks, and luminaries I met that winter was the Greek–New Zealand poet Antigone Kefala. Antigone was studying French literature at Victoria University of Wellington and would move to Australia in 1960, where she published several books of poetry and a poignant memoir of her Wellington childhood. Mindful of Vincent's classical background and his love of all things Greek, I lost no time in telling him about Antigone. Entranced by the name, as I fully expected him to be, Vincent wrote a poem in which he conjures his own Antigone, a synthesis of the classical figure and a woman entirely of his own imagining. In Dunedin, I also met Charles Brasch, the editor of the literary quarterly, *Landfall*. Brasch showed an interest in my poetry and invited me to send him some of my work. When one of my poems was accepted for publication, I urged Vincent to submit something of his, hoping we could make our *Landfall* debuts together. So it was that his "Antigone" and my "To Be Hanged by the Neck" appeared in the same December 1959 issue, our first significant forays into print.

* * *

During the sixty-three years that have passed since I first met Vincent, we have only occasionally found ourselves living in the same place at the same time. Most of our conversations have been during very brief visits in which we have hurriedly caught up on news, recounted tall stories about old acquaintances, discussed our writing, and, more recently, mourned the deaths of mutual friends. Both of us have been haunted by the difficulty of reconciling a strong identification with our homeland with an equally strong sense of being a part of a European tradition of thought, literature, and political critique that, for all its importance to us, was paradoxically not a part of our upbringing but something we adopted and made our own. Sometimes this tension finds expression in geographically disparate images, as in Vincent's poems about Central America; his numerous poems about Greece, both modern and classical; his sonnet sequence on Charles Meryon, the famous French etcher who lived in Akaroa for a while; or his play about Japanese prisoners of war in the Wairarapa. At other times, it shows as a tension between the colloquial banter of, say, his characters Butcher and Baldy, and the "sweet high figure / inside every butcher" that is momentarily illuminated as a redneck lights a cigarette against the wind, "his hands cupping a match / like a yellow stone."[1] Vincent visits William Butler Yeats's grave on the day a bomb kills an innocent boy in Belfast. He takes a fatally wounded thrush from the mouth of his cat. Plato appears among the cockatoos. These incongruities are grist for the poet's mill. But the poet does not seek any moral resolution, for the sparks that fly from these juxtapositions are what makes poetry both necessary and enlightening. "There is something like the glint of a hook, / there is something, love, in that shimmering / vault, trolling too fast to speak of."[2]

*   *   *

In 2014, Vincent and his wife, Helen, were living in Dunedin. After I stayed with them for a couple of days, Vincent and I drove to Central Otago to see our mutual friend Brian Turner at Oturehua. Brian's friend and neighbor, Jillian Sullivan, generously offered Vincent and me her straw-bale house, and that evening the four of us gathered before a roaring fire of pine logs to drink wine and share stories. Though we were all published poets, our interests were as diverse as our personalities. Yet we readily found common ground, Vincent regaling us with hilarious anecdotes, Brian sharing his concerns for the natural environment, threatened by wind farms and irrigated dairy pastures, and Jillian explaining how she had built her house from hay bales, earth, mud, river stones, and timber.

On our first morning in the valley, we clambered into Brian's four-wheel drive vehicle and traveled to the foothills of Mount Saint Bathans to meet Brian's and Vincent's friend Grahame Sydney.

I considered myself fortunate—reunited with two kindred spirits, driving through a breathtaking landscape of tussock plains and snow-covered ranges, *and* about to meet a painter whose work I had long admired. Moreover, I was on the threshold of discovering that my relations with friends, country, and art were all of a piece.

Within seconds of stepping into Grahame's living room, I was introduced to a hale and engaging individual some seven years younger than myself who, without prompting (or so it seems in retrospect), spoke of the postpartum sadness that sometimes oppresses a painter who, having labored on a work for many months, will dispatch it to a dealer or buyer only to rue the day he parted with it. "You writers always have your books," Grahame said, "but we painters have only a photograph or a few catalog details to remind us of what we worked so hard to create, then lost sight of forever." Grahame thought it would be a good idea if paintings could be leased for a few years and returned to the painter from time to time. But prospective buyers had not taken kindly to this idea. "They need to possess the painting," Grahame said. "They want the security of legal ownership. For them, it's often an investment, and they like to feel that no one else can gain access to what they have." I told Grahame that his nostalgia for work that has passed out of his hands reminded me of the Māori concept of the *hau* of the gift—the spirit of the maker or giver that infuses the object so that, as it is transferred or traded far beyond its place of origin, it yearns to be returned one day to where its life began. "I certainly feel this way about New Zealand," I said. Despite having made my home in Australia, Denmark, Sierra Leone, and the United States, I feel a perennial need to touch base with the country where I spent my first and formative years and reconnect with my oldest friends.

As I strolled around Grahame's living room, its shelves crammed with books and walls covered with his paintings, lithographs, and etchings, and its large windows affording a view of the Cambrian Valley and the Hawkdun Range, I was struck by the recurring theme of emptiness and desertion in his work—a group of letter boxes in the middle of nowhere; light from a window falling on a chair that appears to have been only just vacated; a glint of sunlight on the wall of an unfurnished room; a red shed on a tawny plain; a flight of birds in an empty sky. I was also overawed by Grahame's technical mastery, so reminiscent of Chinese art.

"So, Sydney's a realist?" Brian asks in an essay on his friend's painting. "Yes," Brian answers, if that means that "he faithfully records and represents what most of us believe we have seen. I'm not sure about that, personally the more powerful reality is in the feelings his work evokes and releases in me."[3] Continuing this train of thought, Brian questions whether "Sydney's world, his wilderness where the spirit is tested and strengthened by a pure airiness, great space, is almost always unforested?" Again, his answer is edifying: "If you can locate yourself here it is in a forest of loneliness, temperamentally, where you are exposed to yourself and everything else. You need strength of purpose, of character; you need courage to stand up here and not avert the eyes. *Only through distance can you find yourself. Beyond the far blue, gold, or dun hills and mountains, beneath cirrus edged with gold, there's a self to be reckoned with.*"[4]

Such insights would sink in later, when I learned more of the biographical background to Brian's and Grahame's lives in the Maniototo (from the Māori, *Mania-o-toto*—"plain of blood"), and reread Janet Frame's novel, *Living in the Maniototo*, in which an analogy is drawn between a writer's compulsion to explore the innermost mysteries of a person's life and the Central Otago landscape itself, whose surfaces have been stripped away to disclose jagged schist and water-polished graywacke stones. But it was time for a "cuppa," and we sat around a long table as Grahame and Vincent discussed the contemporary art market and poured scorn on art theorists who decree that painting is passé, and realist painting even more so. Though Grahame sells well, he had dispensed with an agent. Art galleries were reluctant to add to their few examples of his work. And art writers largely ignored him.

When we had finished our tea and cookies, Grahame invited us to see his studio—a short walk away from the house. The wind off Mount Saint Bathans was bitterly cold (fresh snow had fallen on the ranges overnight), but I found myself looking up at the cloud-swathed peaks as if I had never seen their like. Only a few times in my life have I experienced this altered state of consciousness. It was as though Grahame's paintings, that had so absorbed me only minutes ago inside the house, had opened my eyes to an outside world that I had allowed myself to take for granted. Landscape and sky were utterly transfigured by the art in the same way that the face of a loved one is transfigured by love.

On the wall of Grahame's studio, I glimpsed a Vermeer reproduction. On his easel was a canvas, just begun, of one of his recurring motifs—a hawk impaled on a barbed wire fence, its freedom to take wing lost for all time. This potential of art to transform our perception of the world—even though, paradoxically, art draws its raw material from some external reality—had been a recurring theme in all my writing: the mysterious interplay of inner and outer realities, and the existential imperative of finding some way of integrating these realities, lest one become lost in another or absorbed in oneself.

I continued to ponder this tension as we drove back to Oturehua across a ceaselessly changing landscape, tussock to pasture, vast river terraces and stone riverbeds, eroded hills above abandoned gold diggings, cottages among trees. That Grahame had so vehemently defended his work against those who would write it off as merely realist[5] made me keenly aware of how difficult it is to sustain one's own vision against all the prescriptions and prejudices that impinge on one's consciousness.

On our return to Oturehua, I went out onto Jillian's porch to drink in the view. A small creek ran through some marshland. Beyond was a stand of pines. On the horizon, the Hawkdun Range defied description, though since words were my métier, I attempted to do just that. Unlike many mountains, the Hawkduns do not rise steeply from the plain or jaggedly become a series of peaks. Rather I was reminded of figures lying on their backs, knees drawn up into their chests, shrouded by snow. The tops formed a tableland under the impress of a cerulean sky in which strange clouds shape-shifted before one's eyes, now flour-covered loaves, now wisps of smoke, now misty plates.

When Vincent joined me, I was moved to ask if he was still a Catholic. I knew he had been raised in an Irish Catholic home, but what had become of his faith over the years?[6]

"I'm not a Vatican Catholic," Vincent said, and he recalled the words of the New Zealand painter Tony Fomison, who said, "I judge a religion by its compassion," regarding it as a means by which one evolves and takes "a journey through life."[7] For Vincent, an institutional order, with its theology and liturgy, was less real to him than religious experience, which may take its point of departure from doctrine but is, more imperatively, grounded in the struggles of our everyday lives—to make ends meet, to survive a broken marriage or the death of a dear friend, to withstand the degrading effects of prejudice, poverty, or willful misunderstanding, and to resist ideologies that do violence to life as it is lived.

"For me," I said, "what matters is not what one believes, or even what one thinks one knows, but the existential question of how one can cross the threshold from our singular and solitary humanity to something greater than ourselves, and to feel not only that this engagement fills us with more life than would otherwise be the case, but that this fusion with otherness remakes and redeems us."

I was thinking, at that moment, of friendship. But I was simultaneously aware of the Hawkduns under their coverlid of freshly fallen snow and their blue shadows; of Grahame's allusions to the hidden histories and past lives he discerned in the seemingly empty land; of Brian's indefatigable commitment to preserving the environment he so loved; of Jillian's devotion to finishing her straw-bale home; of Vincent's celebrations of the divine spark of love in the smallest gestures and most fleeting things ("joy's the word I want, and say it . . . 'Joy' catches the sun").[8]

A question that had been running through my mind in the Maniototo was, Could I live there? I had only to gaze at the mountains to close the gap between my life in America and the life I once led in New Zealand. An occasional vehicle went down the road. A bird piped up in the marshland. A dog barked in the distance. And then the enveloping silence. Grahame Sydney and Brian Turner were at home in this environment and fighting to protect it. But could I endure the isolation without pining to be elsewhere? Vincent had described Brian as being "wedded to the place," a phrase that recalled my own childhood, when, lacking friends, I found solace in the physical landscape, a surrogate society of ethereal presences, even as I yearned for a cosmopolitan world of intellectual companionship far away. Vincent had a similar sensibility, and we talked at length about the wilderness in which Colin McCahon wandered most of his life, his paintings mocked and reviled by critics, as well as by the common man. I told Vincent that I so deeply identified with the plight of men like McCahon, Lowry, and Mason,[9] that when I went to London I would frequent the National Gallery and glimpse their troubled lives in the face of Christ, as painted by Hieronymus Bosch, surrounded by leering bullies—an image echoed in Lovis Corinth's *Ecce Homo*, painted in the last year of his life (1925).

Vincent responded by describing a Titian masterpiece in which Christ, weighed down by a cross on the road to Calvary, looks out at us from the painting as if to ask why we are not coming to his aid.

This sense of vulnerability and bewilderment can be felt in Samuel Butler's writings from the period following his purchase of a sheep run at the Rangitata Forks in 1860. Though the twenty-four-year-old English emigrant is exhilarated by the harsh light, the open horizons, and the prospect of living "beyond the pale of civilization," he experiences moments of desolation, longing to see "some signs of human care in the midst of the loneliness," some glimpse of Europe. Even more onerous is his intellectual isolation. New Zealand seemed "far better adapted to develop and maintain in health the physical than the intellectual nature. The fact is," Butler wrote, "people here are busy making money; that is the inducement which led them to come in the first instance, and they show their sense by devoting their energies to the work." While admiring the shrewd, hardheaded intelligence of the settlers, and their freedom from the pretensions of the old country, he missed his Handel and Bach, and grew weary of conversations about "sheep, horses, dogs, cattle, English grasses, paddocks, bush, and so forth."[10] Isolated in his cob cottage at the Rangitata Forks, he found that "the solitude was greater than I could bear. I felt increasing upon me that dreadful doubt as to my own identity—as to the continuity of my past and present existence—which is the first sign of that distraction which comes on those who have lost themselves in the bush. I had fought against this feeling hitherto and had conquered it; but the intense silence and gloom of this rocky wilderness were too much for me, and I felt that my power of collecting myself was beginning to be impaired."[11]

In Grahame Sydney's paintings, there is a Zen-like acceptance of the contradictions and paradoxes that Butler struggled to reconcile, and that confront you everywhere in New Zealand. The almost deserted Cambrians where Grahame lives was, during the gold rush days of the 1860s and 70s, a populous and boisterous mining town called Welshman's Gully. The predominantly empty and iconic landscapes in New Zealand art galleries are, ironically, evidence of how profoundly generations of painters have peopled those landscapes with their quiet thoughts and secret imaginings.

Not long before he committed suicide, the New Zealand writer John Mulgan wrote to his friend Charles Brasch from Northern Ireland. "What a lonely desolate place NZ seems now. I fell [*sic*] a sense of tragedy in all the people I like there much more keenly than anything over here."[12] Another New Zealand author, Katherine Mansfield, died among Russians, saying she had found her people at last. And toward the end of his life, Tony Fomison elected to do "something few contemporary Pākehā considered. He would undergo the physical trauma of extensive tattooing, and immerse himself in Samoan cultural values and custom, as a bridge towards what he most respected and was drawn to in the Pacific he shared with them. It was not a claim for identity, but for a shared communal bond."[13]

In these words, Vincent sums up the course of action that made me an ethnographer and took me to the remoteness of northern Sierra Leone and central Australia—where not only the physical landscape would leave its imprint on me, but the people whose lives I shared would change me in ways that I could never have been changed had I remained in my natal country. In order to feel at home anywhere, I had to go elsewhere. In order to be someone, I had to become no one. In order to practice art, I had first to learn how to live.

CHAPTER 17

Love and Friendship

Although Plato drew a distinction between *philia* (friendship) and *eros* (passionate love), life rarely conforms to such clear-cut categories. Indeed, it so persistently confounds and overflows them that one sometimes wonders why we insist on deploying them in the first place. While, for some people, platonic and romantic friendships are incompatible, others claim that the spirit of friendship may be consummated in erotic affection. In the Old Testament, when David lamented the death of his beloved friend Jonathan, he spoke of his love as "wonderful, passing the love of women." What happened in history to drain emotionality from friendship, and is it possible that an acceptance of homoerotic love is finally bringing us back to our senses?

Every friendship must be invented, Michel Foucault observes. A desire to be with men, "to share their time, their meals, their room, their leisure, their grief, their knowledge, their confidences" precedes the discovery of how this may be realized sexually, physically, and practically.[1] This is true of both homosexual and heterosexual relationships. The expression of love or friendship does not come naturally to us but must be cultivated through trial and error. This means that friendships sometimes morph into love affairs but sometimes recoil from the very idea of sexuality or even the slightest touch. As Robert Brain observes, "even the formal kiss on the cheek which an Italian gives his friend is looked upon by the Anglo-Saxon as a betrayal of virility."[2]

Ten years after Foucault spoke of friendship as a way of life,[3] the first episode of the television sitcom *Friends* aired on NBC in 1994. In the pilot for the series, friendship was contrasted with family, at the same time as it was celebrated as an alternative form of social life. With friends, you are free; but as with siblings, you are not free to have sex with each other—at least not until season four when Monica and Chandler "do it."

This ambivalence about mixing friendship and sex was also touched on in the second episode of *Seinfeld* (1990) when characters Elaine and Jerry awkwardly negotiate a transition from being a couple to being friends—something that will be comically renegotiated from time to time during the sitcom's nine seasons. In the ninth episode of the second season ("The Deal"), Jerry and Elaine decide to have a sexual dalliance, though with a set of ground rules. However, as their "relationship" develops, they have difficulty maintaining their original friendship.

The 1989 MGM film *When Harry Met Sally* (directed by Rob Reiner) comically documents the metamorphosis of a relationship over several years, beginning with the titular Sally disagreeing with Harry's assertion that men and women cannot be friends because "the sex part gets in the way." At a diner, Harry tells Sally she is very attractive, and she angrily accuses him of making a pass at her. Though their friendship flourishes, it blinds them to their changing feelings for each other, and by the end of the movie they realize they are more than just friends; they are in love. As the ethicist and theologian Gilbert Meilaender wisely concludes, we should not "deny that friendship between men and women—friendships which are not also marked by erotic love—are possible. We ought not, that is, let a theory lead us to deny the reality we see around us"—whether that theory is Harry's or Aristotle's.[4]

That there is no permanent solution to the problem of how friendship, marriage, and romantic love may be combined, made compatible, or kept apart, is evident in the countless stories that the problem has inspired in the popular media, in fiction, and in real life. If friends are not lovers, a friendship can nonetheless be compromised by sleeping with the same woman as in François Truffaut's 1962 movie *Jules et Jim*, based on Henri-Pierre Roché's 1953 semi-autobiographical novel about his relationship with a young writer Franz Hessel and a woman named Helen Grund, whom Hessel married. In Lawrence Durrell's tetralogy *The Alexandria Quartet* (1969), a group of friends become so emotionally entangled that their perceptions of one another become confused. Darley, the English expatriate, comes to wonder if the enigmatic and alluring Justine was his lover, his friend, or neither, and his uncertainty is not alleviated when a mutual friend informs him that Justine's lovers "remained her friends; but more often . . . her truest friends were never lovers."[5] For Darley, the open question is whether Justine's "truest lover would have been the one who could fill both this role *and* that of friend," and in the second book of the *Quartet*, he confides to his friend Balthazar, "Before my love has a chance to crystallize, it turns into a deep, a devouring friendship."[6]

One could go on adducing examples of the ambiguity of love and friend-ship, but what is important, perhaps, is not how this ambiguity can be reduced but rather the light that it sheds on all intimate human relationships. For no matter how avidly we subject them to analysis, creating typologies and vocabularies that give the appearance that life is reducible to language and that feelings can be subjugated to rules, relationships are by their nature dynamic and fluid. Even as I conjure images of my closest friends and try to fathom how I felt about them when I first met them, or what has sustained my friendship with them over time, I come up against the unreliability of memory and the mystery of what attracts us to some people and not others.

Consider my lifelong friendship with Harry St. Rain, who in the eyes of many, myself included, was a young Adonis, destined to enjoy a brilliant career and win the hearts of women, while the likes of me struggled with self-doubt. If I saw in George Bowen (Chapter 14) an image of what I might become, I saw in Harry someone I dreamed of being. Did this mimetic desire have overtones of sexual attraction? Was it that I was physically attracted to Harry and felt that his allure might rub off onto me, or did we simply see in each other qualities we wished we possessed ourselves but had found impossible to cultivate alone?

*   *   *

In my sophomore year at the University of Auckland, I published a poem in a student magazine called *Hippocampus.* The magazine was edited by Fletcher Knight and Harry St. Rain, and though only one issue ever appeared, it was a turning point in my life. After years of isolation, I was suddenly admitted to a literary and intellectual circle that confirmed that I was neither a freak nor a failure.

Harry contributed to *Hippocampus* under an assumed name and seldom appeared on campus. I imagined him as an avatar of Jay Gatsby, who mate-rialized out of the shadows of trees on a summer's night to stand and stare across a body of dark water, then suddenly vanish, leaving a vacuum for oth-ers to fill with innuendo and wild surmise. Did Harry mean to have this effect on people? Did he stage-manage his appearances and disappearances to cre-ate an aura of singularity and mystery? Or was there some dark preoccupa-tion that made him distant without desiring it?

The sketchy details that Fletcher provided only deepened the mystery. The St. Rains were a wealthy but not particularly happy family whose Remuera mansion commanded a view of the harbor and North Shore. Harry had no intimate contact with his father. One night, his father came home late and found Harry playing in his bedroom with his Hornby model train. It was the first time father and son had been alone together, and it would be the last. The boy's father said, "One day you'll get on a train like this. It'll take you far from here, and we'll never see you again." This almost proved prophetic. A few years later, unhappy in the prestigious private school to which he had been sent, Harry escaped to the railway station, climbed into a wagon in the marshaling yards, and fell asleep, waking hours later as the freight train rattled into the Bay of Plenty. Another time, he tried to kill himself by drinking poison. It was only because the poison racked Harry's body so violently that his death was averted; his father happened to be home at the time and heard ominous noises in his son's upstairs bedroom. When he went to investigate, he found Harry's door locked. Realizing something was seriously amiss, he phoned a doctor and Harry was saved. As he lay in hospital recovering from a severely damaged stomach, he read Iris Murdoch's *Under the Net* and wrote a letter to her, confessing admiration and proposing marriage. Murdoch sent a long, handwritten letter in reply, saying that she needed stability in her confused life and had recently married John Bayley. She did not envisage an early divorce.

The first time I visited Harry, I found him ensconced in a Moreton Bay fig tree with his teddy bear and a book.

Since one of Harry's contributions to *Hippocampus* had been an article on Evelyn Waugh, I now found myself imagining Harry, not as Jay Gatsby, but as Sebastian Flyte of Waugh's *Brideshead Revisited*. And in this piece of theater, I cast myself in the role of Charles Ryder.

Perhaps *Brideshead Revisited* does shed some light on Harry's life. Consider that famous passage in which Waugh speaks of the languor of youth and observes that, while all the attributes of youth—ebullience, optimism, illusion, and despair—are also attributes of other times in our lives, languor is something that belongs to youth alone. At no other age does one experience this "relaxation of yet unwearied sinews, the mind sequestered and self-regarding."[7]

Sometimes I thought that Harry was in search of eternal youth. Not in the sense of never aging, but in the sense of being able to recapture at will the way one sees the world when one first opens one's eyes upon it—when everything is offered in abundance, and nothing is asked in return. If Harry thought that living in the present was, as he once put it, "a desperate experiment," it was perhaps because he was infatuated by his vision of a seaborne nymph at his side whose seductive loveliness would stop the passage of time. When Harry contemplated the years ahead, I think he was filled with an immense weariness. When I first encountered Antoine Roquentin in Sartre's *La Nausée*, I was immediately reminded of Harry. What was once a world of infinite promise, filled with the smell of fennel, the taste of couscous, or the glimpse of a Japanese girl bathing naked, has degenerated into a tedious inventory of words. Life is never rarer or more precious than when it is simply lived. Everything is an adventure then, and time loops back on itself, endlessly renewed. But like Roquentin, Harry was convinced that aging erodes this spontaneity. Instead of living, one writes about the lives one has lived. But always from the outside, at one remove, as though through the eyes of someone whom life has passed by, or a voyeur.

Was Harry's attempted suicide a way of avoiding the commonplace? Was death by his own hand to be his last adventure—a gesture toward spontaneity in a life that was already losing its capacity to surprise him? Did he see all too clearly the course his life would run, and did he not wish to live out something so comprehensively preordained? In his *Hippocampus* articles, Harry provides clues as to how these questions might be answered.

He conjures a world of good books, of "wine, intelligent company, and a passion for art." The world of Oxford, possibly, between the wars, "before science students were heard of"—a place of country villages and dreaming spires. Such a "place in the sun," such a place of "love and friendship," Harry argues—"always sheltered, always artificial"—is somewhere most of us have been trying to get to for a long time. Such a place we hope to find in novels. But Waugh won't pander to our dreams. He excites our longings only to frustrate them, shattering our illusions, revealing smoke without fire, a wasteland, a handful of dust. At this moment of disenchantment, Waugh offers the solace of the Catholic faith. But Harry cannot accept either the consolation of faith or the consolation of reason. There is no distraction. Nothing, for him, relieves the bleak prospect.

Harry was also a regular contributor of sardonic letters and political critique to the student newspaper *Craccum*. He signed his articles *Q.E.D.* Until Fletcher told me otherwise, I thought these were the initials of the author's name. Harry's two targets were scientism and romanticism. Seriousness in science and soul-searching in art he found equally abhorrent.

Many of my bohemian contemporaries thought Harry too clever by half. By remaining aloof and anonymous, it was all too easy for him, they argued, to mock the opinions of others, or dismiss them with a condescending shrug. They said that Harry St. Rain could not live up to the perfect and brilliant image

he cultivated for himself, so turned on others, satirizing their foibles, carica-
turing their beliefs, belittling their views. Many regarded his detachment and
disdain as social snobbery. They criticized the way he hid behind a sobriquet
and set himself apart from student affairs. As for me, I found his aloofness both
daunting and captivating. I saw in his splendid isolation a way of making a virtue out of one's loneliness. I read everything he published in *Craccum*, admiring his intellectual precocity and wit. And on the strength of his allusions to
H. L. Mencken, Evelyn Waugh, and Iris Murdoch, I fervently read their books.

My first glimpse—or should I say vision?—of the elusive Harry St. Rain
had been of a tall, tanned individual hurrying through the Gothic cloisters of
the University of Auckland like the White Rabbit.

He was always in haste. He gave the impression that he was not so much
bent on reaching his goal as anxious to leave the campus as quickly as possible.

If he was someone in flight, I, no doubt, in his eyes, was someone mired
or floundering.

I would work in the library for hours on end, industriously researching
essays or struggling with hypothetical proofs, and trying not to meet the eyes
of the woman with whom I had been hopelessly in love for the last year. But
Harry would breeze in and out, his sky-blue shirt unbuttoned to the chest,
confirming my conviction that, though I had never seen anyone like him,
and would never hold my own in his company, he was, in some inexplicable
way, like me.

Perhaps it was the attraction of opposites. I had come of age in a small
Taranaki town and gone to an agricultural high school, where I had failed to
distinguish myself. By contrast, Harry had been blessed with every advantage and had already proved himself academically. While he was articulate,
well-read, and a master of irony, I was tongue-tied and reticent, and passed
my exams only through dogged perseverance. In contrast to Harry, who was
gifted with good looks, intellectual acuity, and confidence, I saw myself as
ill-favored and inferior. Yet, in time, I would come to understand that, just as
Harry set his sights too high, with the result that whatever he did fell short of
his ideal and left him in despair, I started out with such a debased image of
myself and my abilities that whatever I wrote made me feel that I was getting
somewhere, and that one day I might amount to something after all.

CHAPTER 18

Fictive Friendship

Harry St. Rain is a pseudonym, and he is partly imagined. Through my relationship with Harry, who is at once invented and real, I address the ambiguous borderland between intellectual affinity and physical attraction, between friendship and love. Disclaiming that "any similarity to actual persons, living or dead, or actual events, is purely coincidental" affords me a freedom that nonfiction does not allow.

But can a firm line be drawn between fact and fiction?

Whereas modernity likes to distinguish between scientific veracity and superstition, traditional societies contrast ancestral myths, which are held to be true, with folktales, which are admittedly make-believe. But just as scientific knowledge is continually being reshaped, either by the discovery of new facts or the development of new theories, so people of faith claim that their sacred texts contain eternal truths, even though they are continually being reinterpreted.

Doubt and uncertainty are as endemic to human discourse as they are to human relations, whether between strangers who assume no common ground or between friends who claim to know and trust each other unconditionally. This is not only because our situations in life are continually in flux, forcing us to rethink things we took for granted—the climate of our planet, the security of our nation, the constancy of love, the steadfastness of friends. It is also because the viability of our social world depends on binding legal and moral principles, whereas the vitality of our personal lives depends on our freedom to renegotiate these principles when they fail to do justice to our changing circumstances. This dialectic between consensus and critique informs both our public lives as citizens and our private lives as kinspeople, friends, and lovers.

In traditional societies, this tension between binding rules and bending rules finds expression in the counterpoint between myths and folktales. In modern societies, there is a similar tension between the real and the imaginary. Charter myths or constitutional laws uphold the status quo, while works of the imagination foster independence of mind and suggest alternative ways of living and thinking.

The relationship between the personal and the political is echoed in this contrast between creative license and received wisdom. While every friendship reflects virtues that are generally agreed to be "necessary and noble," even Aristotle found that "not a few things about friendship are matters of debate."[1] Like human beings who are all members of the same species yet individually unique, friendship is both one thing and many. By the same token, it is both real and imagined, and it is this ambiguity, as intrinsic to friendship as it is to kinship and love, that is my pretext for turning to fiction in the next chapter ("Reunion").

Fiction also provides a storyteller with an "intrapsychic alibi"[2] for speaking truth to lived experience rather than reinforcing our idealizations and rationalizations about the key relationships in our lives. In claiming that one's characters are make-believe, one is not only relieved of the burden of mirroring the world as others wish it to be, but one is also able to protect from ridicule or shame the real people on whom one's personae are based.

"Reunion" is thus a reworking of reality. The characters are partly invented, the setting partly imagined, and the personal names made up. The story begins, however, in real time, with a real event.

With the onset of the aptly named "novel coronavirus" in early 2020, I felt compelled to take a sabbatical from academic work and write fiction. But why, I asked myself, should I want to escape this new normal rather than study it? Perhaps the answer lay in my enforced isolation, cut off from the friends on whom I relied not only for my sense of self-worth but for my sense of reality as well. These feelings of estrangement were exacerbated when I found myself unable to travel to New Zealand, and email and phone communications with absent family and friends did little to alleviate my homesickness.

Isolation can be profoundly disturbing and can readily lead to paranoid fantasies, conspiracy theories, and suicidal thoughts. But in turning to fiction, I did not feel that I was denying reality; rather, I was engaging with it obliquely. This sense of seeing the world askance was not unlike dying to one life as a prelude to beginning another: Reconnecting with friends with whom I had lost touch. Reviewing my life through theirs. Returning to a road not taken.

CHAPTER 19

Reunion

In the early spring of 2020, I developed a sore throat, persistent cough, and mild fever that confined me to bed for three days. Fearing that I had contracted the COVID-19 virus, I emailed my doctor, only to be advised that in the absence of any tests all I could do was self-isolate and see what happened. I did as I was told, avoiding physical contact with my wife and spending long hours alone, with only a laptop computer to connect me with the world.

During this period, in which I lost track of time, I enjoyed an unexpected reprieve from my ingrained feelings of social inadequacy. Communicating with students and colleagues in writing rather than face-to-face not only restored my self-confidence, it also sharpened my awareness of the degree to which our sense of self reflects the nature of our relations with others.

In Jean-Paul Sartre's play *Huis Clos* (*In Camera*), three flawed individuals find themselves confined in a single room. During the play, they confess their sins to one another and even develop a peculiar love triangle. When Sartre has one of his characters say, "Hell is other people," he intends to remind us that we are so dependent on others for how we see ourselves that when they disparage or snub us we are prone to see ourselves as worthless. Fortunately, being loved or befriended can make us feel that we are in Heaven.

Despite warnings of the health catastrophe about to engulf the world, I was struck by the deceptive calm in the street outside my window. Even though the stock market had crashed, schools and businesses had closed, and international travel was banned, life went on, albeit with an unnerving sense that everything was about to change for the worse. In northern Italy, people sang from their balconies, joining their voices with others in defiance of the social distancing that had been imposed upon them. As they clapped and banged pots and pans together, the cacophony recalled the ancient charivari, when people had recourse to loud noise to mark the suspension of social order and ward off the satanic forces that threatened to fill the void.

On Saint Patrick's Day and during spring break, I heard of revelers ignoring the call to shelter in place and invoking the spirit of eat, drink, and be merry, for tomorrow we die, except they were likely to survive, and it would be others who perished, often alone and in pain, their bodies uncollected for days, and then interred in mass graves. While some were fatalistic, others were in denial, claiming it was all a hoax or attributing the coronavirus pandemic to foreigners, from whom we could be protected by a border wall. As snake-oil salesmen touted remedies reminiscent of the garlic and wildflower garlands people used during the Black Death, we ritualistically washed our hands, obsessively followed the news, or prayed for a medical breakthrough.

During these anxious days, I read Daniel Defoe's *A Journal of the Plague Year*, which begins with rumors that the plague had returned to Holland, whither it had been brought from Italy, the Levant, or Cyprus, or by goods from Turkey. Writing in 1665, Defoe complains that without printed newspapers, everyone was at the mercy of wild speculation. By contrast, I had access to several news channels and could watch the president's daily briefings from the White House, his expressionless minions standing behind him as he fumbled for words, scapegoated the Chinese, abused the media, and blamed previous administrations for the lack of surgical masks, ventilators, testing kits, and treatments. It was as difficult for me as it had been for Defoe to know what was really going on. "It seems," Defoe wrote, "that the Government had a true account of it, and several councils were held about ways to prevent it coming over, but all was kept very private."[1]

I also reread Albert Camus's *La Peste* (*The Plague*), which was already advertised on Amazon as a best seller. Although Camus's novel is sometimes interpreted as an oblique commentary on life in France under German occupation, his insights into the different ways that individuals respond to the prospect of Death's indiscriminate scythe resonated with some of the things I was observing in the United States. Stories were told of people coming together in ingenious ways, reaffirming ties of friendship and kinship, and devoting themselves to the care of the aged and infirm. Other stories documented a rise in cases of domestic violence and suicide. And while some people sank into lethargy or sought distraction, others energetically pursued long-deferred dreams. As one of my older friends, Bjarke, poignantly wrote from Denmark: "I am in good spirits despite being on my own, though there is underlying anxiety given my medical history. I figure, if I get the virus, it's the end, so I am determined to complete my memoir before that happens."

It pained me to think of Bjarke isolated in his house on the outskirts of Åalborg, but when I mentioned his situation to my wife, Pia, she reminded me that Bjarke had children and, even though he was widowed, his family were undoubtedly taking care of him. Perhaps, she said, my concern for Bjarke stemmed from my strong identification with him.

There was more than a grain of truth in her comment, which may explain why I began drafting a series of lectures for the fall that brought together my longstanding interest in the psychology of separation and loss and my research on expatriation and exile. Indeed, had international travel been possible, I would have spent the summer in London, continuing my conversations with Sierra Leone friends who had migrated there during the civil war and whose quandaries of belonging, I now realized, echoed the sense of disconnectedness everyone was now struggling with.

By late March the dogwood and forsythia were flowering, and, walking in the woods with Pia, it was easy to imagine that a semblance of normality was returning to the world. Yet, despite the excited voices of children off from school and out with their parents, it was strange the way we kept our distance from one another, wary of the invisible menace in our midst.

On several successive nights, I woke to sensual dreams that left me with the guilty feeling that I was being unfaithful to Pia. Was it because my weeks of self-isolation had precluded any intimacy with her, or because the pandemic and the mounting fatalities had released in me a primordial urge, not to protect myself but to procreate? The same impulse that moved Giovanni Boccaccio to write pornographic tales during the Black Death in mid-fourteenth-century Italy[2] is echoed in the Swedish physician Axel Munthe's memoir of the 1884 Neapolitan plague, in which he describes his struggle to overcome his erotic desire to kiss a beautiful young nun, Suora Ursula, with whom he was keeping vigil as the abbess of her convent lay dying of cholera. Despite the randomness and pandemonium that appear to prevail whenever life and death are fighting for supremacy, as in pestilence and war, Munthe observes that "the battle is regulated in its minutest details by an immutable law of equilibrium."

> Nature sets to work at once to readjust the balance, to call forth new beings to take the place of the fallen. Compelled by the irresistible force of a Natural Law, men and women fall in each other's arms,

blindfolded by lust, unaware that it is Death who presides over their mating, his aphrodisiac in one hand, his narcotic in the other. Death, the giver of Life, the slayer of Life, the beginning and the end.[3]

My own yearning also precipitated memories of two of my oldest friends. Although I saw Harry occasionally in London, where he worked in publishing, and I spent time with Fletcher on my periodic trips back to New Zealand, these reunions were always brief and somewhat dutiful. Why, then, should I now feel it was imperative that I get in touch with them?

"It's understandable," Pia said. "At times like this, we all long for a time when we felt safe and secure, a time before we went out into the world and had to fend for ourselves. I have been thinking of my parents, who are probably thinking of theirs right now. Of India, Uganda, then England. All those traumatic upheavals in our family's history that sometimes leave me wondering where I belong."

I did not tell Pia that I was feeling homesick for New Zealand, because my bouts of nostalgia deeply unsettled her. She was afraid they might drive me, in a state of dissociative fugue, to quit my job, pull our children out of school, and drag her back to the life she had endured in New Zealand for five years before we moved to America.

After a flurry of emails, Fletcher suggested a reunion. He wanted us to meet in New Zealand as soon as the quarantine was lifted, but Harry demurred. It would mean having to see his family. Though I failed to see how going to New Zealand would oblige him to see people he did not want to see, Pia reminded me that Harry was not the only person who unconsciously conflated home as country and home as family. "Why don't we get together in France," she said. Since we had, for several summers, rented a *mas* (a traditional farmhouse) in Provence, Harry and his girlfriend could drive from London by car. As for Fletcher and Selina, hadn't Fletcher mentioned a wish to revisit Menton, where he spent a year on a writing fellowship? He could kill two birds with one stone.

Mas de la Colinière

It was not until the summer of 2020 that a window of opportunity made it possible for us all to travel to France. Pia and I arrived a day before the others. We wanted to lay in provisions and spend some time with Georges and Marie-France, who had moved out of the *mas* twelve years ago, having decided they were getting too old to manage the vineyard on their own. Renting the house would bring in more income than the winery. After transforming their barn into living quarters, Georges worked to create a self-sufficient lifestyle, growing herbs and vegetables for the local market. While he tended the garden and hunted partridges, hares, and occasionally a wild boar, Marie-France busied herself with the orchard and olive trees and took care of the business of renting the *mas*.

Leaving Marie-France and Pia to chat about children and grandchildren, Georges and I sauntered along the track to the *mas*, where he wanted to show me the renovated kitchen and the solar panels he had installed on the roof. Bemoaning the fact that he was getting too old to do this kind of work unaided, he expressed disappointment that his sons had chosen to live in Marseilles rather than get their hands dirty working on the land. But then, as if to remind himself that he too had once felt the need to leave home in order to find his own way back to it, he quoted the old Provençal adage about the first generation climbing, the second settling, and the third dispersing.

"*Quoi faire,*" he concluded ruefully.

"It was certainly true of me," I said. "I was impatient to leave, and when I did, I thought I'd never look back, let alone go back. *Mais, on fait. On fait toujours.*"

"I doubt that ours will ever come back," Georges said. "Who wants to farm these days? Who can afford to? Though I can't tell this to Marie-France."

When we returned to the barn, Pia showed me a tin box that Marie-France had found when she was cleaning the *mas*. It belonged to our son William, who had taped a label on it. Under the word CHANGE, William had written "Change is Good." Inside the box were several centime and franc coins, some limestone pebbles with curious flaws, and a whittled olive-wood teaspoon. When Marie-France explained how Georges had found the box in the shed beyond the vineyard, Pia had burst into tears, realizing that William must have assumed we would continue to return to la Colinière forever.

"As if nothing would change," she said.

"No," I said, "because he knew everything was going to change and that change was good."

"They grow up so quickly," Marie-France said. "And we are driven ahead of them like geese toward the kitchen door."

Later that afternoon, as Pia and I walked through the orchard toward the hill, Pia said Marie-France was in mourning.

"Georges feels abandoned," I said.

"I can't imagine William and Sally not coming back here," Pia said.

"They'll be back," I said. "This place is as much a part of them as it is of us."

Where a stone terrace had crumbled, a track led up through stunted holm oak and broom toward the summit of the hill. The air was fragrant with thyme, rosemary, and juniper. Scattered among the stones were spent cartridge cases, broken wine bottles, and the remains of a small fire.

"You must be feeling nervous?" Pia said.

"About what?"

"Seeing your friends again. Reconnecting."

"I'm more nervous about you," I said. "You've never got on with Harry. And as for Fletcher—"

"I've always liked Selina. It'll be fine."

At the summit, we stopped to catch our breath. In the distance, the Dentelles de Montmirail resembled a broken comb of ivory. Pia sat on a slab of limestone. She was wearing a white blouse and blue jeans and had tied back her hair. I stretched out on the sun-warmed stones and closed my eyes. I could smell pine straw and dry earth. I heard the buzz of flies and the tinkle of a pebble dislodged as a lizard scuttled into the shadows of the stones. For a moment, I wished I hadn't invited Harry and Fletcher to join us, and wondered why, of all the people I had known and loved, I had felt compelled to renew my friendship with them. Was it, as Pia said, because they were the surviving remnants of my New Zealand self, my youth? Or was it a matter of inertia, like a marriage that is sustained by habit rather than desire?

Returning through the garigue, we debated where we would put everyone. Should we give "our" room to Fletcher and Selina, who would undoubtedly be jet-lagged after their long flight from the antipodes? If we moved into William's old room off the kitchen, we would be well placed for preparing breakfasts. As for Harry and his girlfriend, whose name I kept forgetting, they could have the upstairs room at the back of the house, overlooking the vineyard.

Pont d'Avignon

As Fletcher walked toward me along the railway platform, I was struck by his shabbiness. Was it his winter clothing? Or his weather-beaten face, scruffy beard, and uncombed hair? Or was it because I had never before seen him outside of New Zealand? Out of his element?

He did not respond to my open arms but set down the large suitcase he was carrying and extended his hand which I shook awkwardly. Then I turned to Selina, who had no inhibitions about embracing.

"Where's Pia?" she demanded.

"She thought there wouldn't be enough room in the car for all of us."

"Don't tell me I've put on that much weight!"

"I was thinking of your bags," I said. "It's only a small car."

"Do we cross the Pont d'Avignon?" Fletcher asked and sang the first lines of the famous song.

"There's only four arches left of the original bridge," I said. "Do you want to see them before we head off?"

Fletcher didn't care one way or the other. Selina was eager to see Pia.

Once on the A7, I had to shout to be heard above the buffeting wind, and my attempts at small talk about how impressively New Zealand had managed the pandemic seemed to fall on deaf ears. Unlike Fletcher, however, Selina did her best to respond.

"It got Fletcher down," she said. "He played Patience, watched movies, did cryptic crosswords, and complained about the pointlessness of writing fiction."

I wanted to say that the months of lockdown, and then the flood of anger that brought tens of thousands onto the streets after the killing of George Floyd by a Minneapolis police officer, had precipitated in me a complete disenchantment with academic writing. But Selina's description of Fletcher's passivity troubled me, and I did not want to venture a comparison between his state of mind and my own. Instead, I turned to naming various places they might like to see—the Roman ruins at Vaison, the amphitheater at Orange, the Gigondas vineyards—only for the noise of the wind and of cars overtaking us to sweep my words away. *They must be exhausted*, I told myself. *We can talk later*. And I increased the pressure of my foot on the accelerator.

Within minutes of arriving at the *mas*, Pia took Selina under her wing, leaving me to help Fletcher lug their suitcases upstairs to their room.

"I can imagine writing here," Fletcher said, gazing out the window.

"I thought you said you'd lost interest in writing."

"That was Selina's observation."

I did not press the issue and suggested we go downstairs for drinks.

Pia had set out pâté, tapenade, and water biscuits on the table, together with a bottle of wine. "Help yourselves," she said. "We can sit outside."

Ensconced at a table in the courtyard, and shaded by a large patio umbrella, we raised our glasses and drank to friendship.

The wine brought Fletcher to life. He regaled us with stories of undergraduate escapades and drinking bouts and described the narrow room where he and Harry edited *Hippocampus*. For a moment I was there once more, lounging on the battered sofa, sharing a joint, listening to David Bowie, and watching Fletcher and Harry argue over whether they had enough copy for a second issue of their magazine.

For the first time since meeting Fletcher at the station, I felt my old affection for him returning.

We dined that evening with Georges and Marie-France, sitting at a table under their pergola. Selina was embarrassed by her lack of French, but Pia put her at ease by recounting our own difficulties with the local patois. "Not to mention Georges's dislike of Americans," I added, alluding to his relief when he discovered that, though Pia and I lived in America, we were not American.

Georges laughed and raised his glass. "To Kiwis," he said.

"To Kiwis," I chimed, aware of how presumptuous this appellation might seem to Pia.

It was a cue for Fletcher to extol our national pride in fending for ourselves. Familiar with Georges's philosophy of *faire toi-même*, I told Fletcher that almost everything on the table—the goat's cheese, the wine, the olive tapenade, the liver pâté—was produced locally. Fletcher's eyes lit up. He even attempted to speak French, elated to have discovered a kindred spirit. "I have always wanted to be more self-sufficient," he said. "I dream of a commune somewhere, far from the madding crowd. Of choosing self-isolation before climate change or another pandemic forces us to rely on our own ingenuity to survive."

Water Under the Bridge

I could not sleep. Every couple of hours, I got up and went to the kitchen to slake my thirst. Not wanting to wake Pia, or bother her with what was on my mind, I sat in the semidarkness in my T-shirt and boxers, bare feet on the flagstones, sipping water and wondering whether Fletcher's reserve could be explained, as Pia suggested, as a combination of jet lag and culture shock, or whether he had warmed to Georges not simply because of their common interest in practical matters but because he distrusted what he liked to call "my academic bent." But then it occurred to me that Fletcher and Harry had not met for more than twenty years, and Fletcher might be even more anxious than I was about seeing our mutual friend again.

In the year after completing our bachelor's degrees, Harry flew to London, while Fletcher, who had decided to pursue a master's in anthropology, went to the Tokelau Islands. As for me, I was fueled by an ambition to see the world and transform myself through travel and ordeal. After a year of backpacking through India, Pakistan, and Afghanistan, I ended up in London, so broke and emotionally drained that I was on the verge of asking my parents to cover the costs of a flight back home. Though I was dimly aware that Harry was in London, I had lost my address book in Karachi, and it did not occur to me that I might trace his whereabouts through New Zealand House. After sleeping outdoors in the Victoria Embankment Gardens for two nights and wandering through the city, hungry and hallucinating, I happened on a welfare office for the homeless, where I received vouchers for food and two nights' lodging. As fate would have it, the man who interviewed me was intrigued by my academic background and invited me to apply for a vacant position as a welfare officer.

Within a week, I was handing out vouchers for a bed in a Salvation Army hostel and a meal in a cheap café, and recording the life stories of the homeless people who found their way to our office under the Hungerford Bridge. It was not long before their experiences so enthralled me that I began to entertain the idea of writing a book like Jack London's *The People of the Abyss*, based on his months of sleeping in workhouses in the East End in 1902.

For several months, I rarely spoke to anyone other than these lost souls, and it was, therefore, a coincidence—quite as remarkable as finding work among the homeless—when I ran into Harry as I was emerging from the Underground at Tottenham Court Road one evening.

After repairing to a pub in Soho, Harry described his work at Bayer and Condcliffe and the famous writers he met, adding that he and his fiancée, Annette, were living in one of the Nash Terraces at Regent's Park Gate, thanks to a fortuitous meeting with the editor of *New Society*, who had an apartment there. I had no idea how expensive and famous these houses were and innocently described my one-room apartment in Hammersmith and my work with the homeless, as if our situations were roughly equivalent.

Harry soon put me right. "When I first came here," he said, "I was stunned by the class snobberies. There was no getting away from them, and certainly no way of getting around them. I was asked as a matter of course what school I had attended. That my parents had sent me to the best private school in Auckland did not alter the fact that I was a colonial. My accent gave me away. A single ill-chosen word or phrase would betray me. It was pointless trying to imitate them, and education was no more a passport to their world than wealth."

I was soon to learn that my identification with the homeless gave me no better access to their lives than occupying an apartment in a neoclassical terrace at Regent's Park gave Harry entrée into the world to which he seemed fated to belong.

We saw each other from time to time over the next few months, usually for a pub lunch in the Strand, halfway between our respective places of work. I was always broke, having distributed my meager earnings among the homeless men and women in a self-defeating effort to mitigate my distress at *their* suffering. I would feel ashamed at having Harry buy lunch and quickly wearied of his anecdotes about literary lions and rising stars. We would have had little to talk about had it not been for Harry's fervent interest in my experiences in shelters and flophouses and on the streets. Was he genuinely intrigued by the underworld with which I was becoming familiar and that he was debarred from entering? Did I provide a kind of bridge that allowed him to experience poverty at a safe distance? For he lived, I now realized, through the lives of others. It explained his attraction to Annette and the Home Counties world in which she had been raised. It was the social class Harry's mother emulated, and its other extreme was the degraded world in which I now moved and by which Harry was morbidly fascinated.

One evening, as Harry and I were leaving the Hampstead cinema where we'd gone to see Michelangelo Antonioni's *La Notte*, he made a remark that I would never forget.

In the opening sequence of the film, the dying Tommaso asks, "What should I do? What can I do?" before answering to the effect that his life has been more shadow than substance, that he has lacked the courage to probe things deeply and fully. Harry asked me what I thought of Tommaso's confession. I did not know what to say but was struck by the earnestness of Harry's question and the imploring expression on his face as he waited for me to answer. Should I have told him that our lives are mostly lived in the shadows, that homelessness is a universal condition and not confined to those who have no place to sleep at night?

Despite my disapproval of Harry's philandering, I envied his seductive power over women. But I also saw how his infidelities were affecting Annette, who would sometimes allude to them without realizing she was doing so. She would jokingly tell me she was planning to have an affair. She was in the process of deciding whom it would be with. She wanted someone safe. A short, chubby, jolly, comfortable accountant would be ideal. Someone she could control.

A couple of weeks before Christmas, I had a letter from Fletcher. Things had fallen apart for him in the Tokelaus. He had returned to New Zealand, turned his back on anthropology, and was thinking of coming to London. Could he stay with me?

I leapt at the chance of seeing him, even though I could offer him little in the way of home comforts. Why hadn't he asked Harry for a place to stay? I didn't even have enough money to heat my apartment, and for days on end, I lived on vegetables scavenged from the local market.

The day after Fletcher moved in, we went to see Harry and Annette.

A cold rain was falling as we arrived. Annette opened the door and embraced Fletcher as if he was *her* friend. Harry was sulking, she said. He had shut himself in his study. We were to ignore him; he'd come out in his own good time.

As Annette fixed drinks, Fletcher went to the CD player and put on Joy Division's "Love Will Tear Us Apart." It seemed a perverse and presumptuous thing to do, but the music brought Harry out of his study and he too embraced Fletcher, saying how sorry he was that Fletcher's fieldwork hadn't worked out and his girlfriend had left him.

"May I ask what happened?" Annette said.

During his first weeks in the Tokelau Islands, Fletcher had fallen in love with a young woman, Selina, who worked as a nurse in the local clinic. Several months into his fieldwork, Selina's brother fell gravely ill. When Selina began to arrange for her brother to be taken by sea to Samoa, where he could be properly diagnosed and treated, Fletcher urged her to delay the trip, arguing that Selina's brother was on the mend, though his real motive was to buy time to document the progress of the mysterious illness and its social repercussions. Several weeks passed before another boat arrived, by which time Selina's brother was so ill that Selina no longer trusted anything Fletcher said. When she received news of her brother's death in an Apia hospital, she blamed Fletcher. In a fit of rage, she took Fletcher's field notes and journals and burned them. Fletcher accepted the judgment that had been passed upon him. With his career in ashes, he became desperate to atone for his mistakes and secure Selina's forgiveness.

The following Saturday, as Fletcher and I were discussing whether we had enough money to take the subway into the West End and see a movie, the doorbell rang. It was Annette. Could we buzz her in?

I opened the door of my flat and waited while she climbed the stairs. She was wearing a Burberry raincoat. Her head scarf was crusted with snow.

"Is Fletcher here?" she asked, stepping past me into the room. Then she turned and whispered furtively, "Would you mind if we had some time alone? A couple of hours?"

"It's snowing."

"Please, do this for me."

Moments later I closed the door on them and walked out onto the street, practically blinded by the snow.

I had nowhere to go. Gobbets of wet snow were falling fast. Coatless, I hugged a brick wall for shelter. The cold was creeping into my fingers and toes, and I was infuriated at being turned out of my apartment.

I hung about in doorways, walked the streets, read magazines at the subway station, cursing them both. When I did go back to the apartment, I found them sitting sheepishly at the table. On the carpet was a stain from spilled coffee. I imagined the first clumsy moment of their coming together. Their lovemaking filled me with disgust. But I described my walk in the snow as exhilarating and offered to make them coffee.

Annette said she had to get back to Harry. Fletcher offered to accompany her to the station.

I watched them from the window as they trudged through the snow. She had wanted to avenge herself on Harry, and for some reason I suspected her of wanting to humiliate me.

She might have succeeded in her first ambition, had the lovemaking not been such a fiasco. And she might have succeeded in the second, had she considered the repercussions of my being privy to her betrayal of Harry.

It was the last I saw of her. Not long after she and Harry went their separate ways, I returned to New Zealand, determined to pursue a career in the field that Fletcher had abandoned in his attempt to win back Selina's trust.

Mistral

Harry arrived late in the day, bounding out of his BMW and extending his arms as if he had crossed a finishing line ahead of the field. Overwhelmed by his ebullience and charm, we all laughed, and Pia and Selina held hands as we walked toward the house. All my misgivings faded away, though I found it difficult to talk to his girlfriend, Elle, who was no older than my daughter and clearly bewildered by the company into which she had been thrown.

Fletcher kept his distance. Later, he would confide that we were like actors at a first reading: unfamiliar with our lines and uncertain of the roles we would be called on to play.

To avoid embarrassing Elle, we did not talk about old times but instead exchanged anecdotes about our lives under lockdown or discussed the excursions Pia and I had planned for the coming days.

We dined that evening in the courtyard. I served a *navarin d'agneau* with stuffed capsicums, and as glass after glass of Gigondas wine loosened our tongues, we laughed at Harry's stories and pandered to his egoism. When a hair stylist had commented that his hair was surprisingly thick for a man his age, he bristled, "A man my age! My God, how old did she think I was?"

"Not as old as you are," Elle said, and cheekily informed us that Harry had changed his date of birth to magically make himself younger.

"*Pas vrai!*" Harry exclaimed. But we all knew it was.

Over the next two days, we settled into an amicable routine. After a breakfast of coffee and croissants in the courtyard, Fletcher and Harry retired to their rooms and attended to work-related emails, while Elle took a deck chair into the orchard, stripped to her bikini, and sunbathed behind dark glasses. Selina liked to walk to the village for supplies, sometimes with Pia, then prepare a lunch of fresh baguettes, local cheese, salami, and an arugula salad for our daily picnic at the Toulourenc Gorge. I would use this time to wander through the garigue and find a shaded spot under a pine from where I could survey the countryside, which was so like Cezanne's landscapes near Aix, with farmhouses and cypresses dotting the open fields and pine boughs framing a cloudless sky. Sometimes, I would call on Georges and Marie-France and share an espresso before returning to the *mas*.

The mistral changed everything, blowing out of a clear blue sky, bludgeoning the cypresses, playing havoc with the dry leaves in the courtyard, and driving us indoors for days. With so much dust in the air, we lost interest in swimming at the gorge or eating in the courtyard. Selina no longer enjoyed her daily stroll to the village, and Elle found no pleasure in sunbathing. Though she moved her deck chair to a sheltered corner of the courtyard, she quickly became irritated by the wind and persuaded Harry to take her to Vaison for a couple of days, as if the mistral would not follow them there. Even our sleep was disturbed by a nightlong howling in the kitchen chimney and a loose shutter banging against a wall, and I was mindful of the stories Georges used to regale us with, of frayed nerves and *crimes passionnel* attributed to the mistral. I began to wonder what change it might wreak in us.

In the evenings, we shared news gleaned from websites or social media, or succumbed to boredom and drank. Elle had enjoyed Vaison but was, she said, sick of ruins. I could only guess at what she found so enthralling in her smartphone. Engrossed in rereading *Middlemarch*, Pia was happy to disappear into another century, while Selina struggled with a cryptic crossword, occasionally asking Fletcher for help with an anagram.

Fletcher declared us all party poopers and demanded a moratorium on digital devices. "What did we do before we had cell phones?" he asked. "We *talked* to each other."

"We can talk to each other on our phones," Elle said.

"They were our lifeline during the pandemic," Harry said.

Pia suggested charades. "Or we could play Hunt the Thimble."

There was a long silence.

"Then let's pretend we're back in the nineteenth century," Pia said, "when people had to create their own entertainment."

In the summer of 1816, Mary Shelley, her husband, and some friends were vacationing on the shores of Lake Geneva. One evening, Lord Byron announced that they should each compose a ghost story and recount it on successive nights. As the evening approached for Shelley to tell her story, she became increasingly anxious, though inventing a ghost story was not her only preoccupation, for she had recently read about Erasmus Darwin's experiments with galvanism and the "frightful" effects of "any human endeavor to mock the stupendous mechanisms of the Creator of the world."[4]

"Thus was conceived," Pia said, "the story of Frankenstein."

Fletcher was enthusiastic. Although he rejected the notion that new technologies outraged a divine order, he saw them as inimical to the social order. Harry was not so sure. "Progress is progress," he opined. "Look at the Luddites. Look at the masses who thought the invention of moveable type and the printed book would destroy communal life. We not only survive such changes; we are improved by them."

"There were times during the lockdown," Selina said, "when I thought that life would never be the same again."

"I hoped it would bring us to our senses," Pia said. "That the slate would be wiped clean and we would rediscover the meaning of family and friendship."

"To friendship then," Harry said, and drained his glass.

"And family," Selina said.

"What about the ghost stories?" Elle said.

"Aren't ghost stories rather passé?" Harry said.

"There's another possibility," Pia said, and she described a minor character in Fyodor Dostoevsky's *The Idiot*, a buffoon called Ferdyshchenko, who considered himself blessed with a unique talent for entertaining people.

At a party at which the beautiful Princess Nastasya Philipovna promises to name the man to whom she will give her hand in marriage, her suitors and guests are apprehensive. Ferdyshchenko, however, is in high spirits, laughing loudly for no apparent reason and playing the fool. To liven things up, he suggests a parlor game in which everyone takes turns confessing the most morally reprehensible thing they have ever done. Everyone except Nastasya Philipovna is repelled by the idea of revealing their darkest secrets in front of a man as boorish as Ferdyshchenko, whose shameful admissions could not degrade him further in the eyes of Saint Petersburg society. But lots are drawn, and to his delight, Ferdyshchenko gets to tell his story first.

The incident he describes took place two years earlier, when Ferdyshchenko was a dinner guest at a country house.

After dinner, as the men sat around the dining table drinking wine, Ferdyshchenko went into an adjoining room to ask his host's daughter if she would play something for him on the piano. On a worktable in the passageway was a three-ruble note. Without a second thought, Ferdyshchenko pocketed the money. When the theft was discovered, suspicion fell on Carya, one of the maidservants. In the fuss that followed, Ferdyshchenko feigned sympathy for his hostess and took an active role in trying to persuade the distraught maid to confess.

Later that night he spent the three rubles on a bottle of Lafitte in a local restaurant.

When Ferdyshchenko finished telling his story, Nastasya Philipovna asked what happened to the falsely accused maid.

She was dismissed, and Ferdyshchenko had done nothing to prevent it.

No one felt anything but contempt for Ferdyshchenko. And it was even worse for him when the others related their stories, for in every case the baseness of the misdeed was redeemed by contrition.

"I wouldn't know where to begin," Elle said. "I regret everything."

"It's true," Harry said. "She's the opposite of Édith Piaf. Elle *regrette tout*. She even regrets being with me, don't you sweetheart?"

"Not trivial regrets," Pia said. "Sins of omission or commission. Past mistakes we cannot forget and find it difficult to forgive."

Selina's Story

When Selina volunteered to go first, I feared she was going to tell the story of her brother's death. Instead, she described a book she had read several years ago by an Australian hospice nurse, summarizing the end-of-life epiphanies that hundreds of patients in palliative care had confided to her. Bronnie Ware was not only moved by the clarity with which the dying looked back on their lives but also by the things they wished they had done or not done—the most frequent wish being that they'd had the courage to live a life true to themselves rather than the life others expected of them.

"This book made such a deep impression on me," Selina said, "that I became determined to live in a way that would not make me regret, in my time of dying, the choices I had made or not had the courage to make when I was young and healthy. But like New Year's Eve resolutions, which we make and break with impunity, or the bad habits we get into and cannot change, I could not decide what I needed to do or even if I needed to do anything. I was fulfilled in my work as a nurse. Our children were happy. I bore no grudges and had no regrets.

"The pandemic changed all that. While intensive care wards and emergency rooms in Europe were being overwhelmed, and in America personal protective equipment was in short supply, we felt confident we could cope. Even when I heard reports of people spitting at nurses or verbally abusing them, I put this down to the stress many people were under: people were afraid that we, in New Zealand, weren't as safe and secure in our remoteness as we liked to believe. Besides, being spat on and racially abused were experiences that we Tokelauans were all too familiar with.

"It was the calm before the storm. The national lockdown had been in place for a month, and though the no-visitor policy at the hospital bothered me, I saw the necessity of it. That was until I witnessed an elderly woman being separated from her husband who had tested positive for the virus. She was told to say goodbye to him at the entrance to the hospital, and she walked away as if she had nowhere to go, no one to comfort her, no assurance that she would ever see her husband again. My heart went out to this poor woman. I wanted to run after her. But there wasn't time. We were rushed off our feet. If the sick were going to survive, every second counted.

"I was emotionally drained by the suffering around me and the unrelenting demands of responding to people whose terrified faces betrayed their fear of asphyxiation, or who pleaded with me to phone their loved ones or send messages to them. I've always prided myself on my ability to show empathy while carrying out my professional duties. To see my patients as persons and not simply as sufferers. But then I lost that perspective, and I am not sure that I have recovered it, even now.

"One evening, an elderly Samoan man was brought to the hospital by his wife and children. He was showing all the signs of COVID-19, and since he was diabetic and obese, I feared the worst. It fell to me to explain to the family the seriousness of the situation. They would need to be tested for the virus, then quarantined at home. They would not be able to visit their loved one. Their desperation tore at my heart. The man's wife could not understand the precautions, and though her sons tried to tell her that I was giving them sound advice, she was sobbing so uncontrollably that I began to fear for her well-being. I was also beginning to fear for myself. I was at breaking point. I was losing my self-control.

"Later, when I was intubating the man, I was fighting back tears. I even had to turn away, remove my mask and goggles, and wipe the tears away. I castigated myself for my weakness. Why was I seeing in this man, struggling for breath and clutching at my gown for reassurance, my own father? *This is no time to fall apart*, I told myself. *For God's sake pull yourself together.* But even as I adjusted the ventilator and checked his vital signs, I was composing in my mind what I would say to his family if he passed away, and how I would live with myself if I lost him.

"I did not confide any of this to you, Fletcher. Not because we had decided to sleep in separate rooms, nor because I was too exhausted to talk when I came home from my shift. Finding words for what I was going through had something to do with an unresolved regret at having left home and come to New Zealand all those years ago. Leaving my family in the Tokelaus. Putting off revisiting them during the years I was in nursing school. Not taking our children back to meet their grandparents. Not working hard enough to persuade them to visit us in New Zealand.

"The pandemic separated us from one another. It made us aware of separations we had allowed to happen but could have prevented. The media sang our praises, calling us heroes and celebrating our resilience, but much of the time I felt powerless and alone. That Samoan family still haunts me. I failed them. The man pulled through, but it made no difference to how I felt. It was as though he had died on my watch, and I was responsible for his death.

"Some of the other nurses keep saying, 'We're all in this together.' They said that our greatest strength was our sense of community. But that was

COVID's greatest strength too. It thrived on us being in contact with one another, with our being together."

*   *   *

We were all silent. Then Pia told Selina that no one could have done more than she had. She should not blame herself for events that were not in her power to control.

"But I do blame myself," Selina said, "even though I know I couldn't have done more."

"That you ask so much of yourself is proof of your goodness," Pia said. "It's the loving parent in you. And you would not be the person you are had your parents not imparted that love to you. In you, they are remembered."

Fletcher got up from his chair and crossed the room. He knelt in front of Selina and put his arms around her. He was in tears.

Harry's Story

"I don't have to tell any of you that I never got along with my parents. They sent me to boarding school on the pretext of giving me the best education that money could buy, when the truth was that they wanted me out of the way so that my father could indulge his addictions and my mother could pursue her career. Not once during my childhood can I remember them showing any physical affection, either to me or to each other. And when it came time to discuss whether I would choose medicine or the law, and I told them I wanted to be an essayist, they invoked their shopworn phrase about the importance of one's standing in society. Their hypocrisy was not lost on me. It made me realize that I could not rely on them for moral or financial support and that I would have to make a choice between making my own way in the world or becoming like them. The trouble is, I have never been able to decide whether my choices were free or born of a perverse desire to do what my parents would have seen as lowering my standing in society. Don't get me wrong, I love publishing. That year when we edited *Hippocampus* together was the happiest in my life. You guys thought I had it made. Cash in hand whatever the occasion. A sports car. Success with girls. I don't think you ever realized how meaningless it all was compared to our friendship and our little magazine.

"Fletcher, you once told me you envied my freedom. But I was never really free. I was in thrall to my parents, and almost everything I did was predicated on a determination not to do anything they would have approved of.

"Like you, Selina, I was also haunted. My future was overshadowed by my past. And so, I escaped into the present. I derived vicarious pleasure from the successes of the authors I worked with, had affairs that lasted no more than a few days and nights, made the most of London and felt I belonged there. But there was always something missing. A hole I could not fill. A longing I could not assuage. Despite all the positive things in my life, I am sometimes stricken by the thought that I am not living my real life at all. When I was working on Helmut Borchhardt's memoir of his years in exile, and that 'unbridgeable gap,' he speaks of, 'between oneself and the land of one's birth and upbringing,' I felt that his descriptions of Vienna before the Anschluss echoed experiences of my own.

"It is no secret that I live to excess. Elle will tell you how much she regrets getting into a serious relationship with someone like me. And I don't need to remind you, Fletcher, of the repercussions of my infidelities. Curiously enough, however, I seem immune to remorse. Even though I have terminated so many relationships and disappointed so many people, I feel no regret. I blame my parents, not myself. I have been driven to search elsewhere for the gift of love I should have received from them. I have found its semblance, but its source continues to elude me.

"This isn't much of a story. It's more like a confession. Something I have to get off my chest but can't resolve. I'm sure I've boasted to you guys many times that when I left Auckland and came to London, I swore never to return home. I lied. I did go back, once. My mother had written, saying that my father was seriously ill. My first impulse had been to ignore her. But two days later I was on a flight to Auckland. Was it compassion that changed my mind? Or the sudden realization that my inheritance might be in jeopardy, that sordid boon that had subsidized my lifestyle for so many years?

"The house had not changed. The English garden in which I had wandered as a small child, building bivouacs out of branches, carpeting them with pine needles, was as immaculately tended as ever, though Charteris, the gardener, had retired. The glimpse of the harbor beyond the Abyssinian palms was the same that had once held out to me the promise of another life. But my mother was frail and frightened and pleaded with me not to disappear before I had helped her sort out some legal issues that her lawyer had raised with my father but never resolved.

"I visited my father in hospital. He did not want to talk about his condition, and I was reluctant to answer his questions about my life in London. When he pleaded tiredness and asked me to summon a nurse, I made my getaway. Leaving the hospital, the sunlight dazzled me, and I did not know which way to turn. Should I walk through the Domain or cross Grafton Bridge and head downtown along Symonds Street?

"A tower of red panels and tinted windows occupied the space where my apartment building once stood, and a triangular bed of flowering agapanthus marked the site of the corner apartment where, on summer nights, Melanie and I competed to kill mosquitoes between the pages of library books.

"As I stood on the corner, stunned by the absence of any trace of the place that it still pains me to remember, it occurred to me how easily the materiality of our lives—our homes, our vehicles, our possessions, our bodies—vanishes from the face of the earth, while our thoughts and longings linger, like the spirits of the dead, loath to depart this world for the next.

"In this dark mood, I stepped over the steel barrier at the end of the street and clambered down into the gully. Once a wilderness of rank-smelling plants, broken bottles, and discarded condoms that Melanie called, after Malcolm Lowry's *Under the Volcano*, the *barranca*, a motorway now ran through it, connecting Auckland's northern and southern suburbs. But the *pōhutukawa* where Melanie hanged herself was still there, with its gnarled limbs and braided draperies.

"We had quarreled, and she'd walked out on me. I presumed she'd gone to her mother's place, as she had the last time we broke up, and although, as the days passed, I smelled the putrescence on the air as I walked to the campus, I concluded that a dead cat had been thrown into the *barranca*, along with dead foliage and grass clippings. Then came the police search for a 'missing person' and Melanie's irate sister and mother insisting to the cops that I knew her whereabouts. When an art student stumbled on her remains and the police questioned me for the fourth time, I confessed to having been complicit in her death. In fact, I became so distressed at not being able to explain to anyone how exactly I had connived in the tragedy, that I was referred to a psychiatrist for assessment.

"I don't know where you guys were that summer, but you weren't in Auckland. I can't even remember whether you ever came to our apartment or met Melanie. In any case, I left the city within a week of her funeral, as much to escape the recriminations of her family and friends as to distance myself from the anguish that now possessed me. There was nowhere that did not

bring back unbearable memories—hitchhiking with her to Clearwater for
the festival; her tearing my umbrella from my grasp when it started to rain
and hurling it over a fence into a paddock, berating me for being afraid of a
few raindrops; the week we camped at Matauri Bay, Melanie's body stream-
ing with bioluminescence as she plunged into the blue depths; Spirits Bay,
where we came to blows; the Bay of Islands, where we made up; the times she
turned to stone and the times she opened her soul to me, sharing her terrors.
Though I finally persuaded myself that I was not to blame for her suicide, that
her wild mood swings—clinging to me like a limpet one minute, the next
clawing at me like a cornered animal—were signs of an unhinged mind, deep
down I felt that, with patience, I could have saved her."

*   *   *

As Harry poured himself another brandy, Selina said something about the
need to forgive those who have wronged us and to forgive ourselves when we
have done wrong, but it was clear that listening was all that Harry was asking
of us, and nothing we might say or do would shift the weight of sorrow from
his soul.

In bed that night, Pia asked why some people blame themselves for their
mistakes, and some blame others. "Why do some of us beat ourselves up and
apologize when things go wrong, while others cast about for a scapegoat to
carry away the shame of their own shortcomings?"

"There is something else," I said to Pia. "Something Harry once confided
to Fletcher. Not long after Harry first came to London, he met and became
engaged to someone called Annette Warr-Richards. When Annette discovered that Harry had had a girlfriend who committed suicide, she interpreted
the remorse he felt for what had happened as evidence of an inextinguishable
nostalgia for Melanie and became convinced that this past love would always
overshadow the love Harry had declared for her."

Pia sighed. "My God, is the past ever past?"

When Pia turned away to sleep, I lay awake, trying to reconcile the lost
soul that Harry had revealed to us and the urbane individual that I had always
admired, even though his vanity irked me, and I hated feeling that I was his
inferior. What story would I tell when my turn came? Would I speak of the
guilt and regret my Sierra Leone friends often felt, enjoying advantages in
London that their age-mates, still living in remote villages, could only dream
of? Or would I confess that I, too, was oppressed by a darkness within me

on which I could not shed light? That I had never reconciled my search for somewhere utterly unlike my natal country with my inextinguishable nostalgia for it?

Pia's Story

"If I have thought long and hard about where to begin, it is because my story is so entangled with the stories of my parents and grandparents. The regrets I feel for the mistakes I have made in my life pale in comparison with the regrets I have always felt for the suffering they endured and the price they paid for giving me the opportunities I have had.

"I was born a year after Idi Amin ordered all Indians out of Uganda. My father refused to talk to me about the expulsion, but I read about it at school and even did a project on it. Under my barrage of questions, my mother finally confirmed that our family had come to England penniless and demoralized, with only the clothes on our backs. She said that falling pregnant with me was like a rebirth for her.

"My grandparents emigrated to East Africa in the 1930s, so Uganda was, to all intents and purposes, my parents' homeland. They had, still have, extended family in Gujarat, but these ties have long ago worn thin, which is why my parents did not go to India when Amin expelled them from Uganda but instead chose to join the thousands of others being airlifted to Britain. Although I once visited my grandfather's natal village, I have never felt any deep belonging to India, and for what it's worth, have always called England home. If I sound ambivalent about England, it's because for most of my childhood, I was made to feel like a stranger there, stigmatized as an interloper, just as my parents had been stigmatized in Uganda as *dukawallahs* and bloodsuckers who not only cheated local Africans but also looked down on them. All my life, I have been routinely asked where I am from. When I say 'Leicester,' the next question is always, 'But where are your parents from?' And when I say 'Uganda,' the interrogator is satisfied, even though my parents are not African. Other people assume I am Hindu and give me vegetarian meals, or assume I can't speak English and talk slowly to me as if I'm a child. I've even been taken for Arab and asked for my family recipes for hummus and shawarma, or suspected of being a suicide bomber, so people ask to be seated away from me on airplanes or threaten to call airport security if I continue to insist that my small backpack can easily fit into the overhead compartment.

I have been congratulated on being a strong, liberated, and modern woman and told it is my duty to speak on behalf of the Islamic State or explain the complex politics of the Middle East. I am always a figment of other people's imaginations. I have seldom felt free to simply be myself.

"Throughout my childhood, I lived my life inside out. Either I had to conform to the stereotypes visited upon me or satisfy my grandparents' and parents' expectations that I vicariously realize their thwarted ambitions. I felt that I was expected to make good what they had lost, and somehow compensate them for the suffering they had endured.

"All this changed when I turned sixteen. I became petulant and critical. I accused my father of being a slave to bourgeois values and questioned my mother's decision to waste her life pandering to my father and fretting over her children's futures. Even though I railed against their values, they were so deeply embedded in me that uprooting them almost cost me my life.

"My parents did not want me to date English boys, and my dream of studying English literature at Oxford made no sense to them.

"At seventeen, I was working weekends in a retirement home called the Meadows. Derek was also working there part-time. I lost my virginity to him on a bed in which an elderly woman had died the previous day. Derek was helping me disinfect the room and prepare it for a new arrival. I liked him well enough. We often sat together in the staff room and shared our dreams. I gave myself to him in a moment of madness worthy of Emily Brontë, and when I realized I was pregnant, I told neither Derek nor my parents but saw a doctor who referred me to an abortion clinic. After a long conversation with a counselor, I elected to have the baby and tell my parents that I would give it up for adoption. My mother showed no emotion but made me vow never to tell my father. She said if he found out, it would kill him.

"I left school after completing my A levels, had the baby two months later, and held her in my arms for a few minutes before she was taken from me.

"It was my decision. No one coerced me. Yet I felt I had done something horribly wrong, something unforgiveable. My counselor said that the feelings of regret would soon pass. They were only to be expected in the days after separation, when your hormones and motherly instincts are strongest. As your body heals, so too will your emotions.

"I have never doubted that I did the right thing. When I went up to Oxford that September and got swept away by my studies, my new friendships, and the elation of finally getting away from Leicester, it felt as if Derek and the baby had happened to someone else. But like you, Selina, there was some ineradicable link between giving up my baby for adoption and my grandparents' and parents' loss of their Ugandan home. Lives that might have been. Different futures. Is *regret* the right word for thinking about these paths not taken? Or is it more a matter of idle curiosity? Something that lacks the moral overtones of regret? A sense that life is filled with boundless possibilities, a hopefulness that is always tinged with an awareness that, of all those possible paths, we could only pursue one?"

*   *   *

When no one said anything, Pia began collecting our empty wine glasses. As the others drifted away to their rooms, I helped Pia clean up and stack the dishwasher.

"Do you feel like a walk?" I asked.

"You're not tired?"

"I feel like walking," I said.

It was a moonless night. The track was barely visible.

"You were brave to share all that," I said. "I can't believe that no one responded."

"I didn't expect them to. I didn't even want them to. We remember for ourselves, not for others. I think we return to the past in the hope that repeated exposure to small doses will finally grant us immunity."

I glanced back at the *mas*. It had been swallowed up by the darkness. Even Pia had become a dark presence, and I reached out to her, pressing my hand against the small of her back. She, in turn, put her arm around me.

"Do you think I should have kept my story to myself?" Pia asked. "Elle looked quite distressed."

"Maybe Elle's got a similar story to tell."

We walked on in silence.

"What do you really think?" Pia asked.

"I don't think our stories are ever ours alone. They echo the stories of others, and the whole point of telling them is to make those connections visible. To shatter the illusion that we are the sole authors of our own lives."

"I was thinking of us tonight," Pia said. "Of William and Sally. Of all we have been through, you and me, and as a family. It makes everything else seem like something I have read about. Something I imagined."

Fletcher's Story

That Fletcher elected to share something he had written did not surprise me. After all, he had become a writer, he once confessed, because he had no confidence in his ability to talk off the cuff.

Harry was irked by Fletcher's "cop out."

"For someone who rails against digital technology, this is ridiculous. Why should we have to come up with stories on the fly while you get to compose something on your laptop?"

"Does everyone feel this way?" Fletcher asked.

Pia pointed out that Mary Shelley's story of Frankenstein would have been very different from the story she subsequently expanded and published. Fletcher was simply doing what she had done, only in reverse.

I agreed. It was the story that mattered, not whether it was spoken or written.

We refreshed our drinks and settled into our chairs. Out in the darkness, the wind assailed the house, and the limb of a pine tree scraped against the wall, as if impatient for Fletcher to begin.

*   *   *

For several years now, a small group of us have met for coffee every morning before heading off to our various places of work—me to my studio, Richard to his office, Marian to the Dominion, *and Paul to Te Papa. Spending time together at the beginning of the day was, we decided, an alternative to gathering in a pub after work and squandering time better spent at home.*

Occasionally, we bring along visiting family or friends, though we generally respect an unspoken rule against recruiting more people to our small circle. So, when Richard introduced Hugo Wagener one morning, I was taken aback and a little annoyed.

He was older than any of us but eager to explain that he had been a reader at University College London and had met Richard when he was on sabbatical at the Courtauld. He was recently divorced and, after taking early retirement, had returned to New Zealand to live.

"How long were you in England?" Marian asked.

"Over twenty years."

"So, what's it been like, coming back after so long away?" I asked.

Hugo told us that in all his years in England, he had clung to a memory of a road north of Ashhurst in the Manawatu that wound down from the Pohangina Dome, following the course of a small stream. Years ago, when he lived in the Manawatu, he would drive this road often, sometimes with his family, sometimes alone, but always with a strong sense that this was where he would like to build a house someday. "I always felt at peace there. I thought of this landscape as a man thinks of a woman he loves."

"Is that where you're living now?" Marian asked.

"It's where I imagined living," Hugo said. "But things didn't work out. For the time being, I'm here in Wellington."

"Whereabouts?" I asked.

"I'm renting an apartment in the Wilton valley."

"We're in Wadestown," I said.

"I'm finding it very quiet," Hugo said. "This morning, when I was waiting at the bus stop, there wasn't a soul in sight. The sun was rising. Birds were singing in the bush reserve. Occasionally, a car appeared, and passed. But I felt like Cary Grant, standing on the roadside in North by Northwest, withered cornfields on a dead flat plain under a cloudless sky. Except I knew that nothing was going to happen."

"Well, you happened to find your way here," Paul said.

"Richard has been very kind."

"We may have come into town on the same bus," I said, and suggested we exchange phone numbers in case we didn't meet at the Hangar again.

Later, Richard thanked me. "I thought we were going to get stuck with him. We were never close. I never knew what he taught and still don't. It was decent of you to take an interest in him."

A couple of days later I phoned Hugo and asked if he would like to meet for a coffee and chat.

His eagerness was childlike, but understandable. His routine has been disrupted by the closing of the public library after the earthquake. The library had become a sanctuary of sorts, somewhere to go for a few hours every day and read the Guardian, check his emails, or add a few lines to a Word document he called "What it's like to be alive." When the library closed, he tried to establish a new routine at the Lido, buying a coffee and working on his laptop at a corner table that gave him a direct view of the city council building.

When I asked about his writing project, Hugo said that it was a memoir and asked if I would like to see it and give him an opinion of it.

*I read it that night. At first, I thought it odd that he should write about him-
self in the third person, but soon realized that it is perhaps only by distancing
oneself from painful experiences that one can come to terms with them:*

He sees it in his mind's eye as if it happened moments ago. As if it
was happening again now, and he is a bystander powerless to prevent it. The jet boat careening across the river, airborne before it slams
into the riverbank. The first time he imagines this scene is when the
police officer comes to his house, asking if he is Hugo Wagener and
informing him that his son has been killed in a boating accident. His
response is to blurt out, "This is not possible. There must be some
mistake. My son is staying with the family of a school friend in Wood-
ville. I was in touch with him only this morning."

"It would appear," the officer says, "that your son's friend took the
keys of his father's jet boat without permission and lost control of the
craft at high speed. When it crashed into the river bank, your son
was thrown from the boat and hit his head against a boulder. He died
instantly."

Howls of pain and protest are torn from Hugo Wagener's throat.
He moves through the house like a robot that has gone haywire. He
will not remember telling his wife what has happened. He will leave
it to her to tell their daughter. Nor will he remember anything of the
weeks that follow, for time has been arrested in a moment he cannot get out of his mind. Jonathan, lifeless on a riverbank and a voice
saying *he died instantly*. Though he wakes to this scene night after
night and every day attempts to blot it out, it is indelible. Neither the
well-meaning consolations of friends nor the photo of Jonathan in
his school uniform, smiling at him, can eclipse the image of a dark
stream in a black forest, and his son's abandoned body being slowly
covered with dead leaves.

He is not alone in his grief. His wife and daughter are equally devastated. But they cannot share their feelings, which have occluded
everything that defined their life together. Grief drives them apart.
Hugo's recurring nightmare convinces him that he witnessed his son's
death and could have prevented it. How else to explain the vividness
of what he saw, and its unrelenting recurrence? He is told that this is a
false memory, not untypical of trauma, and that it might be helpful if
he thought of memories not as unbreakable links to an unchangeable

past, but as the raw material from which it is possible to fashion a new beginning. But he cannot give up this link to his son's last moments and insists that this inextinguishable vision contains a message he must decipher. An instruction for what he must do as penance, or what he must suffer as punishment.

As for his wife, Judith, she develops an obsession with home appliances. She purchases a new refrigerator. Within a week, she has found fault with it and has it returned to Harvey Normans and replaced. In quick succession, she orders a bread maker, a pressure cooker, a Dyson V8 Absolute vacuum cleaner, and a Bosch stainless steel oven. Some of her purchases remain in the cartons they came in, stacked in the garage unopened and unused. Hugo says nothing. He is not surprised when Judith tells him that she wants to erase her own life and be with Jonathan, wherever he is.

His colleagues withdraw from him. Or is it that he has turned his back on them? He tells himself that whatever collegiality existed in the past, it was feigned, and everyone is now avoiding him because he smells of death and they fear contamination.

"What do you see in him?" This is the question Richard keeps asking me and that I cannot answer. I cannot bring myself to say that Hugo Wagener reminds me of my father, and though I google Hugo's academic work and skim-read some of it on Amazon, this is not what draws me to him. Perhaps he is affording me a glimpse of the person I might become.

At first sight, Hugo cut a pathetic figure. Hunched. Disheveled. Unshaven. Self-absorbed. And this impression is reinforced the Sunday afternoon he opens his front door and ushers me into his apartment. He seems lost in the gloom. Fumbling in the cupboards for some peppermint tea bags he swears he put there yesterday. Banging the kettle down on the stovetop as if this is a chore he has almost forgotten how to do. I offer to help, but he tells me to sit down at the dining table so he can concentrate. So, I hold my tongue and cast my eyes around the room—the books and magazines on the table, the enlarged photographs of various people taped to the kitchen cabinets, the framed watercolors on the walls.

"You listen to people," Hugo tells me, as we sip our tea. "Where did you learn to listen so well?"

"I'm a writer," I say. "This is what writers do."

I feel guilty. I am a voyeur. Visiting him not because of any deep sympathy for him but for what I can get out of him.

When I ask Hugo to identify the people in the photos, he says they are what is left of his family.

I wonder if he is Jewish and is alluding to the Holocaust.

"My daughter and I are not on speaking terms," Hugo explains. "When I retired, she wanted me to find a place in Sussex, to be close to her. But she held me responsible for the breakup of my marriage and the unhappiness of her mother, and, anyway, I never liked her husband and was already feeling home-sick for New Zealand."

I glance at the vase of agapanthus and hydrangeas at the end of the table. It seems strange to me that someone should bring roadside flowers indoors.

"I have always had flowers on the table," Hugo says. And he confides that when his son died, he could no longer live in a place so deeply associated with him. He applied for an academic position in London, persuaded his reluctant wife to follow him into exile, and tried to put the past behind him.

Being with Hugo was like being in a work of creative nonfiction. He would not have been out of place in W. G. Sebald's The Rings of Saturn, *and I was reminded of that passage in which the German writer describes being way-laid in a labyrinth on Dunwich Heath before finding his way to the house of his friend Michael Hamburger on the outskirts of Middleton. Sebald is over-whelmed by a sense that he once inhabited the house that his friend now occu-pies. The poet's untidy study reminds him of his own. He is convinced that the spectacles, letters, and writing materials on the desk had once been his. And this déjà vu leads Sebald to further imagine that Hamburger's years of exile, in which his German childhood had become reduced to disconnected fragments, no less haunting because they were incoherent, corresponded to his own. Sebald brings his reflections to a close by remarking on his friend's uncanny relation-ship with Friedrich Hölderlin, whom he had translated into English, and how such elective affinities transcend time and space, so that one is sometimes drawn to certain historical figures as though they were kinsmen or close friends. How is it, Sebald asks, "that one perceives oneself in another human being, or, if not oneself, then one's own precursor?"*

The last time I saw Hugo was in the Otari Native Bush Reserve. I was ashamed of myself for having turned my back on him, as if my literary fascina-tion was exhausted and, like Richard, I had no interest in him as a friend. We were strolling along a gravel path, undecided as to whether to go our separate ways or continue walking together. We finally stopped on an elevated foot-bridge from which we could peer down into the radial symmetry of a large tree fern. Hugo remarked how differently things looked from below and above, and how the further you removed yourself from the world, the more orderly it sometimes seemed.

When I asked if New Zealand seemed more orderly to him than England, he laughed. "I don't think anywhere is more orderly than New Zealand. It's our obsession, is it not? Keeping the place tidy. Look at all these native plants, clearly labelled and classified. All in their proper place."

That was it. I do not know what became of him. Whether he found his valley in the hills and made a home there, or returned to England. But I regret my indifference to his fate. It would have cost me so little to have seen him from time to time. The only poetic justice is that the book I began to write went nowhere. And then the pandemic happened, and you could not plan ahead. You lived from day to day, counting on nothing being the same again. I could not bring myself to watch the news, the sentimental mantras about heroic frontline workers and the spirit of togetherness. As Selina said, none of it helped you cope with what you had to do. It was as if time had been fast-forwarded, and everyone, young or old, was suddenly confronted with the imminent possibility of their extinction and the absurdity of what they had taken for granted as normal.

My Story

When Fletcher concluded his story about Hugo Wagener, Harry said something about not being one's brother's keeper. Although I did not expect him to explain what he meant by this remark, it helped me decide on the story I would tell.

*   *   *

During the year Pia and I spent in West Africa, the success of my fieldwork depended entirely on the assistance of one exceptional person—Braima. He was my translator, teacher, and boon companion, and though I paid him a living wage, I incurred a moral debt that I have never been able to repay. When Braima died in 2012, this sense of personal indebtedness became a painful reminder of all that we in the affluent West owe the peoples we ruled over and robbed blind for centuries. While I see no point in crying mea culpa and beating myself up about this, I believe that if anthropology has a future, it must come to terms with its past.

Pia and I were living in a house that Braima found for us within a week of our arrival in the remote town that was to be our base. After my first six months of fieldwork, I was exhausted by the demands of local farmers to help them get their produce to market or drive family members to a clinic some twenty miles to the south. More pertinent, perhaps, was my growing sense of being in a place where I had no place. I observed local life but played no active role in it, and I began to resent my lack of autonomy. When the rains came, I spent less time in remote villages and turned my attention to transcribing oral traditions with Braima's help, or simply hanging out with Pia. One morning, Braima turned up at the house to continue the work we had been doing the previous day. I was weary of small talk and had little appetite for the laborious tasks of transcription and translation. Pia brought us tea and turned on the radio. She wanted to catch the BBC news. An interview with Iris Murdoch was in progress, and Murdoch was saying that a good person is not necessarily someone who *does* good to others but someone who abstains from visiting his or her desires onto them, thereby allowing them to come into their own. In the company of such a person, she said, one often experiences such peace and self-fulfillment that it seems as if a divine gift has been bestowed. This gift is the essence of the good.

As Murdoch continued to elaborate on what it means to open up a space in which others can find their voice, or experience themselves as subjects rather than objects, I became aware of Braima's discomfort. Yet I was the one who should have been feeling uncomfortable, not just because Murdoch's remarks were directly relevant to the subject of friendship but because the perverse pleasure I was taking in obliging Braima to listen to something of interest to me, but probably of little interest to him, contradicted the goodwill that I liked to associate with our relationship.

That night, after closing the shutters and bolting the door, Pia and I undressed and climbed into bed. I remember the smell of our palliasse and the pinging of the iron roof as it contracted in the night air. As we were talking softly before sleep, we heard voices. We stopped talking and waited for the visitors to summon us.

It was Braima and his wives.

I shouted that we were in bed.

I should have got up and let them in. Made them feel welcome. Sat in amicable silence, which was all that local protocol required. You did not ignore visitors, whatever the circumstances, and you certainly did not ignore your friends. But ignore them we did, and they remained on the porch for half an hour, talking amongst themselves and occasionally knocking discretely as if to remind us they were still there.

Then they went away.

I apologized to Braima the next day, but my remorse lingered like a wine stain. It made me deeply ambivalent about academic anthropology which, by fetishizing language, fosters the illusion that our descriptions of the world mirror its inner reality. And it made me determined not to fall under the spell of magical thinking, like those who think the pandemic can be wished away with words or who tell themselves they are immune to the virus.

"But a lot of people have not turned a blind eye to what is happening," Fletcher said. "They have done something about it. They have corrected course, changed their ways. Isn't this what you have done over the years, helping Braima, putting his sons through college? And isn't this connected to the way you understand ethnography—your argument that it offers us a way of seeing the world and oneself from a displaced point of view?"

"I used to think so," I said. "Perhaps I still do. But what of the risks we run of getting it all wrong? It's all too easy to persuade ourselves that we know another person simply because they do not question our assumptions."

"Selina questioned mine," Fletcher said, "and thank God she did."

We were all tired, and I was probably not the only one to feel that our stories of regret and reckoning were indulgences that neither salved our consciences nor set old wrongs to right.

Cabin Fever

When I came into the kitchen, Harry was there, spooning coffee grounds into the French press.

"I'm driving Elle to Avignon," he said. "She's going stir crazy, and our stories make her feel as if she's got nothing to say for herself. She has friends in Paris she can stay with for a couple of days. I'll join her there."

I said I was sorry but understood.

We waved them off that afternoon. Then, like survivors from a shipwreck, Pia and I and Fletcher and Selina sat in the courtyard, taking stock.

Unabating, the wind thrashed the cypresses beyond the sheltering wall, as if reminding us that our time was also up.

"I found it interesting," Fletcher said, "that all our stories had one thing in common. We all feel we have failed someone who mattered deeply to us."

"Did Hugo matter to you?" I asked. "And what about Harry? He seems to feel that his parents failed *him* and that he owes them nothing."

"He seems very caring toward Elle," Selina said.

"I wouldn't want him to think he has to come back," Pia said. "Perhaps we should have made it clear to him that he should feel free to take the train to Paris with Elle."

"Selina and I were thinking of leaving in a couple of days," Fletcher said. "Harry offered to drive us to Avignon before he heads off to Paris."

Over the next two days, I felt despondent, as if I had hoped that something would transpire during our time together, but nothing had happened. Although it was a relief not to wake every morning to conversations about what we would do for the day and where we would eat in the evening, there were moments when I found the absence of my friends unbearable. I felt particularly bad about my failure to reach out to Harry; and though Fletcher had made Pia and me promise that we would visit Selina and him in New Zealand, I knew that if I made the journey home, it would be alone.

Pia's mood was very different. "I feel as though I've just arrived here," she said. "Now that the wind is dropping, the place feels like it did last year, when William and Sally were with us. No distractions, no stories of regret, no more overindulging food and wine."

"It was you who got us started on sharing stories of regret," I said.

"I thought it would clear the air," Pia said.

"You can't have a confession without a confessor," I said.

"Isn't that what friends are for? To listen? To lighten our loads?"

I did not want to argue with Pia. I went walking in the garigue, picking my way along stony paths, across outcrops of limestone, my shirt snagged by the contorted branches of oaks and stunted pines. I remembered how Sierra Leone villagers would sometimes blurt out confessions to crimes they were not guilty of, simply to lift a cloud of suspicion that had fallen over their community, and for a moment I regretted having come to Provence rather than returning to West Africa, or to New Zealand. Had leaving my homeland years ago been a kind of suicide, dying to one life in order to be born to another? But if I had not met Pia, what would my life have been like?

My reverie was suddenly interrupted by the panicked rush of wings as a flock of white and grey pigeons took flight, banked around the shoulder of the hill, and settled back into the scrub. I looked around, trying to identify what had startled them. But the only sound was the incessant "stitching" of cicadas in the dry grass.

I headed back to the *mas*.

I did not share my thoughts with Pia, and she, for reasons of her own, kept herself from me, our backs turned to each other in bed that night as we lay sleepless and silenced by the absence of the wind.

Waking at first light, I left Pia asleep and made my way to the kitchen, bare feet on the terra-cotta tiles, and filled the kettle, placing it on the stove.

As I waited for the kettle to boil, I heard Pia close the door of the shower, then the sound of splashing water. After placing two brioche buns in the microwave to warm, I turned on the radio, already tuned to Radio Luxembourg. Instantly, the kitchen was filled with music. It took my breath away. I stood stock-still, fearing that the slightest movement would break the spell. As I was standing in the middle of the kitchen, listening, Pia came from the bathroom, as mesmerized as I was by the song. Neither of us said a word. Pia had a white towel around her, globules of water on her shoulders and neck. We stood together as the music transported us to a distant landscape, one moment steeped in shadow, the next in light, the voice of the singer by turns exultant and bereft.

As the song came to an end, Pia touched her forefinger to her lips, wanting to hear the title of the song. "Zajdi Zajdi." A Macedonian folk song. But who was the singer?

"Nadya, Natania . . . something," Pia said. "I didn't quite get it."

As the announcer introduced the next piece and I turned down the volume, Pia began to dry her hair, her hand holding the compressed towel against the side of her head as if she had momentarily forgotten herself and the music held her entranced.

I stepped toward her and kissed her bare shoulder.

"I love you," I said.

"And I love you too."

Renewal

The pandemic was often spoken of as "unprecedented" or "crazy," as if people were oblivious to the famines, wars, and natural disasters that had plagued human history and the tragedies that had punctuated their own lives. I was drawn into online conversations about racial inequality, and how the Far Right appeared to welcome the pandemic as an accelerant of societal collapse or as a portent of the Apocalypse. At the *mas de la Colinière*, our conversations had been very different, and as the mistral hammered our shuttered house, we had confessed to events that had confounded us, times we had wounded others or been wounded. And we had asked ourselves how the past could be redeemed. Ostensibly more political than the rest of us, Harry talked about Kate Raworth's "doughnut economics," in which every citizen's minimal needs would be met—for health care, education, food, shelter, gender equality, housing, energy, income, and political voice. I felt that the doughnut was a metaphor for Harry's life. Instead of wealth unevenly distributed, the question for him was of love withheld. Selina thought otherwise: "How can you expect love and friendship between people if some are deprived of even the most basic opportunities for eating healthy food, drinking clean water, getting an education, or affording decent housing? How many people are as privileged as we are, holidaying in the South of France, indulging our stories of regret?"

I had no answer to Selina's question. I didn't want to argue against revolutionary action. But I was belatedly discovering that my own interest was in the revolutions that occur within us.

When I wrote to Bjarke, my friend in Denmark, about my preoccupations, he said he now realized that his memoir was a magical attempt to revisit his early life, not because he wanted to relive it but because he wanted to savor the excitement, the promise, and vibrancy of a time when he thought he would never die. While he could recall long-ago events and people with great vividness, they seemed to have become leached of all affect, as if emotional memories did not last as long as visual ones. He spoke of pieces of music that become indelibly associated with significant moments in one's life. "Years later," he said, "you listen to one of these old songs in the expectation that it will give you back that moment, in all its pain or joy. The music is familiar, but it is also strangely devoid of the meaning you hoped to find in it. It's like a battery that has lost its charge. It is the same battery you've been using for years, but suddenly it is lifeless and useless, though you cannot bring yourself to throw it away.

"I am also finding it strange," Bjarke continued, "to wake every morning in the house to which my parents brought me and my siblings every summer when we were children, only to feel that I am the sole survivor of a shipwreck. But, unlike Robinson Crusoe, I cannot summon the will to rebuild my life from the materials I have salvaged."

Bjarke's poignant words reawakened in me a memory of when I was eight or nine, and my family was making its annual visit to Fussell's farm to select our Christmas goose. May Fussell must have been in her thirties at the time and was one of my mother's closest friends. Ebullient and given to gales of uproarious laughter, she had driven us from Moabite to the farm in her V-8 Ford and had laid out her best china for an afternoon tea in the sitting room. The room was lined with bookshelves on which were stacked hundreds of *National Geographic* and *Popular Mechanics* magazines, evidence of "Auntie" May's father's penchant for all things American, and possibly the source of his pioneering initiative of planting *Pinus insignis* in the gullies of his farm and milling the timber. He also built a New England–style water mill that generated electricity for the house and sawmill.

As the adults poured their tea and served themselves date scones or slices of pavlova cake, my sister and I were told to "go out and play." My sister was three years older than I was and more adventurous, and I trustingly followed her into the pine plantation not far from the house. Suddenly, the summer light was dimmed. Pine boughs soughed and creaked overhead. And the pine straw under my bare feet was soft and warm. I imagined we were Hansel and Gretel, wandering deeper and deeper into a place of danger. But then I saw the lake, glistening beyond the dark and closely packed trunks of the trees. We did not reach it. We turned back. Perhaps we had been promised pavlova cake as a reward for "being good." But I had been rewarded by a glimpse of an enchanted elsewhere, beyond the claustrophobic world of my hometown. That vision would never leave me, though it ceased to be a vision of my future and became nostalgia for my past.

As for Fletcher, he made a clean break with his former life, repudiating fiction and buying a piece of land in the Burnett Range, where he and Selina embraced the challenges of life without electricity and the internet. Selina found nursing work in Golden Bay and wrote to Pia about their bees being ravaged by wasps and viruses, and opossums causing havoc in the vegetable garden. But it was all worth it, Selina concluded, which led Pia to ask me if Georges and Marie-France would say the same about their struggles.

"Or Harry about his," I said, mindful of his recent email, confessing his unresolved quarrel with his parents, even though both were dead:

After all these years, I still find it shocking that I can't recall my father ever speaking kindly to me or showing even a flicker of physical affection. But one winter day stands out in my memory. For some reason we were in the garden together, and he pointed to the twin cypresses that framed our view of the harbor. "Did you know I have names for these trees?" he asked. "I call the one on the left 'Peace' and the one on the right 'Prosperity.'"

I was too young to know what he meant by this, and naively asked why Peace was not at tall as Prosperity. I cannot remember his answer, or even if he gave me one.

What was it with our parents: their anger and sadness; why did their comfortable Kiwi life so disappoint them? My unhappy recollections have been sharpened by reading [Bruce] Springsteen's autobiography—decades spent in battle with his father: a familial misery that runs through decades of his life. I also read recently of Frederick the Great, whose every action was calculated to enrage his father. I think my every action was calculated to displease my father; unfortunately, it also distorted my life. Frederick handled it better. Turning that unhappiness into art—as so many of us try and, mostly, fail to do.

A couple of months after receiving Harry's email, I flew to London to look up Sierra Leone friends. Harry insisted I stay with him.

He buzzed me up to his third-floor apartment and was waiting for me on the landing as I climbed the last few steps to his door. Treating me like a traveler who has been caught in a storm, he relieved me of my sodden overcoat and showed me my room. "You must be dead beat," he said. "If you want to crash, go ahead. We can talk later."

"I'm more famished than anything," I said. "If you've—"

"Say no more. We'll walk to Smithfield. There's an Italian place I know you'll like."

I had expected to find Harry in bad shape. Drinking heavily. Incommunicado. But here he was, as happy as Larry, his sky-blue shirt unbuttoned at the chest to show off his artificial tan, as if it were summer rather than the dead of winter.

Over shrimp scampi with linguini, Harry pressed me for news of Fletcher.

After describing Fletcher's aerie in the Burnett Range, I admitted to envying him. "In fact," I said, "I have been thinking of returning to New Zealand myself."

"For good, you mean?"

"That's the problem. I'd probably wind up like Hugo in that story Fletcher shared with us in France. Anyway, Pia would never hear of it."

"So, let me get this straight. Pia is your wife and New Zealand is your mistress, and you think you have to choose between them?"

I laughed.

"*La règle du jeu*," Harry said.

"Or like Richard Somers in D. H. Lawrence's *Kangaroo*," I said, "wearying himself to death struggling with the problem of himself and calling it Australia. Only in my case, it's New Zealand?"

"The past goes by many names," Harry said. "You think of it as another country. I think of it as my childhood. In either case, it's largely imagined." Harry reached for the bottle and made to fill my glass, but I placed my hand over it.

"I was sorry to hear about Elle," I said.

"I think I imagined her too."

"Is there someone else?"

"I told you my parents died, didn't I?"

"You did. I'm sorry."

"Within months of each other. My father was ill for years, but I thought my mother was indestructible. It seems that life without my father was no life at all. Anyway, I have inherited a small fortune; hence this apartment."

*　　*　　*

Snow was falling when I returned to the café at Smithfield Market the next day. Revived by an espresso, I was soon on the street again, making my way toward London Bridge. At the Central Criminal Court building of the Old Bailey, I stopped to read the inscription over the great portal—*Defend the Children of the Poor and Punish the Wrongdoer*. It occurred to me how easy it was to slip through the net, as my supervisor at the welfare office for the homeless used to say, and I recalled with what terrible suddenness one could fall or be felled, like Icarus tumbling out of the sky in Bruegel's great painting, the promise of life slipping through one's fingers because of the betrayal of a spouse, the loss of a job, the onset of illness, or simply the machinations of those who do not think you deserve to live.

I pushed on through parishes where the plague decimated the poor in 1665 and at last returned to Farringdon, where Harry suggested we dine in a Greek restaurant in Soho and afterward repair to the Groucho Club for drinks.

I felt like a stranger in Harry's world, though not to him. I did not envy Fletcher's life at Golden Bay, though I envied the way he had reinvented himself and found his true vocation. Similarly, for all the years I had spent in

Sierra Leone and all the books I had written about life there, I remained a
stranger to everyone except Braima and his brothers, and their families. And
when I thought of Pia and our children, it was as clear as day that belonging
was not, at heart, an attachment to a place or a possession or even a name, but
a bond with those one loved.

All for One, and One for All

The phrase "All for one, and one for all" is so well worn and so frequently invoked to promote the model of a federal republic (it is the unofficial motto of Switzerland) that its relevance to friendship is sometimes overlooked. Even in the context of Alexandre Dumas's 1844 novel *The Three Musketeers*, the heroic ideal of uniting to defeat a common enemy or fight for justice barely touches on the personal costs that such principled loyalty entails.

In his celebrated movie *The Wild Bunch*, director Sam Peckinpah makes it very clear where his loyalties lie.

Following a failed bank robbery in a Texas town called Starbucks in 1913, five outlaws cross the border into Mexico. Their botched attempt to rob the bank (they had been ambushed by a gang of bounty hunters) and their growing awareness that "it's time to get another game" lead to a showdown that pits the two younger outlaws, Tector and Lyle, against their aging leader, Pike, and his sidekick, Dutch, who believe in sticking together through thick and thin. "We started together—we'll end it together," Pike declares. "When you side with a man, you stay with him, and if you can't do that, you're like some animal. You're finished. We're finished. All of us!"

The fifth outlaw is a young Mexican man called Angel. When Angel is captured and tortured for stealing guns from General Mapache, a brutal officer in the Mexican Federal Army who has been pillaging villages to feed his troops, Pike and his men must decide whether to risk their lives by going to Angel's rescue.

Mapache has two hundred well-armed men.

Pike and his three companions attempt to barter Angel's life for gold. Mapache rejects their offer.

Later that day, when Pike repeats his request, the now drunk Mapache slits Angel's throat in front of him. In the bloodbath that ensues, everybody dies.

When I first saw this movie, I was struck by the confluence of two different ways of understanding friendship—as a purely personal relationship or as an abstract principle, a moral virtue. It's not that Pike and his fellow outlaws go to the rescue of Angel because he is a close friend. Regardless of any sympathy they may feel for his plight, it is the principle of solidarity that counts. You have given your word. You have taken an oath. You have "sided" with a person, and if you cannot remain true to that allegiance "you're like some animal. You're finished."

I was again reminded of *The Wild Bunch* when, not long ago, a friend of mine with whom I had been sharing some of my reflections on friendship asked me an intriguing question. "How is it that we sometimes remain friends with people we do not particularly like, who have seldom shown any interest in us, or what we do? And why do we sometimes not befriend people with whom we have a lot in common?"

When I asked this friend, Sejal, if she had anyone in mind, she said, "Yes, I have a friend from childhood who, for reasons unknown to me, was so mean to me in our youth that it's a wonder we are still friends. It's almost as if she has forgotten the way she once treated me. But I love her, for reasons I don't fully understand. Is it better to be in a flawed relationship than no relationship at all? And what do we make of the fact that, though we have many friends, we choose to stay in touch with those who did not reciprocate our affections?"

Having known Sejal for several years, I asked if her loyalty to this "friend" was less a matter of liking or love and more a matter of principle—for Sejal was, after all, a remarkably principled person.

"I suppose I think about friendship in the way I practice law," she replied. "When I am representing a client, I don't need to know what made them break the law or seek my counsel. I extend them some grace. I do the same with my friends."

For Sejal, honoring her friends meant honoring the principle of friendship, as though the ideal of friendship could enable one to sustain a relationship with someone who failed to reciprocate one's affection, while the mutual affection, care, and trust experienced in another friendship, or in a passing moment, was sufficient to confirm that generalized ideal.

I took Sejal's comments as a salutary reminder of how complicated friendship is, and how irreducible. Even when one can identify a trait that seems synonymous with "friendship," such as mutuality or trust, every friendship, like every intimate relationship in life, not only fluctuates but falls short of the moral ideal one would like it to affirm. And I thought fleetingly of George Bowen, with whom I felt almost no mutuality yet kept in touch with for forty years, sympathizing with his failing health, his loneliness, and his political pessimism. Was I in some oblique way comparing notes with someone I might easily have become?

In exploring this "subjective in-between," Hannah Arendt reiterates Aristotle's idealist conception of *philia politike*—a friendship "without intimacy and without closeness" that makes possible a common world.[1] But in giving priority to the value of friendship for the *res publica*, Arendt downplays the psychological complexities of friendship. Paradoxically, her emphasis on love of the world (*amor mundi*) means that the personal friendships that meant the world to her found no place in her political philosophy.

In a similar vein, Brijen Gupta's vision of an intentional community (Chapter 2) overlooks the differences and divisions among the individuals who would comprise this utopian collective. Inasmuch as this group is united solely in the vision of its leader, it is not an organic community at all, and though Brijen invokes the idea of friendship to give it the appearance of moral coherence, none of its members were close friends.

By contrast, Montaigne focuses on a personal friendship whose uniqueness disqualifies it from being politicized. Its essence is love, and it, therefore, bears comparison with love of one's child or spouse.

How can this tension between personal and political conceptions of friendship be resolved?

For Keti Ferenke Koroma (Chapter 3), the personal and the political are not opposed but complementary. Both speak to the relational nature of human existence. In Kuranko thought, relations between kin, affines, friends, and neighbors are likened to the paths that connect houses, compounds, villages, and chiefdoms, and everyday life involves a continual flow of gifts, goods, and greetings along these paths. Paths bring people together in the common cause of sustaining life.

Since one never moves through life alone, the Kuranko sometimes speak of friendship as a kind of accompanying. Personal liking or agreement is less important than steadfastness, which may explain why visiting a village neighbor does not require earnest conversation or even small talk but achieves its goal of amicability through sitting together in silence. As with Ferenke's story of the two friends who embark on a trading venture together, or with Peckinpah's movie about a bunch of outlaws who stick together to the bitter end, the story of my friendship with Harry and Fletcher is the story of three friends who started out with a shared ambition to become writers. Although we wound up traveling different roads (writing ethnographies, writing fiction, editing books), our companionship was sustained less by personal affinities than by each being able to offer the others a means of periodically getting a measure of himself. In the beginning, however, our friendship was a coincidence of choice.

Ferenke and Aristotle both underscore this point.[2] If common goals are to be achieved, be they making money to marry, writing books, or creating a viable community, they must be freely chosen, not externally imposed. While ties of kinship and in-law relationships entail obligations and duties, friendships encourage people to think for themselves, exercise moral judgment, and find their own paths toward common goals.

Soldier's stories of friendship under fire are particularly relevant here, for, as Les Cleveland shows, the "dark laughter" of comrades in arms scorns regimentation, ridicules authority, eschews heroism, and even holds idealism in contempt (Chapter 11). Soldiers take comfort in knowing that their friends will risk their lives to ensure that no fellow soldier is left wounded or dead on a battlefield, even if they disobey orders in choosing to do so. Here, no hard-and-fast distinction can be made between personal friendship and friendship as a principle. The friend may be someone with whom one identifies deeply, like Ted Scherer for Les Cleveland, or simply someone with whom one undergoes the same experience, in the same place, at the same time, like age-mates who endure initiation together, classmates at school, roommates at college, coworkers on the factory floor, or soldiers in the same outfit.

This sheds light on my friendships with Noah Marah, Vincent O'Sullivan, Harry St. Rain, and Fletcher Knight, and the way these friendships deepened over many years. We had interests in common, to be sure, but the raw experience of enduring the vicissitudes of life was what bound us together.

The suffering of friends may awaken us to our common humanity. In the other's misfortune, the fragility of our own good fortune is made apparent, and the possibility of sharing the same fate becomes suddenly very real. *There, but for the grace of God, go I.* Such, I suspect, was the case with the character of Ahmadpour in Kiarostami's film *Where Is the Friend's House?* (Chapter 7), and with Keith Ridler, who supported me in the wake of my first wife's death (Chapter 12). They recognized in my distress a possibility for themselves, just as I would come to recognize in Galina Lindquist's reckoning with life (Chapter 15) my first wife's experience of facing death.

We tend to explain our responsiveness to others, particularly those we are close to, with morally weighted words like *sympathy* and *empathy*. I prefer the more neutral term *intersubjectivity* because it suggests that we are immersed in the lives of others long before we have any emotional, moral, or conceptual views on the matter. Quite simply, from the outset of our lives, it is through others that we know, see, find, lose, and recover ourselves.

This sense of being implicated in the lives of others and of accompanying others through life is captured in the metaphor of navigation. We do not cross the stormy seas of life as individuals. Like the Polynesian navigators who sailed thousands of miles across the southern oceans, guided by their knowledge of subtropical weather systems, star constellations, and ocean currents, we find our way through life with our friends. Each has their own expertise to contribute, depending on the exigencies of our ever-changing situations. Our different talents and temperaments complement rather than contradict each other, enhancing our chances of survival.

There must have been a moment in my early childhood when I realized that I could choose my relationships and could "make friends." Rather than suffer the world into which I had been thrown, I could vicariously enter other worlds and be transformed.

At first, I reached these other worlds through books and movies. Old volumes of my father's *Chums* and *Boy's Own Paper* took me to fabulous places, while *King Solomon's Mines* transported me to a mythical Africa, and *Beyond the Great Wall* reincarnated me in Manchuria, where I learned to ask, "How many seeds in a watermelon?" and sagely reply, "Many."

But when I made friends, books and films ceased to be ends in themselves. Where I had once imagined becoming a heroic loner—a drover, train driver, or conjurer—adventures with friends like DKD now became the source of my fulfillment. Through these childhood friendships, I passed into another incarnation and lived a life parallel to the one into which I had been born.

My adult friendships with Harry St. Rain, Sofka Zinovieff, Noah Marah, and Te Pakaka Tawhai all reiterated this yearning to remake myself, not in the image of another, but as a participant in a world beyond myself. In some cases, writing brought us together; in other cases, anthropology was our common concern. But in every instance, there were other factors, as elusive as trace elements in the earth or the terroir of a wine that encompasses the soil, climate, and topography of the region in which the wine is produced.

If I have learned anything from interleaving scholarly essays on friendship with memories of some of my closest friends, it is that no typology can do justice to the way in which different elements combine and permute in a relationship over time. What is foregrounded in one context will be backgrounded in another, in the same way that a conversation will switch from topic to topic, or our daydreams wander from one thing to another without any evident rhyme or reason.

Rather than create historical sequences in which one form of friendship comes to supplant its precursor, I prefer to see friendship as a fuzzy concept, like fate or love, that offers many potential meanings and tactical uses. Like Walt Whitman's Self, friendship "contains multitudes," none of which distills the essence of the subject, which appears differently according to the lens through which we view it.

Because *friendship* is a relational term, it must be understood relationally.

In his essay on Subject and Object, Theodor Adorno argues that every individual subject (e.g., a friend) entails a general subject (e.g., friendship). The terms *friend* and *friendship* are both "patently equivocal," and these concrete and abstract nouns bear comparison with figure and ground in a continually shifting Gestalt, or a wheel inside a wheel.

This helps us understand why Brijen Gupta's commitment to social justice on the one hand and his yearning for a small circle of friends on the other cannot be reconciled. In Hannah Arendt's case, her commitment to a form of government whose authority derives entirely from the people (the *res publica*, the "people's concern") is often at odds with her personal quest, as a conscious pariah, for an oasis in the desert of public life.

If public and private interests cannot always be reconciled, it is not surprising that groupings based on shared goals or a common cause are often riven by interpersonal rivalries, power struggles, and factionalism. A commune in New Zealand or a village in West Africa may be bound together by common interests or a common charter without, however, being a society of friends. This ambivalence about social existence finds expression in the Bambara view that being with others "is not an ideal; it is a necessity to which men must adapt and adjust themselves." Social life is like a bulb of garlic. "The cloves continue to cling to each other although all are equally evil smelling. It is the same with men and their communities."[3]

In an interview with the *Guardian* published on September 25, 2021,[4] the climate activist Greta Thunberg was asked whether there was a sense of solidarity among her fellow activists.

"Definitely," she replied. "We have daily contact. We don't just campaign together, we are also friends. My best friends are within the climate movement."

Asked if she could ever be friends with a climate denier, she responded less certainly. "Erm, yeaaaah. . . . I mean in one way we're all climate deniers because we're not acting as if it is a crisis. I don't know. It depends on the situation."

I admired Thunberg's frankness. It brought me to reflect on my oldest friendships in which shared interests only partially explained our sense of amity. When I consider the causes we espoused, such as ending the war in Vietnam or ending sporting contacts with apartheid South Africa, I am struck by how often I disliked many of the individuals with whom I shared identical political goals, and how many of my closest friends poured scorn on my activism. Friendships, like love affairs, do not necessarily begin or end in accord.

But they do involve choice, which brings me back to the distinction anthropologists draw between kinship and friendship. Whereas friendships are freely chosen, kinship is defined by predefined roles and obligations. If, as existentialists argue, our lives are only viable if we can strike a balance between our need to act upon the world and our need to accept or endure the ways in which the world acts upon us, then kinship becomes a metaphor for all that we have to do in order to live, while friendship becomes a complementary metaphor for the sense of freedom without which our lives lack purpose and vitality. This is not to say that friendship is never institutionalized. In school settings, teachers often enjoin rather than oblige their students to "be friends." Among the Kuranko, as in many patrilineal societies, relations with one's mother's brother tend to be as informal as relations with one's father are formal. While one is free to banter playfully with one's maternal uncle, snatch the cap from his head and food from his plate, and even abuse him in jest, this is not prescribed behavior, and one will only act in these ways if intimacy and familiarity already exist between uncle and nephew. Friendship is not born ex nihilo. Nor can it be explained by circumstance or psychology. It emerges in the subjective-in-between, a source of personal fulfillment and a model of social viability—one of the many ways we create worlds we call our own within the wider worlds to which we belong and are beholden.

NOTES

Note to epigraphs: Paul Auster and J. M. Coetze, *Here and Now: Letters 2008-2011* (New York: Penguin, 2008).

Prologue

1. *Billboard Magazine* 11, no. 35 (1999): 40.

2. Howard wrote me on October 12, 2021: "The fascinating structural tension you mention immediately reminds me of something in Adorno: 'Already by then [at the time of the correspondence of Stefan George and Hugo von Hofmannsthal] friendship out of simple sympathy and taste was no longer possible, even between people of the most extraordinary productive power, but instead only on the basis of binding common knowledge: friendship out of solidarity, which embraces theory as an element of its praxis' ('George und Hofmannsthal' [1942], *Zur Dialektik des Engagements*, p. 47—cited in Susan Buck-Morss, *The Origin of Negative Dialectics*, pp. 299–300). This passage would apply nicely to the Benjamin-Adorno relationship."

3. Theodor Adorno, *Minima Moralia: Reflections from Damaged Life*, trans. E. F. N. Jephcott (London: Verso, 1974), 18.

4. Jacques Derrida, *The Politics of Friendship* (London: Verso, 1997).

5. Raymond Carver, *No Heroics, Please: Uncollected Writings* (New York: Vintage, 1992), 218.

6. Michel Foucault, "Friendship as a Way of Life," in *Ethics: Subjectivity and Truth*, ed. Paul Rabinow, trans. Robert Hurley and others (New York: New Press, 1997), 138.

7. Aristotle, *Eudemian Ethics*, trans. Brad Inwood and Raphael Woolf (Cambridge: Cambridge University Press, 2013), 140 (1241b).

8. Mary Wollstonecraft, *A Vindication of the Rights of Woman: With Strictures on Political and Moral Subjects*, ed. C. H. Poston (New York: W. W. Norton, 1988), 30.

9. Aristotle, *The Nicomachean Ethics*, trans. David Ross (Oxford: Oxford University Press, 1980), 228 (1166a). Jean-Jacques Rousseau also praises friendship as a feeling rather than a moral ideal and emphasizes the compassion we feel for a suffering friend and the consolation that friend derives from our care. John Warner, "Bad Education: Pity, Moral Learning, and the Limits of Rousseauan Friendship," *Review of Politics* 74 (2014): 243–66.

10. Alan Bray, *The Friend* (Chicago: University of Chicago Press, 2003), 43–44. Bray also cites Shakespeare's "boundlessly beautiful sonnet 29" in support of his argument that homosexuality is always a logical, though not necessarily desirable, element in both cross-sex and same-sex friendships.

11. Dirk Baltzly and Nick Eliopoulos, "The Classical Ideals of Friendship," in *Friendship: A History*, ed. Barbara Caine (London: Routledge, 2014), 2.

12. Agnes Brandt, *Among Friends? The Dynamics of Māori-Pākeha Relationships in Aotearoa New Zealand* (Göttingen: V&R unipress, 2013), 120–23.

13. Michael Jackson, *How Lifeworlds Work: Emotionality, Sociality, and the Ambiguity of Being* (Chicago: Chicago University Press, 2017), 139. For an illuminating account of friendship between brothers-in-law, see Robert Brain, *Friends and Lovers* (Frogmore, UK: Paladin, 1977), 174–75

14. Plato, *Lysis*, in *Plato's Dialogue on Friendship: An Interpretation of the* Lysis, *with a New Translation*, by David Bolotin (Ithaca, NY: Cornell University Press, 1979), 215a6–b2. See also Lorraine Smith Pangle, *Aristotle and the Philosophy of Friendship* (Cambridge: Cambridge University Press, 2003), 20.

15. R. D. Laing, *The Divided Self* (Harmondsworth, UK: Penguin, 1965), 26.

16. Maurice Merleau-Ponty, *Phenomenology of Perception*, trans. Colin Smith (London: Routledge, 1996), 354.

17. Colin Duriez, *The Oxford Inklings: Lewis, Tolkien and Their Circle* (Oxford: Lion Hudson, 2015), 82.

18. Titled "Mythopoeia," the poem involves Philomythus ("lover of myth"—i.e., Tolkien) persuading Misomythus ("hater of myth"—i.e., Lewis) not to see the world materialistically, but in the light of religion and myth.

19. Duriez, *Oxford Inklings*, 120–21.

20. Jean-Paul Sartre, *Saint Genet: Actor and Martyr*, trans. Bernard Frechtman (New York: George Braziller, 1963), 49.

21. T. S. Eliot, *Points of View* (London: Faber and Faber, 1941), 25–26. See also Jorge Luis Borges, *Other Inquisitions 1937–1952*, trans. Ruth L. C. Simms (New York: Simon and Schuster, 1964), 108.

22. Michael White, *Maps of Narrative Practice* (New York: W. W. Norton, 2007), 129. White's concept of "re-membering" is borrowed from Barbara Myerhoff's essay, "Life History Among the Elderly: Performance, Visibility, and Re-membering," in *A Crack in the Mirror: Reflexive Perspectives in Anthropology*, ed. J. Ruby (Philadelphia: University of Pennsylvania Press, 1982), 99–117.

Chapter 1

1. Elisabeth Young-Bruehl, *Hannah Arendt: For Love of the World* (New Haven, CT: Yale University Press, 1982), xii.

2. Young-Bruehl, *Hannah Arendt*, xiv.

3. Hannah Arendt, "We Refugees," *Menorah Journal* 31, no. 1 (1943): 61–77; Arendt, "The Jew as Pariah: A Hidden Tradition," *Jewish Studies* 6 (1944): 99–122.

4. Hannah Arendt, *Men in Dark Times* (Harmondsworth, UK: Penguin, 1973), 168.

5. Arendt, "Jew as Pariah," 107.

6. In a 1964 interview, Arendt described the "special warmth" that existed among Jewish people when they were dispersed and without a state, and she argued that this pariah status, "this standing outside of all social connections," "this sense of being an emigrant in one's own homeland," paradoxically generated an intellectual spirit of open-mindedness. Hannah Arendt, "What Remains? The Language Remains: A Conversation with Günter Gaus," *The Portable Hannah Arendt*, ed. Peter Baehr (New York: Penguin, 2003), 3–22, 17.

7. Hannah Arendt, *Men in Dark Times* (Harmondsworth, UK: Penguin, 1973), 16. Her remark was first made in her speech on receiving the Lessing Prize in Hamburg in 1959.

8. Theodor Adorno, *Critical Models: Interventions and Catchwords* (New York: Columbia University Press, 2005), 292.

9. Arendt, "What Remains?" 3–4.

10. Hannah Arendt, *Lectures on Kant's Political Philosophy*, ed. Ronald Beiner (Chicago: Chicago University Press, 1982), 42; Friedrich Nietzsche, *Thus Spake Zarathustra*, trans. Walter Kaufmann (Harmondsworth, UK: Penguin, 1978), 313.

11. Hannah Arendt, "What Is Existenz Philosophy?," *Partisan Review* 13, no. 1 (1946): 36.

12. Arendt, "What Is Existenz Philosophy?," 37; Hugo von Hofmannsthal, "Moments in Greece," trans. Tania Stern and James Stern, in *The Whole Difference: Selected Writings of Hugo von Hofmannsthal*, ed. J. D. McClatchy (Princeton, NJ: Princeton University Press, 2008), 87.

13. Hannah Arendt, introduction to *Illuminations*, by Walter Benjamin, trans. Harry Zohn (New York: Schocken Books, 1969), 11–13.

14. Arendt, *Lectures on Kant's Political Philosophy*, 43.

15. Friedrich Nietzsche, *Beyond Good and Evil: Prelude to a Philosophy of the Future*, trans. Judith Norman (Cambridge: Cambridge University Press, 2002), 42; see also Jacques Derrida, *The Politics of Friendship* (London: Verso, 2020).

16. Hannah Arendt to Karl Jaspers, letter, January 29, 1946, in *Hannah Arendt/Karl Jaspers Correspondence, 1926–1969*, trans. Robert Kimber and Rita Kimber (New York: Harcourt, Brace, Jovanovich, 1992), 29.

17. *Hannah Arendt/Karl Jaspers Correspondence*, 31.

18. Arendt to Jaspers, postcard, February 28, 1955. In *Hannah Arendt/Karl Jaspers Correspondence*, 256.

19. Arendt to Jaspers, postcard, March 26, 1955. In *Hannah Arendt/Karl Jaspers Correspondence*, 257.

20. Cited by Stephen Miller, "Eric Hoffer Revisited," *News from the Republic of Letters* 1–11 (1997): 13.

21. Mary McCarthy, quoted in the editor's introduction to *Between Friends: The Correspondence of Hannah Arendt and Mary McCarthy, 1949–1975*, ed. Carol Brightman (New York: Harcourt Brace, 1995), xvi.

Chapter 2

1. Keith McPherson Buchanan was a prolific writer and polemicist who helped develop the Victoria University of Wellington's Department of Geography as a center of innovative research and writing on Asia and the Third World in the early 1960s. As a radical geographer, socialist, champion of the dispossessed, and unrelenting critic of orthodoxy, capitalist regimes, and power elites, Buchanan made a powerful case against some of the dangerous trends that were shaping the late twentieth-century world.

2. In 1964, though not yet a U.S. citizen, Brijen was arrested for civil disobedience in Tougaloo, Mississippi.

3. Hannah Arendt, *The Human Condition* (Chicago: Chicago University Press, 1958), 242.

4. Agehananda Bharati, *The Ochre Robe* (Seattle: University of Washington Press, 1962), 244. See also *The Tantric Tradition* (London: Rider, 1965).

5. See William A. Gerhard and Brijen K. Gupta, "Literature: The Phenomenological Art," *Man and World* 3, no. 2 (1970): 102–15.

6. R. L. Nigam joined the DAV (Dayanand Anglo-Vedic) English faculty while Brijen was at Banares Hindu University. They became lifelong friends.

7. Ram Manohar Lohia (1910–67) was an Indian freedom fighter and a socialist political leader who helped establish the Congress Socialist Party in 1934 and wrote numerous articles on the feasibility of a socialist India.

8. Cārvāka (also known as Lokāyata) is a materialist, skeptical Indian philosophy that eschews religious foundations. It is named after its founder, Cārvāka, author of the Bārhaspatya-sūtras.

9. Ramana Maharshi (1879–1950) inspired Paul Brunton's *In Search of Secret India* (1934).

10. Born in 1898, Nixon joined the Royal Flying Corps and served in a fighting squadron during the First World War. "His direct experiences with the death and destruction of warfare filled him with a sense of futility and meaninglessness. . . . After the war Nixon enrolled in King's College at Cambridge University to study English literature. There he discovered Buddhism, being particularly attracted to the life story of the Buddha. Like many others interested in Buddhism at that time, Nixon became involved with the Theosophical Society." David Haberman, "A Cross-Cultural Adventure: The Transformation of Ronald Nixon," *Religion* 23 (1993): 217–27.

11. J. A. Chadwick (1899–1939) was educated at Cambridge and became a fellow of Trinity College.

12. Gertrude Emerson Sen (1892–1983) was a geographer and explorer, and the author of *Voiceless India* (1934).

13. As George Orwell observes, Gandhi's struggle was not against sexuality per se, but against intimate and preferential attachments that, by their passionate and exclusive nature, prove inimical to the service of God and humanity. Orwell, "Reflections on Gandhi," *Partisan Review* 16, no. 1 (1949), 85–92.

14. Orwell, "Reflections on Gandhi."

15. Thomas Merton, *Turning Toward the World: The Pivotal Years*, ed. Victor A Kramer (San Francisco: HarperSanFrancisco, 1996), 291.

16. Thomas Merton, *Dancing in the Water of Life: Seeking Peace in the Hermitage*, ed. Robert E. Daggy (San Francisco: HarperSanFrancisco, 1997), 259.

17. Bernard McGinn, "Withdrawal and Return: Reflections on Monastic Retreat from the World," *Spiritus* 6, no. 2 (2006): 149–72.

18. Pendle Hill was established in Wallingford, Pennsylvania, in 1930 as a Quaker study center designed to prepare its adult students for service both in the Religious Society of Friends and in the world. The founders envisioned a new Quaker school of social and religious education that would be "a vital center of spiritual culture" and "a place for training leaders." "Pendle Hill's Origins and History," Pendle Hill (website), accessed November 2021, https://pendlehill.org/explore/vision-mission-values/pendle-hill-beginnings/.

19. Perhaps the most renowned historian of his time, Toynbee's focus was the rise and fall of civilizations. Unlike Oswald Spengler, who regarded decline as inevitable, Toynbee argued that a society's longevity and vitality depended on how creatively it responded to physical and social challenges within. That civilizations so often sink into a slough of nationalism, militarism, and despotism led him to argue that "civilizations die from suicide, not by murder."

20. The phrase is from Thomas Merton, *Dancing in the Water of Life: Seeking Peace in the Hermitage*, ed. Robert E. Daggy, vol. 5 of *The Journals of Thomas Merton* (San Francisco: HarperCollins, 1997), 243.

21. Scott Milross Buchanan was an American educator, philosopher, and foundation consultant, renowned as the founder of the Great Books program at St. John's College, at Annapolis, Maryland. Brijen first met Buchanan in 1954 and was introduced to the Toynbee seminar by him. Brijen regarded Buchanan as one of his greatest mentors.

22. McGinn, "Withdrawal and Return," 153.

23. Arthur Koestler, *The Yogi and the Commissar, and Other Essays* (London: Cape, 1945), 10–11.

24. "Because of its inherent worldlessness, love can only become false and perverted when it is used for political purposes such as the change or salvation of the world." Arendt, *Human Condition*, 52. See also, Hannah Arendt, "'What Remains? The Language Remains': A Conversation with Günter Gaus," in *The Portable Hannah Arendt*, ed. Peter Baehr (New York: Penguin, 2003), 16.

25. Cf. Adorno's critique of the "liturgy of inwardness" in his *Jargon of Authenticity* (London: Routledge, 1964).

26. Of Arendt's youthful love affair with Martin Heidegger, Elzbieta Ettinger suggests that "it underwent many transformations over the years. To say that it turned into a friendship is to say both too much and too little, though both Arendt and Heidegger might have called it just that." Ettinger, *Hannah Arendt/Martin Heidegger* (New Haven, CT: Yale University Press, 1995), 1.

27. Walt Whitman, *Leaves of Grass* (New York: Fowler and Wells, 1855), 4.

Chapter 4

1. Hortense Powdermaker, *Stranger and Friend: The Way of an Anthropologist* (New York: W. W. Norton, 1966), 260–262. A critical reading of the essays in a special issue of *Etnofoor* on the theme of friendship raises this issue yet again. Tessa Diphoorn and Eva van Roekel, eds., "Friendship," special issue, *Etnofoor* 31, no. 1 (2019).

2. I allude here not to Shakespeare's *The Tempest* but to Octave Mannoni's study of the psychology of the unequal power relationship between colonizer and colonized, and by extension between anthropologist and key informant. Mannoni, *Prospero and Caliban: The Psychology of Colonialization* (Ann Arbor: University of Michigan Press, 1990).

3. Michael Jackson, *The Kuranko: Dimensions of Social Reality in a West African Society* (London: C. Hurst, 1977). *Ferensola* (lit. "town of twins") was traditionally used to signify a political alliance between two different polities. In 1977, the term became an image of the unity of all Kuranko people in the common cause of achieving political representation in Sierra Leone's central government.

Chapter 5

1. Aristotle, *Eudemian Ethics*, trans. Brad Inwood and Raphael Woolf (Cambridge: Cambridge University Press, 2013), 126 (236b3–6).

2. Denis Johnson, *Train Dreams* (New York: Farrar, Straus and Giroux, 2002), 63–64.

3. Michael Jackson, *Paths Toward a Clearing: Radical Empiricism and Ethnographic Inquiry* (Bloomington: Indiana University Press, 1989), 102–18.

4. Lucien Lévy-Bruhl, *Primitive Mentality* (Boston: Beacon Press, 1966). Rane Willerslev, *Soul Hunters: Hunting, Animism, and Personhood Among the Siberian Yukaghirs* (Berkeley: University of California Press, 2007), 106.

5. Curiously enough, a Warlpiri informant named Minjina recounted the same story to A. Capell in 1952, and with the same mimetic mastery that Zack possessed. Capell speaks of Minjina's "wealth of eloquence that only a recording machine could have preserved, and of action which would have demanded a ciné camera." A. Capell, "The Wailbri Through Their Own Eyes," *Oceania* 23, no. 2 (1952): 130. Minjina was the paternal grandfather of the Aboriginal painter, Michael Jagamara Nelson. Vivien Johnson, *The Art of Clifford Possum Tjapaltjarri* (East Roseville, New South Wales: Gordon and Breach Arts International, 1997), 12.

6. Maurice Merleau-Ponty, *The Visible and the Invisible*, trans. Alphonso Lingis (Evanston, IL: Northwestern University Press, 1968), 122–23.

7. Willerslev, *Soul Hunters*, 190–91.

8. Eduardo Kohn, "How Dogs Dream: Amazonian Natures and the Politics of Transspecies Engagement," *American Ethnologist* 34, no. 1 (February 2007): 7.

9. Deborah Bird Rose, *Dingo Makes Us Human: Life and Land in an Aboriginal Australian Culture* (Cambridge: Cambridge University Press, 1992), 176–77.

10. Steven Feld, "They Repeatedly Lick Their Own Things," *Critical Inquiry* 24, no. 2 (1998): 446–47.

Chapter 6

1. Johann Wolfgang von Goethe, *Elective Affinities*, trans. R. J. Hollingdale (Harmondsworth, UK: Penguin, 1971), 52–53.

Chapter 7

1. K. E. Løgstrup points out that "we do not become aware of the sovereign expressions of life until a failure or conflict or crisis disrupts our immediate preoccupation with the needs of the other." Kees van Kooten Niekerk, introduction to *Beyond the Ethical Demand*, by K. E. Løgstrup (Notre Dame, IN: Notre Dame University Press, 2007), xx, xviii.

2. Jane Bennett, *The Enchantment of Modern Life: Attachments, Crossings, and Ethics* (Princeton, NJ: Princeton University Press, 2001), 3.

3. Edmund Husserl, *Ideas: General Introduction to Pure Phenomenology*, trans. W. R. Boyce Gibson (New York: Collier Macmillan, 1962), 93.

4. Husserl, *Ideas*, 99–100.

5. Husserl, *Ideas*, 103.

6. This is precisely where Emmanuel Levinas parted company with Husserl.

Chapter 9

1. D. W. Winnicott, *Playing and Reality* (Harmondsworth, UK: Penguin, 1974), 17.

2. Aleksandar Hemon, "The Aquarium: A Child's Isolating Illness," *New Yorker*, June 13 and 20, 2011, 50–62.

3. Maurice Merleau-Ponty, *Phenomenology of Perception*, trans. Colin Smith (London: Routledge, 1996), 355.

4. In a television interview with MSNBC's Ari Melber, author Fran Lebowitz declared, "A friend is what you think a friend is. Whatever your idea of a friend is, that's who your friend is." Fran Lebowitz, interview by Ari Melber, *The Beat*, MSNBC, July 22, 2021.

Chapter 10

1. Christopher Lasch, *The Culture of Narcissism: American Life in an Age of Diminishing Expectations* (New York: W. W. Norton, 1979).

2. Billy Moss, an officer in the Coldstream Guards, was Leigh Fermor's collaborator in the kidnapping.

3. Deborah Devonshire, "Patrick Leigh Fermor," in *In Tearing Haste: Letters Between Deborah Devonshire and Patrick Leigh Fermor*, ed. Charlotte Mosley (London: John Murray, 2008), xv–xvi. There are two minor errors in this account: the guerillas reached Mount

Ida *three* days after the kidnapping, and Leigh Fermor read *five* stanzas of Horace's *Ad Thaliarchum* (*Odes*, 1.9).

4. Patrick Leigh Fermor, *A Time of Gifts* (New York: New York Review of Books, 2005), 86.

5. Maurice Cardiff, *Friend Abroad: Memories of Lawrence Durrell, Freya Stark, Patrick Leigh-Fermor, Peggy Guggenheim and Others* (London: Radcliffe Press, 1997), 19.

6. Patrick Leigh Fermor, *A Time to Keep Silence* (New York: New York Review of Books, 1982), xvii. Even in his youth, Leigh Fermor had experienced the attraction of monastic life, describing in *A Time of Gifts* his visit to the Benedictine Abbey at Göttweig, where an Irish monk "of immense age and great charm" showed the young wayfarer around. "I envied his airy and comfortable cell, his desk laden with books, and his view over the mountains and the river." Leigh Fermor, *A Time of Gifts*, 187.

Chapter 11

1. New Zealand even had a word for the vice of braggadocio, a word not heard so much these days—*skiting*.

2. Les Cleveland, *The Iron Hand: New Zealand Soldiers' Poems from World War Two*, (Wellington: Wai-te-Ata Press, 1979), 11–12. In his poem, "The Long Way Back," Cleveland writes of the same moment: "A week ago the other survivors / Carousing rowdily in Rome / Declined to join this excursion" (51). Les Cleveland, *The Songs We Sang* (Wellington, NZ: Editorial Services, 1959), 51.

3. John Mulgan, *Man Alone* (Hamilton: Paul's Book Arcade, 1949).

4. Mulgan, *Man Alone*, 6–7.

5. Cleveland, *The Iron Hand*, 11–12.

6. Cleveland, *The Iron Hand*, 12.

7. Cleveland, *The Iron Hand*, 12.

8. Cleveland, *The Iron Hand*, 12.

9. Cleveland, The Iron Hand, 12.

10. Les Cleveland, "An Assiduous Industry," *New Zealand Books* (June 1997), 15.

11. Les Cleveland, "Soldiers' Songs: The Folklore of the Powerless," *New York Folklore* 11, nos. 1–4 (1985): 79. See also Les Cleveland, *Dark Laughter: War and Song in Popular Culture* (Westport, CT: Praeger, 1994).

12. Cited in Athol McCredie, "The Social Landscape," in *Witness to Change: Life in New Zealand*, ed. John Pascoe, Les Cleveland, and Ans Westra (Wellington: *PhotoForum*, 1985), 52.

Chapter 12

1. Though it echoes Keith's account of his father's experience, the preceding paragraph is drawn from Gavin Mortimer's account of the liberation of Celle and of Belsen. *Stirling's Men: The Inside History of the SAS in World War II* (London: Weidenfeld and Nicolson, 2004), 322–24.

2. Martha Gellhorn, cited in Caroline Moorehead, *Martha Gellhorn: A Life* (New York: Vintage, 2004), 284.

3. Moorehead, *Martha Gellhorn*, 284.

4. This was confirmed by a remark Keith made after reading my account of Dunc in Belsen. "As for Dunc's Belsen recollections, yes, they are what he told Gavin Mortimer, but not what he told me exactly: we'll have to revisit this next time we're at table—the private recollection is far less distant."

5. Keith Ridler, "If Not the Words: Shared Practical Activity and Friendship in Fieldwork," in *Things As They Are: New Directions of Phenomenological Anthropology*, ed. Michael Jackson (Bloomington: Indiana University Press, 1996), 244.

Chapter 13

1. Te Pakaka Tawhai, "He Tipuna Wharenui o te Rohe O Uepohatu" (master's thesis, Massey University, Palmerston North, NZ, 1978), 51.

2. Tawhai, "He Tipuna Wharenui," 49.

3. Sir Apirana Ngata, cited by Ranginui Walker in *He Tipua: The Life and Times of Sir Apirana Ngata* (Auckland: Penguin, 2002), 297.

Chapter 14

1. J. M. Coetzee and Paul Auster, *Here and Now: Letters 2008–2011* (New York: Penguin, 2013), 2.

2. Meyer Fortes, *The Web of Kinship Among the Tallensi* (London: Oxford University Press, 1949), 163.

3. Margaret Trawick, *Notes on Love in a Tamil Family* (Berkeley: University of California Press, 1990), 159.

4. Agehananda Bharati, *The Light at the Center: Context and Pretext of Modern Mysticism* (Santa Barbara, CA: Ross-Erikson, 1976), 161.

5. Joyce Johnson, *Minor Characters: A Beat Memoir* (London: Virago, 1983), 237.

Chapter 15

1. Galina Lindquist, *Conjuring Hope: Healing and Magic in Contemporary Russia* (New York: Berghahn, 2006), 192.

2. Lindquist, *Conjuring Hope*, xiv.

3. Galina Lindquist, "In Search of the Magical Flow: Magic and Market in Contemporary Russia," *Urban Anthropology* 29, no. 4 (2000): 315–57.

4. Lindquist, *Conjuring Hope*, 199.

5. Lindquist, *Conjuring Hope*, 80.

6. Lindquist, *Conjuring Hope*, 229.

7. Maurice Merleau-Ponty, "From Mauss to Lévi-Strauss," in *Signs*, trans. R. C. McLeary (Evanston, IL.: Northwestern University Press, 1964), 119.

8. During Galina's last field trip to Tuva, she was brutally informed by a local woman healer that she had cancer. Feigning great distress, the healer offered not only to cure Galina's cancer but also to collaborate in writing a book with her. In a posthumously published paper, Galina describes the overwhelming dread this diagnosis caused her, and how—when she had recovered her equilibrium—she came to value the insights that this traumatic episode had given her into how healers work by intimidating their clients, asserting their authority, and inspiring belief in their powers. But as for accepting the healer's offer, Galina speaks of this moment as a baptism of fire: "I must admit that I was not prepared to go that far: the face of the Other as the face of death was too much for me." Galina Lindquist, personal communication with the author, 2007.

9. Gillian Rose, *Love's Work: A Reckoning with Life* (New York: Schocken Books, 1995).

10. D. W. Winnicott, *Home Is Where We Start From* (New York: Norton, 1986), 66.

11. Maurice Merleau-Ponty, *Phenomenology of Perception*, trans. Colin Smith (London: Routledge), 316.

12. Merleau-Ponty, *Phenomenology of Perception*, 359.

Chapter 16

1. Vincent O'Sullivan, *Being Here: Selected Poems* (Wellington: Victoria University Press, 2015), 33.

2. O'Sullivan, *Being Here*, 97.

3. Brian Turner, "Humanity and Nature: Thoughts on the Art of Grahame Sydney," in *The Art of Grahame Sydney*, by Grahame Sydney and contributors (Dunedin: Longacre, 2000), 94.

4. Turner, "Humanity and Nature," 94; emphasis added.

5. Kevin Ireland speaks of Grahame Sydney's "painterly 'truth'" as "a kind of fabricated realism" in which "bravura skills . . . are deployed only incidentally to represent place and time, *for his purpose is always to record an inner journey.*" Kevin Ireland, "Grahame Sydney," in *Grahame Sydney Down South: Recent Paintings 2001–2011* (Porirua, NZ: Pataka Museum of Arts and Cultures, 2011), 6; emphasis added.

6. In a recent poem titled "Not included in the footnotes," Vincent declares that he is "a Catholic as much by repute as by mundane choice." *Being Here: Selected Poems* (Wellington, NZ: Victoria University Press, 2015), 214.

7. "Tony Fomison Talks with Denys Trussell," *Elva Bett Gallery Newsletter*, no. 7 (November 1978): 1, 3. Cited in Vincent O'Sullivan, "You Could Tell Them This," in Mark Adams, *Tony Fomison a Portrait of the Artist 1971–1990*, ed. Kriselle Baker, Collector's Edition (Parnell, NZ: Baker and Douglas, 2014).

8. Vincent O'Sullivan, "On the odd eventful morning," in *Us, Then* (Wellington, NZ: Victoria University Press, 2013), 100.

9. Bob Lowry was a New Zealand book designer, typographer, and printer whom I worked for in 1962, until he was driven out of business by bankruptcy and illness, and subsequently committed suicide. The poet R. A. K. Mason was Lowry's contemporary.

10. Samuel Butler, *A First Year in Canterbury Settlement*, ed. A. C. Brassington and P. B. Maling (Auckland: Blackwood and Janet Paul, 1964 [1863]), 48, 59, 50, 35.

11. Samuel Butler, *Erewhon or Over the Range*, ed. Hans-Peter Breuer and Daniel F. Howard (Toronto: Associated University Presses, 1981), 74.

12. John Mulgan to Charles Brasch, letter, postmarked August 20, 1940. A copy of this unpublished letter is in the possession of Vincent O'Sullivan who let me read it in 2014.

13. O'Sullivan, "You Could Tell Them This," 8.

Chapter 17

1. Michel Foucault, "Friendship as a Way of Life," in *Ethics: Subjectivity and Truth*, ed. Paul Rabinow, trans. Robert Hurley and others (New York: New Press, 1997), 136.

2. Robert Brain, *Friends & Lovers* (Frogmore, St. Albans: Paladin, 1977), 9.

3. Michel Foucault, "Friendship as a Way of Life," in *Ethics: Subjectivity and Truth*, ed. Paul Rabinow, trans. Robert Hurley and others (New York: New Press, 1997).

4. Gilbert Meilaender, "When Harry and Sally Read the *Nicomachean Ethics*," in *The Changing Face of Friendship*, ed. Leroy S. Rouner (Notre Dame, IN: University of Notre Dame Press, 1994), 185–86.

5. Lawrence Durrell, *Justine* (London: Faber and Faber, 1957), 96.

6. Lawrence Durrell, *Balthazar* (London: Faber and Faber, 1958), 132.

7. Evelyn Waugh, *Brideshead Revisited* (Harmondsworth, UK: Penguin, 1951), 77.

Chapter 18

1. Aristotle, *The Nicomachean Ethics*, trans. David Ross (Oxford: Oxford University Press, 1980), 193 (1155a).

2. George Devereux, "Art and Mythology, Part 1: A General Theory," in *Studying Personality Cross-Culturally*, ed. B. Kaplan (New York: Harper and Row, 1961), 378.

Chapter 19

1. Daniel Defoe, *A Journal of the Plague Year* (Mineola, NY: Dover, 2001), 1.

2. "I intend to relate one hundred tales or fables or parable or stories—whichever you choose to call them—as they were told ten days by a band of seven ladies and three young during the time of the recent plague." Giovanni Boccaccio, prologue to *The Decameron*, trans. G. H. McWilliam (London: Penguin, 2004), 1.

3. Axel Munthe, *The Story of San Michele* (London: Hodder Headline, 2004), 125–26.

4. Mary Wollstonecraft Shelley, *The Annotated Frankenstein* (Cambridge, MA: the Belknap Press of Harvard University, 2012), 12.

Coda

1. Hannah Arendt, *The Human Condition* (Chicago: Chicago University Press, 1958), 243.

2. Aristotle, *Eudemian Ethics*, trans. Brad Inwood and Raphael Woolf (Cambridge: Cambridge University Press, 2013), 137 (1232b).

3. Dominique Zahan, *The Bambara* (Leiden: E. J. Brill, 1974), 5.

4. Simon Hattenstone, "The Transformation of Greta Thunberg," *Guardian*, September 25, 2021.

INDEX

CPSIA information can be obtained
at www.ICGtesting.com
Printed in the USA
JSHW022251080223
37493JS00004B/5